THE INTEGRATION OF MODERN IRAQ

CROOM HELM SERIES ON THE ARAB WORLD

Edited by P.J. Vatikiotis

PALESTINE IN THE ARAB DILEMMA

Walid W. Kazziha

THE INTEGRATION OF MODERN IRAQ

EDITED BY ABBAS KELIDAR

CROOM HELM LONDON

Croom Helm Ltd, 2-10 St John's Road, London SW11

British Library Cataloguing in Publication Data

The integration of modern Iraq.
1. Iraq – History
I. Kelidar, Abbas
956.7 DS70.9

ISBN 0-85664-510-9

Printed in Great Britain by offset lithography by
Billing & Sons Ltd, Guildford, London and Worcester

CONTENTS

THE INTEGRATION OF MODERN IRAQ

INTRODUCTION

This work deals with some important aspects of development in the fields of history, politics and economics in modern Iraq. It arose out of an interdisciplinary seminar organised by the Near and Middle East Centre of the School of Oriental and African Studies, which was held in June 1977. The concern of the contributors was, for each of them, to examine a particular feature or a specific problem in their own field of interest, without any preconceived notion or an established procedure of approach. The result has been remarkable and extremely illuminating for students of modern Iraqi society. The chapters have indicated a pattern of continuity and change in the social, political and economic evolution of the country. In many ways what happened in the country since the foundation of the modern state of Iraq has been a reflection of the political hopes, aspirations and ideological orientation of the ruling élite.

The modern state of Iraq was set up in 1920, in a country where the social structure was so fragmented that it was practically impossible to have a general agreement among its various and divergent components on common basic fundamentals which could provide the essential guidelines for the new social structure. The absence of an indigenous source of authority acceptable to the social groups meant that the British Mandatory authorities were able to propose a Sharifian prince – Faisal – to head a constitutional parliamentary system of government under a hereditary monarchy.

Under this system the way to national integration was by the selection and appointment of local notables and educated young Effendis to government posts. This form of nation-building was started by Sir Percy Cox, who was appointed British High Commissioner in Baghdad in 1920, when he set up the Arab Executive Council as the nucleus of a national administration. A prominent member of the major communities that made up Iraqi society was appointed as Minister on this council. The method was enshrined and became the normal practice for all government appointments. However, the aspirations and ambitions of the Sharifian politicians who dominated the political process accentuated the difficulties towards national integration by their constant reference and express desire to seek the disestablishment of the new state, and seek its merger in a larger whole yet to be created, constituting the Arab nation. Mr Shikara explains the grounds on which these claims were made, as well as the obstacles that faced Faisal and his supporters in their quest for Arab unity and a bigger domain. Mr Adhami examines the same problem in its internal dimension. The pluralist system of representation proposed by Cox also served as the basis on which members of the Constituent Assembly and subsequent Parliaments were selected and elected. Parliamentary government in Iraq had inauspicious beginnings and it was soon discredited, not only because it had perpetuated the division among religious and ethnic communities, but also as a living indictment of the democratic system as it worked in Iraq. The political radicals of the 1930s and 1940s were able to condemn the whole edifice as a British creation and a sham that ought to be abandoned.

The various vicissitudes to which the new state was subjected become the focus of the contributions by Mr Hemphill, Mr Kopietz and Dr Pool. To maintain the unity of the country, the creation of an organised coercive force at the disposal of the new state became imperative, so that any challenge to its authority – and there were many – could be put down. Mr Hemphill, therefore, takes up the task of explaining the processes by which the Iraqi army was created. He also undertakes an assessment of the social and political factors that influenced its development.

The disenchantment with the system of government as it was operated in Iraq compounded the failure to evolve a uniform political loyalty and allegiance to the state of Iraq, and was further aggravated by the radicalisation of Iraqi politics under the impact of the European ideologies rampant in the 1930s, which had a direct impact on the evolutionary processes which characterised Arab politics at the time. Political aspirants who felt deprived of appropriate channels to vent their political demands found willing allies among the freshly recruited rank and file of the armed forces. Dr Pool attempts to trace the manner by which the Sharifian political élite was transformed into a ruling class with a vested interest in the economic resources of the country. The fact that this kind of transformation could only proceed by virtue of the exercise of power at the disposal of the central government served only to reinforce the alienation of the population, and widen the gulf separating the rulers and their subjects. Mr Kopietz examines all these processes in the internal politics of Iraq from the European viewpoint. The perception of the European powers, namely Britain, who had a direct and immediate interest in Iraq, and Nazi Germany, who was determined with some Arab goodwill to supplant Britain's dominant position in the region, is, of the various political upheavals in the country, of considerable relevance to the understanding of Iraqi political attitudes and the events which took place.

The contributions by the economists are of far-reaching importance in view of the huge development programme which Iraq has been attempting for the last thirty years. The direct impact of investment has meant a change not only in the economic structure but also in the nature of the economic relationship which prevailed under traditional modes of production. This change has been rather haphazard and accompanied by many of the problems associated with rapid economic growth, despite governmental planning and the exercise of administrative control. Mr Issa and Mr Jomard highlight these effects through their examination of the distribution of national income for 1971, and the complex and vexing question of internal labour migration respectively. Professor Penrose and Dr McLachlan direct their attention to the vital and complementary fields of economic activities: agriculture and industry. Iraq is primarily an agricultural country attempting to industrailise at an extremely fast pace – a process which has been characterised as 'explosive development'. While Dr McLachlan concentrates on some features of development in the agricultural sector, outlining the resources available and assessing future prospects, Professor Penrose takes up the delicate problem of industrial policy, examining the methods employed in the management of the nationalised industries. Both chapters point out the highly significant need for a number of prerequisites for a successful development programme of the kind which Iraq has been undertaking.

The aspects of the economy dealt with in these papers mark a turning-point in the political evolution of Iraq. State control of economic resources in the Middle East is not an abnormal phenomenon. The role of government in this area has been growing with a consistency that has been matched only by the increase in the revenues derived from oil. In the case of Iraq this has been of considerable importance. Iraq has not simply been seeking an increase in its oil revenues but also asserting its total control over the industry. To this extent Iraq has been one of the leaders amongst the oil-producing countries to call for the nationalisation of its oil resources. This clamour for nationalisation has come as a direct result of the radicalisation of Iraqi politics in which both the Iraqi Communist Party since the early 1930s and the ruling Baath Party since the mid-1950s played no mean part.

Despite the fact that the structure of political power and the nature of rule in Iraq has continued to be largely authoritarian, and in many ways personal, these parties have exerted considerable influence on the adoption of a certain semi-revolutionary political terminology in which the ideology of various groups has been couched. The influence of the Soviet Union on the hearts and minds of young people in Iraq, and the example it set up for economic development, should not be underestimated.

When the state was established in 1920, for most Iraqis the model to be emulated was that of the advanced countries of Western Europe. After the Second World War, however, the constitutional parliamentary system as practised in Iraq could not accommodate or deal with the social, economic and political discontent prevalent among a new generation of disgruntled Iraqis. Revolution and radical notions of nationalism became the order of the day. The example of the Soviet Union could not but serve to make such a revolutionary-military régime conscious of the importance of totalitarian control. Thus from a parliamentary system of government the country has come to look to the East European method of setting up a National Front of progressive nationalist and patriotic political parties and groupings under the domination not so much of the Communists, but the Baathists. Some manifestations of the reaction to this trend are discussed by Dr Jawad, who offers a brief outline of the history of the Kurdish problem of Iraq, and the assertion made by Kurds of both their contributions to radical notions of ideology and their claim to autonomy and ultimate nationhood. Dr Kelidar examines a more extreme reaction, and indicates the extent to which ideology could provide a motivation for violent political action by focusing attention on the politics of the Communist movement of Iraq and the role played by one of the most influential radical writers, Aziz al-Haj.

1 THE ELECTIONS FOR THE CONSTITUENT ASSEMBLY IN IRAQ, 1922-4

M.M. al-Adhami

The occupation of the three Ottoman provinces, Basra, Baghdad and Mosul, which were together known as Mesopotamia or Iraq, was completed by British troops in October 1918. For the disparate indigenous population of these provinces, an Iraqi nationality had hardly developed. Men felt the ties of loyalty to their tribes and religious leaders, or to their town and region, but not to their country. This was because the state of Iraq did not exist as a political entity before 1920. Also, there were no political parties, but groups who were called by some British officials 'extremists'. They were against the British Mandatory administration, demanding the establishment of an Arab state in Iraq to be headed by one of the Sharif Husain's sons. In 1919, they established a secret party called Haras Al-Istiqlal (Guards of Independence), supported by the Shii religious leaders in the holy cities, Najaf, Karbala and Kazimain.[1]

On 3 May 1920, the British Mandate for Iraq was announced in Baghdad. It meant that Iraq became a British responsibility before the League of Nations. For Iraqis, the Mandate was a cover for domination. Its announcement caused great agitation.[2] Secret meetings of the anti-British Mandate leaders were held, where they decided to set out the demands concerning the future of the country which they presented to the Acting Civil Commissioner, A.T. Wilson, for transmission to the British government. For this task fifteen delegates, 'Mandubin', were chosen in one of the big gatherings in al-Haidar Khana mosque in Baghdad,[3] and on 2 June they presented Wilson with a document in which they demanded the immediate formation of a convention for Iraq, to be elected in accordance with the Turkish Electoral Law. It was envisaged that the Assembly would represent the whole of the country, sitting in Baghdad to draw up proposals for a national government in Iraq as promised in the Anglo-French declaration of 1918.[4] In his reply, Wilson promised to urge the British government to expedite matters as much as possible.[5]

Delegates were chosen, also, in Karbala, Najaf, Hilla and Shamiyya. They presented to their local Governors a similar document to the one drawn up in Baghdad.[6]

The British authorities in Iraq announced on 21 June 1920 that Sir Percy Cox, who subsequently became British High Commissioner, would be in Baghdad in the autumn and would be authorised to set up a council of state under an Arab president and a General Elective Assembly, freely elected by the population of Iraq. It was made clear that he was entrusted to prepare an organic law, in consultation with the General Elective Assembly, as provided under the terms of the Mandate.[7] The anti-Mandate movement insisted on an immediate convention of the Assembly and objected to the delay until autumn.[8] However, the British authorities invited, on 12 July, the former Iraqi deputies of the Ottoman Chamber and the former Senators (al-Mab'uthan) to meet in council and discuss the electoral basis of the General Assembly elections.[9] The anti-Mandate movement emphasised their previous demands and tried to convince the former deputies not to accept the invitation, but they failed.[10] In Gertrude Bell's words, 'The Nationalists' party have set their face against the scheme which they look upon as an attempt on our part to cut the ground from under their feet.'[11] Therefore, Muhammad al-Sadr, Yusif al-Suwaidi and Jaafar Abu al-Timman, three out of five members of the delegates' executive committee, refused the membership which the former deputies' committee offered them during their second meeting. Nationalist agitation was renewed in Baghdad. But their movement was suppressed, and Martial Law was announced. This signalled the end of Haras al-Istiqlal as a party.[12]

The Electoral Committee proceeded with its meetings to revise the Turkish Electoral Law. Meanwhile, Sir Percy Cox proclaimed on 11 November a provisional Council of State under Abd al-Rahman al-Naqib's presidency.[13]

On 4 November 1920, the Electoral Committee submitted its revision of the Turkish Electoral Law to the High Commissioner, who put it before the government for consideration. The main revision drawn up by the Council of State was that a special representation be accorded to the tribes as well as to the non-Muslim communities in Iraq.[14] They also decided that the Electoral Law of the General Assembly should be known as 'The Provisional Regulation of the Constituent Assembly Elections'. On 16 December 1920 the Council ratified the proposals.[15]

The lapse of three months without the inauguration of the General Elective Assembly encouraged the anti-Mandate organ *al-Istiqlal* to become more hostile, both towards the provisional government and towards British policy.[16] The newspaper was suspended on 10 February 1921. The anti-Mandate leaders, including some delegates – Mandubin

– were rendered passive,[17] though violent anti-British posters had appeared on the walls of Baghdad.[18] It was also reported that several tribes were contemplating a revolt against the government.[19] All these obstacles, plus the evidence that attempts would be made to force the Assembly, if convened, to make anti-British declarations,[20] convinced the High Commissioner and the Cairo Conference, called by Winston Churchill, Colonial Secretary at the time, to decide among other things the future of Iraq,[21] postponed the elections of the Constituent Assembly. The Conference nominated Prince Faisal, who had been forced out of Syria, to be ruler of Iraq. The anti-Mandate movement demanded that Faisal should be elected as King through the Constituent Assembly[22] but the government decided to hold a referendum.[23]

In the referendum the anti-Mandate movement made their approval of Faisal conditional on the convention of the Constituent Assembly within three months' time, beginning from the date when Faisal assumed his official duties.[24]

In his accession speech, King Faisal promised that his first task would be to proceed with the elections and the convocation of the Constituent Assembly, which would draw up a Constitution and ratify the Anglo-Iraqi Treaty.[25]

Under the monarchy a Council of State had become the Cabinet. The main task for the new government was the negotiation of the Anglo-Iraqi Treaty. For the British the treaty was the embodiment of Britain's obligations as a Mandatory for Iraq. It would also serve to protect British interests in the country, by reformulating the terms of the Mandate as a treaty with the state of Iraq.[26] For Iraq the treaty meant the abrogation of the detested Mandate.[27]

The divergence of views prolonged the negotiations until 25 June, when the Iraqi Cabinet, under British government pressure, accepted the treaty, while a great agitation against the Mandate and the treaty was spreading in the country, led by the anti-Mandate movement which acquired fresh impetus.[28] King Faisal, who had been in constant contact and sympathised with the anti-Mandate movement in Iraq, withheld his consent to the resolution of the Cabinet.[29] He told the High Commissioner that if he accepted the treaty, his fall would be certain. He was convinced that the Constituent Assembly would repudiate both him and the treaty.[30]

The resolution of the Cabinet to accept the treaty meant that the Constituent Assembly would have to be convened to give its decision.

Following the resignation of Jaafar Abu al-Timman, the anti-Mandate movement representative from the Cabinet in protest against the acceptance of the treaty, it appeared to the anti-Mandate movement that under these new circumstances, it would be difficult to hold free elections without any interference from a British-dominated Iraqi government. Therefore, a meeting was called in Najaf, on 27 July, at which a statement was drawn up demanding the dismissal of the Cabinet, and threatening to boycott the elections if the political situation in the country continued on the same course.[31] In Baghdad, a petition addressed to the King was circulated throughout the city for signatures; it expressed the determination to procure complete independence, reject the treaty, and resist the holding of elections,[32] whose regulations had been published, in May 1922.[33] The proceedings of Najaf and Baghdad precipitated a crisis in the Cabinet, whose members resigned on 14 August, as they felt that they did not posses the King's confidence.[34]

Two anti-British political parties, Hizb al-Watani al-Iraqi (Nationalist Party), whose secretary was Jaafar Abu al-Timman, one of the fifteen delegates in 1920, and Hizb al-Nahda (Awakening Party), had been established in the second week of August 1922.[35] Sayyid Muhammad al-Sadr was the moving spirit of the anti-British parties. He appealed to the Iraqi nation, five days after the Cabinet resignation. in the newspaper *Al-Mufid*, to reject the Mandate and the treaty and asked for the postponement of the Constituent Assembly elections until the situation had improved sufficiently to prevent abuses in the elections.[36] On the anniversary of the King's accession, 23 August 1922, the two parties organised a demonstration in the courtyard of the King's palace to express their new attitude. A speech was delivered in the presence of the King's representative, in which the underlying reasons for demanding Constituent Assembly elections the year before were outlined, and yet it was concluded that the elections were not favourable now.[37] The representatives of the two parties presented the King with a protest, which had been published on the same day in their newspapers. It attacked British policy in Iraq, and demanded an end to British influence in the administration. They also demanded the establishment of a Cabinet whose members would be sincere patriots, and that no treaty should be concluded or negotiations entered into until the Constituent Assembly met, its members having been freely elected.[38]

The King, on the same day, suffered from a sudden attack of appendicitis, which required an immediate operation.[39] This, with the government non-existent, allowed the High Commissioner to take over formal authority in the country. He restrained the opposition movement by arresting and deporting its leaders, suppressing its press and parties, and ordering an aerial bombardment of the anti-Mandate sheikhs and their tribes.[40]

While Faisal was convalescing, Churchill, on 29 August, instructed the High Commissioner to induce al-Naqib to form a moderate government, ostensibly to carry on the routine work of administration, subject to the King's subsequent approval. The Cabinet should publish the treaty forthwith, and it should be made clear to the King that Britain would not allow its policy to be wrecked by his obstinacy. He indicated that 'If we decide to go on with the elections, al-Naqib's government would, of course, instruct all Arab and British officials to use their influence as far as is proper to secure acceptance of the treaty.'[41] On 2 September, Churchill asked Cox to demand from Faisal endorsement of the actions that the High Commissioner had taken during the King's illness and agreement to consult the High Commissioner and to act upon his advice in the formation of his Cabinet. On 14 September, he emphasised that both the King and his Cabinet should work enthusiastically for the treaty's passage through the Constituent Assembly.[42]

In order to keep his throne safe, and because he felt the end justified the means, King Faisal acquiesced to the High Commissioner's terms.[43] Therefore, the formation of a new Naqib Cabinet took place on 2 November, which reaffirmed the last Cabinet's treaty approval. The treaty was published on 13 October 1922.[44] A royal decree was then published on 21 October, providing for the elections of the Constituent Assembly to begin on 24 October.[45]

The Election

In the regulations of the Constituent Assembly elections, Iraq was divided into 14 Divisions, or *liwas*. Every liwa was regarded as 'an electoral college', such as Baghdad liwa, Basrah liwa, etc. The administrative head of the liwa was called 'Mutasarrif', and the liwa contained several numbers of administrative units based on the large towns called *qada*. The qada consisted of several administration units based on small towns and villages called *nihiya*.

The representative for the Constituent Assembly was chosen, by indirect elections, in the following manner. The primary elector, who should be a male and not less than 21 years old, elects a secondary elector, who should be a male, not less than 25 years old. The latter elected the representative to be a member of the Constituent Assembly. This member should be a male not less than 30 years old. The elections were by secret ballot, conducted by supervising committees in the qadas. These committees were elected by representatives of their locality.

The Constituent Assembly consisted of one hundred representatives, distributed as follows:

(1) between 1-3 tribal representatives from each liwa;
(2) between 1-2 Jews and Christians from Baghdad, Basra and Mosul liwas;
(3) from the inhabitants of towns and villages, such a number of representatives as was proportional to the number of primary electors.

The sheikhs of the tribes domiciled in each liwa should nominate double the number of their representatives. If they did not agree over the required number, the names of candidates would be communicated to the secondary electors of the liwa, who would elect the requisite number of representatives from among the candidates. This meant that the tribes could not participate in the elections as primary or secondary electors.[46]

Elections passed through two stages. The first stage lasted from 24 October 1922 until the second half of January 1923, when the elections reached a standstill for reasons that will be dealt with below. The second stage started when the elections were renewed on 12 July 1923, only after strenuous efforts were made by British authorities, King Faisal and the Iraqi government.

The First Stage

On the same day as the royal decree signalling the start of the elections, secret instructions with the King's approval were being sent to the Mutasarrifs informing them that it was their duty to explain clearly to the people the necessity of selecting candidates who would ratify the treaty.[47] The administrative inspectors in the liwas had also been ordered to push their Mutasarrifs to secure the election of such candidates.[48] In the meantime, a contrary declaration to the secret instructions from the Minister of the Interior to the Mutassariffs was published in the newspapers, instructing all government officials to adopt an attitude of complete neutrality during the elections.[49]

As the elections started, political parties were banned except the government party, Hizb al-Hurr (Free Party), and no one was nominated as a candidate for the elections for the opposition groups. In fact, the atmosphere of the elections was rather dull. Two weeks after the election campaign started, the Shii ulama, under the leadership of

Sheikh Mahdi al-Khalisi, and with the support of anti-Mandate elements who had not been included in the High Commissioner's action against their leaders in the preceding August, intensified the opposition of the previous summer. In Najaf, Karbala and Kazimain, they issued (Fatwas) to the Muslims of Iraq, forbidding participation in the elections, as it was against the wishes of the nation.[50]

Unsigned notices urging the people to obey the Fatwas were circulated as well.[51]

As soon as the Fatwas were issued, the electoral committees in the holy cities resigned and the elections came to a standstill.[52] In fact, the overwhelming majority of Shiis abstained from participating in the elections. Copies of Fatwas were extensively circulated in Iraq.[53] In Baghdad they called on Jews and Christians to join their Moslem brothers in boycotting the elections.[54] Meanwhile, the formation of the supervising committee failed in Baghdad,[55] and threatening letters from a 'supreme-committee of the secret societies of Iraq' were received by the members of the new committee.[56] In Hilla the elections reached a deadlock,[57] and the Mutasarrif of Mosul informed the Ministry of the Interior on 28 December 1922 that the committee had no more desire to continue, and the people started to avoid the elections, as the influence of the Shiis' Fatwas and other notices had affected Sunnis in Mosul.[58]

Decrees from Christian religious leaders were circulated in Mosul as well, urging members of their communities to support the unity of the nation by boycotting the elections.[59] In some other liwas, the elections were proceeding slowly, but came to a standstill by January 1923.

Efforts were made to conciliate the ulama,[60] but they declared that the Fatwas would remain in force as long as the country remained under martial law. They demanded guarantees for the freedom of the press and public meetings; withdrawal of the Administrative Inspectors from liwas, and the return of the deportees from exile, as well as the reconvening of the suppressed parties.[61]

On 16 November, one week after the issue of the Fatwas, al-Naqib's Cabinet resigned, as King Faisal was annoyed with the government party, Hizb al-Hurr, for its failure to launch an energetic campaign in the election. Abdul Muhsin al-Saadun formed a new Cabinet on 20 November 1922. The new Cabinet, with the approval of the High Commissioner, announced the release of the deportees,[62] and on 8 December 1922 the Council of Ministers resolved to reconvene the two nationalist parties, al-Watani and al-Nahda.[63] These procedures were not adequate to prevent the standstill of the elections.

It was not only the Fatwas which hindered the preliminaries of the elections. Many people feared that the registers of the elections might be used for purposes of conscription.[64] The other reason was the limited number of tribal representatives to the Constituent Assembly, which led the sheikhs to fear they would be overwhelmed by townsmen.[65]

For the Kurdish areas, such as Sulaimaniyya, Arbil, and other Kurdish qadas in the Mosul and Kirkuk liwas, most of these areas were not under British troops and Iraqi government control when the elections started. The position of Kurdistan in Iraq was unsettled.

The High Commissioner was instructed by the Colonial Office not to interfere militarily in Kurdistan. Therefore he withdrew his troops from Sulaimaniyya liwa,[66] most of the Arbil liwa and parts of the Kirkuk liwa. The British thought that with the co-operation of Sheikh Mahmud Barazanji, who led the rising of 1919 in Kurdistan, the control of Kurdish areas could be regained, but as soon as he arrived in Sulaimaniyya from exile, he began to co-operate with Turks who were demanding the restoration of Mosul Willayat. Then, Sheikh Mahmud declared himself as king of an independent Kurdistan.[67] These areas, therefore, were out of the electoral machinery in its first stage.

Efforts to Renew the Elections

The whole Kurdish question had changed with the disappearance of the idea of an independent Kurdish state in Asia, following the failure to ratify the Treaty of Sèvres.[68] This allowed the British troops to re-occupy the Kurdish district in the north of Iraq. Sulaimaniyya town remained, with British approval, in Sheikh Mahmud's hands. All other Sulaimaniyya qadas were united to the Arbil and Kirkuk liwas.[69] In the meantime, the British and Iraqi governments announced their recognition of Kurd rights within the boundaries of Iraq, and their intention to set up a Kurdish government within these boundaries.[70] On 11 July 1923, the day before the elections were renewed, the Iraqi government resolved that all Kurdish districts should be given, before participating in the elections, three assurances:

(1) that no Arab officials should be appointed in them;
(2) that the Arabic language should not be made a compulsory language;
(3) that the rights of all communities should be duly safeguarded.[71]

These procedures in the Kurdish areas, and the reduction of the period of the Anglo-Iraqi Treaty of 1922 from twenty years to four by a protocol signed on 30 April 1923 between Iraq and Britain,[72] encouraged the High Commissioner and Iraqi government to take advantage of these developments. An election campaign arranged for King Faisal to visit Mosul on 21 May,[73] and the southern liwas during 18-29 June (Kut, Amara, Basra, Nasiriyya, Diwaniyya and Hilla).[74] On every occasion during his tour, King Faisal pointed out the danger of further delay in carrying out the elections.[75] A week before King Faisal left Baghdad, the High Commissioner had said that at no time since the establishment of the provisional government had any form of martial law prevailed in Iraq.[76]

With regard to the boycott movement leaders, they announced that the country was still under the control of the British Administrative Inspectors.[77] On 18 May 1923, notices were posted up in Kazimain, reminding the people of the existence of the anti-election Fatwas, and explained that the government wanted to bluff the people when it signed the protocol. It stated that King Faisal was shortly going to the north and south of the country to push the elections, so the people should beware.[78] In June, new Fatwas were circulated throughout the country. They declared that the decree banning the elections was still in force.[79] The Iraqi government, armed with the amendment in the Penal Code which had been passed on 9 June, giving the right to deport foreigners for political offences, resolved, in special meetings, to renew the elections after the king's tour, and to deport the foreigners who were opposing the elections.[80] Thus the government deported, on 26 June, Sheikh Mahdi al-Khalisi and his family, regarding them as Persian subjects.[81]

As a protest to the deportation, the Persian ulama in Najaf organised a general voluntary exodus of Shii priests to Persia. The Persian government protested at this, but the Iraqi government assured the Persians that the ulama would be allowed to return to Iraq after the Constituent Assembly had finished its work, except for Sheikh Mahdi al-Khalisi.[82]

Thus the British and Iraqi governments, after all these efforts, were able to renew the elections with the existence of a weak boycott movement, whose leaders' return from exile was conditional on a gurantee that they would not resist government policy.[83] The Colonial Office sent its official consent to renew the elections in Iraq, and asked the High Commissioner what procedure he proposed to adopt with regard to Kurdish districts.[84] He explained that the Kurds had quietly settled down.[85] All Mutasarrifs in the liwas gathered that the elections could be renewed without great difficulty.[86]

The Second Stage

The electoral machinery was set in motion on 12 July. The political parties held divergent attitudes at this stage, and Hizb al-Nahda stood aside as a spectator to the elections. Hizb al-Watani split. Some of its leaders, like Jaafar Abu al-Timman and Hamdi al-Pachachi, insisted that they should continue the boycott.[87] The other leaders, such as Ahmad al-Shaykh Dawood and Mawlud Mukhlis, participated in the elections as members of the opposition, but as individuals rather than as a party.[88] In other wards, King Faisal's supporters in the party preferred to go into the election. Abd al-Ghafur al-Badri, the editor of the nationalist organ, *al-Istiqlal,* joined the latter group.

Two main difficulties faced the preliminary procedures of the elections at this stage. The first was the tribes and the second was the activities of the remaining boycott elements, which were not as efficient as they had been before.

1. The tribes

The regulation of the elections regarded the tribes as a minority and gave them twenty seats out of one hundred in the Constituent Assembly, while they were the majority in the country. The sheikhs found this unjust. Furthermore, the electoral committees found it very difficult, and sometimes impossible, to distinguish the urban sector from the tribes,[89] since as minority representation was accorded to the tribes it prevented the latter from registering themselves as primary electors. The Administrative Inspector in Hilla liwa explained to the Adviser of the Ministry of the Interior that 'all the inhabitants of the Middle Euphrates are cultivators. They are also tribes-men.'[90] In fact, the large tribal section in Iraq embraced most of the agrarian population.[91] This question was of great importance, and therefore the Council of Ministers resolved on 9 August 1923, that the right to elect tribal representatives did not prevent tribesmen from participating in the elections and voting with the urban population in the ordinary way.[92] The sheikhs took advantage of this decision and registered their tribesmen by the thousand.[93] At the end of August, when the High Commissioner went on tour in the southern part of Iraq, he found satisfactory progress in the elections had been made from Baghdad to Basra.[94]

In the north, where the Kurds and Turkoman lived in Arbil, Kirkuk and Mosul liwas, some reluctance to participate appeared at first, on account of the old fear of conscription.[95] This fear had prevailed from the first stage of the elections in many parts of the country, towns and villages. The assurance from the government that the registers would not be used for conscription set these doubts at rest.[96] In Kirkuk, the main cause for hesitation in participating in the elections was the uncertainty as to whether the special conditions accorded to the Turcoman minority, when the inhabitants accepted inclusion in Iraq, would thereby be jeopardised. These privileges were that the Turcoman language – Turkish – should be the official language in Kirkuk, and the officials should be local men. The High Commissioner, in his visit to Kirkuk, assured them that these privileges would not lapse, unless the inhabitants decided voluntarily to dispense with them. A similar promise was put on record by the Ministry of the Interior. The elections, then, were carried out without further difficulty.[97]

2. The Activity of the Remaining Boycott Movement

On the second day after the resumption of the elections, anti-election notices were posted up in Kazimain bazaar. They declared that the reason for forbidding the elections was now religious rather than political.[98] It was to protest against the deportation of the ulama. These notices were quickly removed by the police;[99] similar difficulties in Najaf and Karbala had been overcome and supervising committees were formed.[100] In Hay, a qada of the Kut liwa, a very few primary electors attended to elect the secondary electors and, of these, the large majority – 817 electors – had put into ballot boxes papers declaring that the elections were *haram* (forbidden by the religious law) instead of noting the nominees' names.[101] To overcome this, a clerk was appointed to write the nominees' names for electors. The Mayor of Hay was held responsible for the boycott and for attempting to delay the elections. He was dismissed from his post.[102] In Hilla there was a great reduction in the numbers of voters. The arrest of Sayyid Abd al-Hakim, one of the Shii ulama representatives, settled the problem.[103] In Baghdad, some supervising committee members received threatening letters ordering them to resign,[104] but, with the exception of this and other two minor incidents, the elections of the secondary electors were quietly conducted. In the meantime, the dispute between the anti-treaty elements who had participated in the elections and the moderates was continued. King Faisal's supporters, who had been installed as Mutasarrifs or in other administrative posts, were helping their previous comrades in the al-Watani party. Mawlud Mukhlis, Mutasarrif of Karbala was accused by the Ministry of the Interior of interfering in the elections in favour of the opposition.[105] His announcement that the elections were entirely free and that the people could choose any candidate they preferred was regarded by British officers as a great play between the opposition and the King's clients.[106] In Mosul, the Administrative Inspector declared to the Adviser of the Ministry of the Interior that without the active backing of the Mutasarrif, Rashid al-Khuja, the opposition could not have attained their prominent position, which would affect the secondary elections on behalf of anti-treaty elements.[107] It seems that King Faisal adopted this sort of policy to reconcile the Shiis and the anti-treaty elements after the suppression of their leaders. In other words, his object was to placate the discontent against himself, and to regain his prestige as an acceptable king to his people. He even contacted, personally and secretly, the deportees' ulama to let them back to Iraq.[108] This policy led him and his colleagues to collide with the British, who were anxious to get a pro-treaty majority in the Constituent Assembly. On 31 August 1923, the High Commissioner wrote to King Faisal accusing him of endeavouring to allow the anti-treaty element in many parts of the country to get a majority in the Constituent Assembly. He warned King Faisal that this attitude should be changed the following week, and the government must declare that its policy was to ratify the treaty by the Constituent Assembly. He added that the government should notify the people of its pro-treaty candidates and guarantee their election.[109] King Faisal, in his reply, denied this accusation and emphasised that his objective was to ratify the treaty.[110] On 25 September, the Prime Minister, Abd al-Muhsin al-Saadun, declared in the newspaper *al-Iraq* that Iraq would be in a very critical situation if the treaty was not ratified. He asked the secondary electors to take this matter into account when electing the members of the Constituent Assembly.[111] On 9 October the Administrative Inspector in Mosul informed the Ministry of the Interior that the moderates had gained a majority. He declared that these results would have been the opposite if nothing had been done by the government.[112]

The policy of King Faisal concerning the reconciliation of the Shiis and the anti-treaty movement was one of the main factors which led to a crisis between King Faisal and his Prime Minister, whose Cabinet had deported the Shii leaders. On 15 November 1923 the King accepted his Prime Minister's resignation, and Jaafar al-Askari formed a new Cabinet two weeks later.[113] At the insistence of King Faisal, the Cabinet contained two Shiis, one of whom was the carrier of the ulama's letters to the King.[114] A deputation of leading Shiis of Baghdad declared to the King that they would loyally support the new Cabinet.[115] A few months later, all the exiled ulama were allowed to return to Iraq, except for Sheikh Mahdi al-Khalisi. They had undertaken to refrain from interfering in politics.[116]

The Elections of Members of the Constituent Assembly

During the elections of the secondary electors, the Adviser of the Ministry of the Interior, Cornwallis, urged, on 11 September 1923, every Administrative Inspector of the liwas to telegraph the names of candidates who were recommended by the Administrative Inspector himself and the Mutasarrif as suitable candidates who would vote for the treaty.[117] All Administrative Inspectors, with the approval of their Mutasarrifs in each liwa, sent in reply the recommended names of the candidates.[118] After consideration of these names, the Adviser of the Ministry of the Interior sent the Inspectors a list of proposed candidates for each liwa on 8 February 1924, to be elected as members of the Constituent Assembly. The same list was sent to the Mutasarrifs as well. The adviser explained that the fidelity of each candidate to the policy of the government had been guaranteed by himself or King Faisal or the Prime Minister. He added,

> Certain candidates who are commonly presumed to be extremists have been put forward on the guarantee of His Majesty, the Prime Minister or Ali Bey Jawdat [Minister of the Interior], both because they trust them and because they consider it politic to include them in the Assembly.[119]

This term 'politic' meant that the policy of the King towards the anti-treaty elements was accepted by the British now, as long as they did not have a majority in the Assembly, and would safeguard the popularity of King Faisal. Furthermore, some of these anti-treaty elements would be elected even though the government or the British did not favour them, because of their popularity or the prestige which they had gathered among their colleagues, or amongst the tribes.

As a result of the previous campaign against the existence of the Administrative Inspectors in the liwas, the British were very cautious not to incur the charge of unjustifiable influence. Therefore, the Adviser instructed the Inspectors that their activity should be amongst those whose loyalty to the British was proven. He asked them to give their assistance to the Mutasarrifs where their influence, in some questions, was larger than that of the Mutasarrif, but generally they should confine their activities to the minimum.[120]

On 25 February the elections of the representatives of the Constituent Assembly were carried out without a hitch, except in Mosul, which was overcome before the elections started.[121]

In the elections, comparing the results with the list of government candidates, 74 out of 98 government candidates were elected. Fifteen of them were anti-treaty elements, and five of the latter were not enrolled in the government candidates list. No doubt the government interfered in the elections in favour of its list, but it is very difficult to assess the extent of overt interference, or whether the Mutasarrifs and other government officials rigged and abused the ballot boxes during the elections or during the sorting-out of the ballot papers. Nevertheless, the following points could shed some light on these questions.

In the Shii district, Kuzimain, Abd al-Jabar al-Khayat, who was Christian had 32 votes, and Manahim Danial, who was a Jew had 26, while the popular Shii leaders received less than them. For example, Jaafar Abu al-Timman had 19 votes, Abd al-Husain Chalabi 16, and Abdal Ghani Kuba 14 votes. Furthermore, Sasun Hiskail, who was a Jew, gained two votes more than Abdul Ghani Kuba, and four votes more than Sayyid Muhammad Ali Hibat al-Din, who had 12 votes. This Madbata (electoral statement) of Kazimain was not signed by the supervising committee in Kazimain.[122] Nafi al-Urfali, a member of the supervising committee in Baghdad, rejected, in his notice on the original Madbata of the Baghdad liwa's delegates, the Kazimain Madbata, as it was not signed. He demanded to scrutinise the ballot papers of Kazimain,[123] but was refused.[124]

A petition was written, in which some people in Baghdad complained of the rigging of the elections in their Mahala (district). These petitions were rejected by the authorities.[125]

The newspaper *al-Istiqlal* wrote, on the occasion of the first parliamentary elections, on 20 October 1924, that everybody knew that there had been rigging and abuse in the Constituent Assembly elections.[126]

The biographies of those who had been elected as members of the Assembly show that the majority of them were grey-haired landowners, middle-aged merchants and members of the old families. About one-third of them were sheikhs of tribes. Six of the delegates were lawyers. Four ex-members of the Ottoman Chamber were elected. Three of the fifteen delegates, who had demanded the convention of the Assembly, became members of it. Six out of the members of the electoral committee, who had formulated the electoral law, were elected. Some officers who were serving with King Faisal in Syria were elected as well.

These statistics mean that the educated elements composed the minority as compared with a majority consisting mostly of illiterates or the uneducated, but this does not mean that the latter would not be active in the Assembly defending their opinion or interests.

Notes

1. Muhammad Mahdi Al-Basir, *Tarikh al-qadiyya al- Iraqiyya* (Baghdad, 1924), Vol. 1, pp. 33, 75, 99-111.

2. A.T. Wilson, *Mesopotamia, A clash of loyalties, 1917-1920* (London, 1931), pp. 251-5; Percy Cox, 'Historical Summary' in *Miss Bell, Letters* (London, 1927), Vol. II, pp. 535-6.

3. al-Basir, *Tarikh al-qadiyya,* Vol. 1, p. 149; Wilson, *Mesopotamia,* p. 255; Elizabeth Burgoyne, *Gertrude Bell, From Her Personal Papers, 1914-1926* (London, 1961), p. 137.

4. A.T. Wilson, Baghdad, to India Office, 3 June 1920 (letter) No. 65A in FO 371/E606Q; *The Baghdad Times,* 3 June 1920;

5. A.T. Wilson, Baghdad, to India Office, 3 June 1920 (letter) No. 65A in FO 371/E6060.

6. al-Basir, *Tarikh al-qadiyya,* Vol. 1, pp. 156-7; Abdul Razaq al-Hasani, *al- Iraq F.T. Dawray al-Ihtilal wa al-Intidab* (*Iraq during Occupation and Mandate*) (Syria, 1935), Vol. I, pp. 98-100.

7. *al-Iraq,* 21 June 1920; A.T. Wilson, Baghdad, to India Office, 20 June 1920 (Tel.) No. 7432 in FO 371/E7286.

8. al-Basir, *Tarikh al-qadiyya*, vol. 1, p. 178; Gertrude Bell, *Review of the Civil Administration of Mesopotamia* (London, 1920), p. 141.

9. A.T. Wilson, Baghdad, to India Office, 9 July 1920 (Tel.) No. 8284 in FO 371/E8486; *Al-Iraq,* 12 July 1920.

10. Sulaiman Faidi, *Fi ghamrat al-nidal (In the Centre of the Struggle)* (Baghdad, 1925), p. 248.

11. Bell, *Personal Papers,* p. 149.

12. al-Basir, *Tarikh al-qadiyya,* Vol. 1, p. 145.

13. *al-Iraq,* 15 November, 1930; *al-Sharq*, 15 November 1920; New Policy in Mesopotamia in FO 371/E9926.

14. *Annual Administrative British Report to the League of Nations, 1920-1922,* p. 8, in Office of the High Commissioner; Intelligence Report, secret, Baghdad, 31 December 1920, No. 4 in FO 371/E2904 (later Intelligence Report).

15. *Qararat Majlis al-Wizara al-Iraqi (The Resolutions of the Iraqi Council of State)* 13 November 1920 – 27 June 1921, secret, pp. 29, 33-4.

16 *al-Istiqlal,* 31 December, 1920, 2, 19 January, 2, 9 February 1921.

17. Intelligence Report, 13 January 1921 in FO 371/E3824 and CO 730 1/10115, *British Report to the League, 1920-1922*, p. 7.

18. F.W. Ireland, *Iraq. A study in political development*, p. 239.

19. Ireland, *Iraq*, p. 292.

20. Ibid.

21. The Secretary of State of the Colonial Office, Winston Churchill, called a conference in Cairo in March 1921, after the creation of a separate Department for Middle East Affairs in the Colonial Office, to discuss the interests and responsibilities of Britain abroad. Percy Cox attended the Conference. See *British Report to the League 1920-1922*, p. 10.

22. *Dijla,* 27, 28 June, 4 July 1921; *al-Falah,* 5 July 1921; *Lisan al-Arab,* 15 July 1921.

23. Percy Cox to Colonial Office (Tels.) 9 July 1921, nos. 280, 281 in FO 371/E8130; *British Report to the League, 1920-1922*, p. 4.

24. Intelligence Reports, 15 July, 1 August 1921, nos. 17, 18 in FO 730/ E1061, E10162.

25. Cox, Baghdad, to Colonial Office, 25 August 1921 (Tel.) No. 422 in FO 371/E9854; *al-Iraq,* 23 August 1921.

26. Cox, Baghdad, to King Faisal, 21 March, 7 May 1922 (letters) in File No. 29 in the National Archives, Baghdad.

27. *Lisan al-Arab,* 24 February 1922; *al-Istiqlal,* 12, 24 May 1922.

28. Colonial Office to British Cabinet, September 1922 (Iraq Treaty Correspondence) secret, No. 4178 in FO 371/E9258; Bell, *Personal Papers,* pp. 275-8.

29. Bell, *Personal Papers,* pp. 285, 278; *British Report to the League, 1922-1923,* p. 14.

30. Cox, Baghdad, to Colinial Office, 31 March 1922 (Tel.) No. 182 in FO 371/E3613.

31. *al-Mufid,* 8 August 1922; *British Report to the League, 1922-1923,* p. 16.

32. *British Report to the League, 1922-1923,* p. 16.

33. Ibid., p. 17; all Baghdad newspapers, 2, 3 May 1922; Intelligence Report, 15 May 1922, No. 10 in FO 371/E5937.

34. *British Report to the League, 1922-1923,* pp. 16-18.

35. *British Report to the League, 1922-1923,* pp. 15-16.

36. *al-Mufid,* 19 August 1922.

37. *al-Mufid,* 25 August 1922; Cox, Baghdad, to Colonial Office, 25 August 1922 (Tel.) No. 597, confidential, in CO 730 File 24/E42741.

38. *al-Mufid,* 23 August 1922; al-Basir, *Tarikh al-quadiyya,* Vol. 2, pp. 414-16.

39. Cox, Baghdad, to Colonial Office, 25, 26 August 1922 (Tels.) No. 598, 604 in FO 371/E9258.

40. Cox, Baghdad, to W. Churchill, 26 August 1922 (Tel.) No. 607 in CO 730 24/42829.

41. Churchill, London, to Cox, 29 August 1922 (Tel.) No. 492 in CO 730 24/E43043.

42. Churchill, London, to Cox, 2, 14 Septemberm 1922 (Tels.) Nos. 503, 524 in FO 371/E9258.

43. Cox, Baghdad, to Churchill, 10, 17 25 September 1922 (Tels.) Nos. 643, 654, 678 in FO 371/E10470; Bell, *Personal Papers,* p. 297.

44. *British Report to the League, 1922-1923,* pp. 23-5.

45. Ibid., p. 26; *al-Iraq,* 21 November 1922; Intelligence Report, 1 November 1922, No. 21, para. 1032 in FO 371/E13087.

46. *al-Hukuma al-Iraqiyya, Qanun Intikhab al-Majlis al-Ta'sisi* (Baghdad, 1923). (The Law of the Constituent Assembly Elections).

47. Intelligence Report, 1 November 1922, No. 21, para. 1046 in FO 371/E13087.

48. Bell, *Personal Papers,* p. 301.

49. *al-Iraq,* 21, 24 October 1922.

50. The Original Fatwas and their copies are in Envelope No. 49, File 115/S/1/4, National Archives, Baghdad.

51. Ibid.

52. Intelligence Reports, 1, 13 December 1922, 15 January 1923, Nos. 23, 24, 2, paras. 1157, 1204, 56 in FO 371/E14415 E14636.

53. Intelligence Report, 13 December 1922, No. 24, para. 1204 in FO 371/ E14636.

54. Ibid.

55. Intelligence Reports, 1 December 1922, 1 January 1923, Nos. 23, 1, paras. 1158, 12 in CO 730 26/63011, and 37/5193.

56. Intelligence Report, 15 January 1923, No. 2, para. 57 in CO 730, File 38/ 8360.

57. Ibid., para. 56.

58. Mutasarrif of Mosul to Ministry of Interior, Baghdad, 28 November 1922 (letters), No. 9198, File No. 10/B-2 in Ministry of Interior, Baghdad.

59. Ibid., enclosure of a copy of the Christian Fatwa and the decree of the supervising Committee in Mosul dated 25/12/1922 (No. 18).

60. Intelligence Report, 13 December 1922, No. 24, para. 1206, FO 371/ E15636; Ireland, *Iraq,* p. 392.

61. al-Basir, *Tarikh al-quadiyya*, Vol. 2, p. 485; *al-Istiqlal*, 1 June 1922.
62. *al-Iraq*, 2, 20 February 1923; *al-Asima*, 20 February 1923; *Qararat*, January–March 1923, secret, p. 84.
63. *al-Waqa i al-Iraqiyya (The Iraqi Official Gazette)*, 8 December 1922, p. 15.
64. Intelligence Report, 13 December 1922, No. 24, para. 1210 in FO 371/E14636; *British Report to the League, 1922-1923*, p. 26.
65. *British Report to the League, 1922-1923*, p. 8; Ireland, *Iraq*, pp. 391-2.
66. Cox, Baghdad, to the Iraqi Prime Minister, 1 October 1922 (letter), File No. 2/4 III in Ministry of Interior, Baghdad.
67. *British Report to the League, 1922-1923*, pp. 36-7; *British Special Report to the League*, p. 255.
68. *British Report to the League, 1922-1923*, p. 38.
69. *British Report to the League, 1923-1924*, p. 30.
70. Ibid., p. 38.
71. *Qararat*, July-September 1923, secret, p. 27.
72. *British Report to the League, 1923-1924*, p. 7.
73. *al-Istiglal*, 23 May 1923; *British Report to the League, 1923-1924*, pp. 8-9.
74. *British Report to the League, 1923-1924*, p. 10; *al-Istiqlal*, 19 June 1923.
75. *British Report to the League, 1923-1924*, p. 10.
76. *al-Asima*, 10 June 1923; *al-Istiqlal*, 11 June 1923.
77. al-Basir, *Tarikh al-qadiyya*, Vol. 2, pp. 489-90, 501..
78. Criminal Investigation Department, Baghdad, to Ministry of Interior, 18 May 1923 (Special Report, secret and urgent), No. S.B./4545, File S/1/4/2, Serial No. 114 in National Archives, Baghdad.
79. CID, Baghdad, to Ministry of Interior, 11, 16 June 1923 (Special Report, secret and Urgent), File No. s/1/4/2, Serial No. 114 in National Archives, Baghdad; *British Report to the League, 1923-1924*, p. 9.
80. *British Report to the League, 1923-1924*, pp. 10-11.
81. High Commissioner, Baghdad, to Colinial Office, 27 June 1923 (Tel.) No. 338 in FO 371/E6758; *al-Iraq*, 25, 27 June 1923; *British Report to the League, 1923-1924*, pp. 10-11.
82. *British Report to the League, 1923-1924*, pp. 11-12.
83. *British Report to the League, 1923-1924*, p. 30.
84. Colonial Office to Acting High Commissioner, 7 June 1923, (Tel.) No. 261 in CO 730, file 48/28508.
85. Acting High Commissioner, Baghdad, to Colinial Office, 16 July 1923 (Tel.) No. 370 in CO 730 41/35625.
86. Letters from the Mutasarrif of the liwas to Ministry of the Interior dated between 24 June and 9 July 1923, files S/1/4/9, Serial No. 142, S/1/4/E Serial No. 119 and S/1/4/j Serial No. 183 in National Archives, Baghdad.
87. al-Basir, *Tarikh al-qadiyya*, Vol. 2, pp. 511-612; al-Hasani, *al-Ihtilal*, Vol. 2, p. 32.
88. al-Basir, *Tarikh al-qadiyya*, Vol. 2, p. 512; *al-Iraq*, 27 June 1923.
89. Administrative Inspectors, Diwaniyya, Dulaim, Hilla, to Adviser of Ministry of Interior, 22 July, 31 July, 11 August 1923 (Memo – Confidential), Nos. 257, C/B130, 142, Files 10/2/2 in Ministry of Interior, Baghdad, S/Y4/H Serial No. 121 and S/1/4/J Serial No. 142 in National Archives.
90. Administrative Inspector, Hilla, to Adviser of Ministry of Interior, 11 August 1923 (Memo – confidential), No. S/63, File S/1/4/J, Serial No. 142 in National Archives, Baghdad.
91. *British Report to the League, 1923-1924*, p. 14.
92. *British Report to the League, 1923-1924*, pp. 14-15.
93. Ibid., p. 15.
94. Ibid., p. 14.
95. *British Report to the League, 1923-1924*, p. 14.

96. *British Report to the League, 1923-1924,* p. 14.
97. *British Report to the League, 1923-1924,* p. 14.
98. CID, Baghdad, to Adviser of Ministry of Interior, 13 July 1923 (Special Report – secret), No. S.B./1148, File S/1/4/2, Serial No. 114 in National Archives, Baghdad.
99. Ibid.
100. Adviser of Ministry of Interior, Baghdad, to High Commissioner, 8 July 1923, No. C/1427, File S/1/4/k, Serial No. 122 in National Archives, Baghdad.
101. Intelligence Report, 20 September, 1923, No. 18, para. 665 in CO 730, File 42/48109.
102. Election Report No. 4, p. 7.
q 103. Administrative Inspector of Hilla to Adviser of Ministry of Interior, 27, 29 August 1923 (Memo-secret), Nos. S/74 and S/76, File S/1/4/J, Serial No. 142 in National Archives, Baghdad.
104. Intelligence Report, 9 August 1923, No. 16, para. 580 in CO 730, 41/43775.
105. Ministry of Interior to Mutasarrif of Karbala, 1 September 1923 (Tel.) No. 13517, File S/1/4/K, Serial No. 122 in National Archives, Baghdad.
106. Mutasarrif of Karbala, to Ministry of Interior, 2 September 1923 (letters), No. 6532, File S/1/4/K, Serial No. 122 in National Archives, Baghdad.
107. Administrative Inspector of Mosul, to Adviser of Ministry of Interior, 17 July, 4 September 1923 (Memo and Election Report, secret) Nos. 291, 348, File S/1/4/B, Serial No. 156 in National Archives, Baghdad.
108. Bell, *Personal Papers,* p. 321.
109. High Commissioner Henry Dobbs to King Faisal, 31 August 1923 (letter – secret) No. 1519, File C/7/J, in National Archives, Baghdad.
110. King Faisal to High Commissioner Henry Dobbs, 3 September, 1923 (letters) File C/7/J in National Archives, Baghdad.
111. *al-Iraq,* 25 September 1923.
112. Administrative Inspector of Mosul to Adviser of Ministry of Interior, 9 October 1923 (Memo - secret), No. 381, File S/1/4/B, Serial No. 156 in National Archives, Baghdad.
113. *al-Waqa i al-Iraqiyya,* 19 November 1923.
114. Intelligence Report, 1 December 1923, No. 23, para. 830a in CO 730, File 43/60035.
115. Bell, *Personal Papers,* Vol. 2, p. 321.
116. *British Report to the League, 1923-1924,* p. 13.
117. Adviser of Ministry of Interior to Administrative Inspectors in liwas, 11 September 1923 (Tel., very secret) No. C/1974, File SB/28 (secret) in Ministry of Interior, Baghdad.
118. All the recommendations are in File SB/28 (secret) in Ministry of Interior, Baghdad.
119. Adviser of Ministry of Interior to all Administrative Inspectors, 6 September 1924 (memo – very secret), No. S.O./41, File SB/29 (secret) in Ministry of Interior, Baghdad.
120. Adviser of Ministry of Interior to all Administrative Inspectors, 10 February 1924 (memo – very secret), No. S.O./49, File No. S. 13/28 (secret) in Ministry of Interior, Baghdad.
121. Intelligence Report, 6 March 1924, No. 5, para. 154 in FO 371/e2498
122. Qaimmaqam of Kazimain, to Mutasarrif of Baghdad, 25 February 1924 (memo – secret), No. 799/1/5. Enclosure: election statement of Kazimain qada, File 1/15 in Ministry of Interior, Baghdad.
123. Election statement of Baghdad liwa, File 1/15 in Ministry of Interior, Baghdad.
124. Amin al-Asima (Mayor of Baghdad) to Ministry of Interior, 28 February 1924 (letter) No. 613/M-11, File 10/A-2 in Ministry of Interior, Baghdad.

125. Amin al-Asima to Ministry of Interior, 8 September 1924 (letters), No. 220/29/228, File 10/A-2 in Ministry of Interior, Baghdad.

126. *al-Istiqlal,* 20 October 1924.

2 FAISAL'S AMBITIONS OF LEADERSHIP IN THE FERTILE CRESCENT: ASPIRATIONS AND CONSTRAINTS

A. Shikara

This descriptive historical study can be divided into two sections: the first will deal with Faisal's attitudes and role within the context of the Arab nationalist movement in the period between the preparation for the popular (1916) Arab revolt to the conclusion of the 1930 Anglo-Iraqi Treaty relationship, and the second will deal with Faisal's aspirations and efforts between 1930 and 1933 to realise his cherished immediate objective of Iraqi-Syrian unity.

1. Faisal's Attributes and Attitudes and his Role as an Arab Leader 1913/14-1930

The formation of Faisal's pan-Arab attitudes and leadership aspirations can be traced to the era of political communication between the Arab nationalist societies and the Sharif of Mecca, Husain ibn-Ali, prior to the First World War. Faisal visited Damascus in late March 1915, where he met members of the two main secret Arab nationalist societies (al-Fatat and al-Ahad). As a result of his visit, an 'Arab Protocol' was drawn up, including the conditions upon which the Arabs pledged their support to Britain in her war against Turkey. Also, as recorded by the prominent Arab historian George Antonius, the Protocol defined the basic Arab demands upon which they would join forces with Sharif Husain. Hence, the Damascus Protocol deserves to be quoted in full because it laid the basis for the later ill-fated Anglo-Arab negotiations (best known as the McMahon-Husain correspondence) on the question of Arab independence under Sharifian suzerainty, within the context of Anglo-Arab alliance:

> The recognition by Great Britain of the independence of the Arab countries lying within the following frontiers:
>
> North: The line Mersin-Adana to parallel 37°N. and thence along the line Birejik-Urfa-Mardin-Midiat-Jazirat (Ibn Umar)-Amadia to the Persian frontier;
>
> East: The Persian Frontier down to the Persian Gulf;

South: The Indian Ocean (with the exclusion of Aden, whose status was to be maintained);
West: The Red Sea and the Mediterranean Sea back to Mersin.

The abolition of all exceptional privileges granted to foreigners under the Capitulations.
The conclusion of a defensive alliance between Great Britain and the future independent Arab state.
The granting of economic preference to Great Britain.[1]

During his visits to Damascus and Constantinople in 1915 and 1916, as his father's emissary, Faisal was seen increasingly by many nationalists as the only acceptable candidate to lead the Arabs in their great popular revolt of 1916. Furthermore, Faisal was commended and recommended by a number of British officials. Thus his wartime British companion-in-arms, Colonel T.E. Lawrence, characterised him as the 'leader who would bring the revolt to full glory'.[2] Certainly, during the 1916 Arab campaign Faisal displayed his rare qualities of leadership when he successfully managed to negotiate with various tribal factions and hence established consolidated tribal alliances in support of his cherished objective – Arab emancipation from Ottoman oppressive rule. The climax of the campaign came in 1918 when the Arab forces, with effective Allied co-operation, drove the Turks out from all Syrian territory. Soon after the entrance of the first Arab contingent to Damascus, Faisal issued his proclamation of an independent Arab government for the whole of Syria. In 1919, Faisal's efforts to build up a base for his political power in Syria was manifested in his encouragement of and guidance for the activities of the Iraqi and the Syrian members of al-Fatat who organised a political party called the Arab Independence Party. He attempted to direct his support into the channel of orderly constitutional procedure.[3] Hence, elections were held in all parts of Syria including the zone under the direct French suzerainty to establish a National Congress in Damascus, which eventually came into existence on 2 July 1919. Henceforth the Congress started to be known as the General Syrian Congress (al-Mutamar al-Suri al-Amm). This Congress passed a set of resolutions considered to be the embodiment of the most cherished Arab national aspirations. G. Antonius summarised them in the following order:

(a) recognition of the independence of Syria, including Palestine, as a sovereign state with the Amir Faisal as King; recognition of the independence of Iraq;

(b) repudiation of the Sykes-Picot Agreement and the Balfour Declaration and of any plan for the partition of Syria or the creation of Jewish Commonwealth in Palestine;

(c) rejection of the political tutelage implied in the proposed mandatory systems, but acceptance of foreign assistance for a limited period, provided it did not conflict with national independence and unity, preference being given to American or, failing American, to British assistance;

(d) rejection of French assistance in any form.[4]

These resolutions represented a more realistic assessment of the Arab political situation at that time and henceforth reflected a retraction on Faisal's original position and his attitudes in January 1919 at the Peace Conference in Paris. During the Paris Conference, Faisal expressed his total commitment to his father's attitudes and approach in reviving the Caliphate system:

> The first leaders of Arab political nationalism, particularly Sharif Husain [sic] of Mecca, envisaged, immediately before and during the First World War, an Arab State rising out of the dissolution of the Ottoman Empire, built around an Arab Muslim King and on Muslim foundations.[5]

The geographical boundaries of such a kingdom would cover vast territories, from the line of Alexandretta to Persia, southwards to the Indian Ocean. Nevertheless, the rivalries and the interests of the great powers, particularly France and Britain, blocked the realisation of Hashimite ambitions.

On 8 March 1920, the Syrian Congress passed resolutions reaffirming Arab aspirations as expressed in the July 1919 resolutions. Meanwhile, in another meeting, the Iraqi Congress passed a similar resolution concerning Iraq where Amir Abdullah (Faisal's brother) was to be its first monarch.[6] All those Iraqis, as well as Syrians, who gathered in 1920 in Damascus, clearly recognised the fact that Arab independence and unity in the form expressed at the Paris Conference were just not attainable or realistic any more. Thus the decisive factor determining the future of the Arab lands and Arab people would be made by France and Britain rather than solely by Arab Amirs or kings. Nevertheless, Damascus resolutions represented the nationalist popular will which would only be acceptable to the Arab national movement. Along this line, Faisal furnished the two great powers with assurances that Arab independence and unity would be to the advantage of the Allied powers as well as the Arab world. Despite that, he was strenuously rebuked by both Britain and France. Eventually, the latter, considerably irritated by Faisal's proclamation of the Syrian kingdom under his own leadership, decided to expel him. Clearly the era of mandatory systems, following the decisions of the Supreme Council at San Remo on 25 April 1920, had delayed the satisfaction of Arab national aspirations — independence and the unity of their nation whether in the form of an Arab confederation, or in a limited arrangement in the form of a United Arab Kingdom similar to the previous short-lived experience in Syria.

Since his installation as the new Hashimite King of Iraq on 23 August 1921, till his last days as an active ruler, Faisal devoted considerable time and energy to establishing a relatively stable and integrated community in Iraq as a vital factor in his struggle to achieve the country's political emancipation. However, his preoccupation with Iraq's domestic affairs did not at all change his cherished dynastic ambitions in the Arab world, and more particularly in the Fertile Crescent.

On Iraq's external affairs, one can, generally speaking, distinguish two major streams of thought – the pan-Arabist and the Iraqi moderate.[7]

The pan-Arabist advocated an aggressive external policy to the effect of helping other Arab countries in their twin struggle for independence, and later for their unity. Hence, the relative political independence of any Arab country would be viewed as an integral part of the Arab struggle to achieve political emancipation. The Iraqi stream of thought advocated an independent Iraqi external policy, for Iraq has its own peculiar internal conditions as a pluralistic community (i.e. a Shii community and a Kurdish community, as well as other ethnical and religious minorities). Furthermore, the country was bound by a special treaty of alliance with Britain. The so-called Iraqi school pledged co-operation with other Arab countries, but only on the understanding that each would maintain its identity and independence.

Faisal showed great sympathy with both main streams, but he found certain fundamental weaknesses in each:

> As an Arab who took active part in the various stages of the Arab nationalist movement, in Istanbul, Hijaz, and Syria, he naturally sympathised with the pan-Arab school and hoped to achieve the

independence and unity of all the Arab countries. But as the architect of the Iraqi State he hesitated to follow the hazardous foreign policy advocated by the pan-Arab school, which would expose Iraq to danger.[8]

To achieve political independence as his cardinal aim, Faisal tended to marry his conception of Arab nationalism with a European-styled *realpolitik*, and for that he took a realistically moderate and a compromising approach, as explained by Hans Kohn:

> Faisal . . . was one of the best examples of the effects of Europeanization . . . he succeeded in mediating between Europe and the unruly nationalism of his followers, and won and kept the confidence of both sides in the course of an obstinate and lengthy struggle.[9]

Faisal strongly believed that effective Anglo-Iraqi friendship and co-operation established on a mutual basis would eventually serve the interests of both parties. Hence, he regarded the 30 June 1930 Anglo-Iraqi Treaty as the corner-stone for protecting Iraq's independence, and certainly the basis of an extended Anglo-Arab friendship. Meanwhile, other Iraqi nationalists felt the treaty had introduced more shackles on the country's real sovereignty, and henceforth was an impediment to Iraq's real independence. They argued that Iraq was not yet fit to be independent, particularly as Britain had remained a powerful force influencing and directing Iraqi foreign and defence policies. Also, during the negotiations for the 1930 Treaty, Faisal showed an awareness that the indefinite prolongation of the treaty's duration would perpetuate British as well as French hegemony in Iraq and in Syria respectively, and eventually obstruct the proposed Iraqi-Syrian unity.[10]

Admittedly, in appreciating the significance of the Anglo-Iraqi Treaty relationship, Faisal was supported mainly by his close associates, such as General Nuri al-Said, General Jaafar al-Askari and Rustam Haidar. Though many Iraqi nationalists suspected and strenuously opposed the treaty, it was seen in the eyes of many Arab nationalists as a corner-stone for their countries' independence. Hence, it was greatly and enthusiastically welcomed by them, particularly when compared with their own deteriorating political situations in Syria, Palestine and Egypt.[11]

2. The Iraqi-Syrian Scheme as an Operational Immediate Objective 1930-3

Faisal remained strongly committed to achieving his relatively long-term cherished political objective of a confederation of Arab independent states, including Iraq, Syria, Transjordan, Palestine and the Hijaz. Independence was the necessary condition for any country wishing to become a member of the proposed confederation. However, for Faisal the first immediate aim would be to help Syria gain her political emancipation, and soon after, her unity with Iraq.

A. Kelidar was right in stating that Faisal 'could not readily forget his old capital, nor did his supporters – Iraqis as well as Syrians who continued to campaign for Syrian independence'.[12] He was optimistic (according to Nuri al-Said's statement in September 1932, given to a member of the staff of the Colonial Office) that within the next three years Syria would be emancipated from the French Mandate.[13] Nevertheless, Faisal was under no illusions that the French would attempt to circumscribe the limits of Syrian independence unless the pressure from the nationalist movement mounted considerably, to force the French to completely relinquish their Mandate from all of Syria. Accordingly, Syria would be treated on similar terms as those granted to Iraq.

The trend towards the unification of the Arab countries of the Fertile Crescent was strengthened by the influx of many exiled Arab nationalists. For them, Baghdad was the natural outpost which would help satisfy their aspirations in the independence and unity of their divided and fragmented country, Greater Syria (Bilad al-Sham). Hence, they earnestly sought the unity of Greater Syria and Iraq under Faisal's leadership. For Faisal, the Fertile Crescent unity has enormous advantages of not only sustaining the shaky foundations of Iraq's independence, but would in the not too distant future enhance his own position in the Arab world. J. Malone clearly identified the advantages of his unity to Faisal:

> Faysal was convinced of the advantages to be gained by mobilising the Sunni majority to end the precarious nature of Baghdad-based minoritarian governments; he recognised that a greater Arab majority would reduce the Kurdish problem to manageable proportions, and he knew the value of Syrian entrepreneurial skills, intellectual attainments and diversified resources. He knew too, that he could combine all these resources in an association latterly made attractive by the prospect of Iraqi oil resources.[14]

To establish an Iraqi-Syrian unity, rapprochement should be promoted with the main Arab countries, particularly those in the Fertile Crescent. However, the pro-Sharifian Syrian nationalists (i.e. Shakib Arsalan, Ihsan al-Jabiri, etc.) were very keen on seeing the dynastic feud between the Hashimite and the Saudis terminated. Certainly the meeting, organised by the British, between Faisal and Ibn Saud on board H.M.S. Lupin on 21 February 1930, settled some of their deep dynastic differences, and other salient points have been summarised by H.C. Sinderson Pasha in the following manner:

> The clauses of the draft agreement, nineteen in all, included mutual recognition of the independence of the two countries; the exchange of diplomatic representatives; the outlawing of tribal raiders; the extradition of refugees or fugitives from justice; the establishment of a permanent frontier commission; an undertaking to settle disputes arising from the interpretation of the treaty by arbitration only; compensation to Iraq for damage caused by Nejdi raiders, and, in the event of claims not being satisfactorily settled before the close of the Haj (annual pilgrimage to Mecca), an arbitration court to be held at Kuwait consisting of five members, one being British, for their settlement; the acceptance by Nejd of Iraq's point of view concerning frontier posts; and, in the event of agreement not being reached within six months, the dispute to be referred to a five-man court whose decisions should be binding. A final clause granted pardon to Ibn Mashur and other refugees on their liberation by Iraq.[15]

This agreement helped ease the tension in the area. Only four months had elapsed since the conclusion of the 1930 treaty when Iraq's Prime Minister, Nuri al-Said, announced the intention of his government to work for the establishment of an Arab alliance (al-Hilf al-Arabi) between Iraq, Transjordan, the Hijaz and Najd.[16] In the spring of 1931, Nuri embarked on a much-publicised visit to Transjordan, Palestine and also Egypt, during which he explained his proposed plan and urged that all the Arab states would some day work much more closely together. The outcome of his visit was the conclusion in 1931 of a number of treaties of friendship, bon voisinage and extradition.[17]

Meanwhile, Faisal was fully cognisant of the need to translate pan-Arab aspirations into reality by the process of convening Arab conferences. Through these summit meetings Faisal's plan of unity would be clarified and gain legitimacy all over the Arab world. Within this context, Faisal sent Yasin al-Hashimi as his special envoy in a visit to the Arab countries (i.e. Jerusalem, Cairo and Damascus) in order to propagate the need to convene an Arab conference (congress) in Baghdad. While he was in Jerusalem, al-Hashimi spoke in an interview with the representative of *al-Jami'a al-Islamiyya* the Muslim League newspaper in Palestine, about the initial essential aim for convening such a congress: 'If the [proposed] Arab Conference succeeds in awakening the nation and making it realise [sic] its defects and the dangers surrounding it, it will have accomplished the first part of the task [? before it].'[18] The Congress would also provide Faisal with a favourable form for demonstrating the reality of Iraq's independence, thereby weaning the Arabs from the suspicion of Iraq pursuing an excessively pro-British policy.

Apart from Cairo, Faisal's proposal of an Arab congress was met with enthusiastic welcome in the countries of the Fertile Crescent. But the congress eventually failed to convene largely due to the Great Powers' opposition.[19]

When coming to analyse the proposed scheme, one could not escape the conclusion that the political structure had not been clearly defined either by Faisal or by his close associates (pro-Sharifians). Hence, though the objective was crystal clear in the mind of Faisal and the pro-Sharifians, nothing substantial was revealed. As Humphrey says:

> Whether this is to be done by uniting them under his own rule or by placing another member of his family on the Syrian Throne and then bringing the two countries into close alliance, I do not think he [Faisal] has yet decided, though certainly the first alternative would find greater favour with him. His objective is fixed, but the means whereby it is to be obtained are likely to be adapted to the tendencies of current events.[20]

A clearer definition of the political structure of an identical unity project came later in 1942, when Nuri al-Said, Iraq's prominent Prime Minister, submitted a proposal of Arab unity on federal lines to Mr Casey, the British Minister of State in the Middle East.[21] However, during Faisal's reign, the vital thing was how to assert his leadership in the Fertile Crescent in the face of inter-Arab dynastic and personal rivalries. A serious challenge to Faisal came from his own older brother, Abdullah (the ruler of Transjordan). Abdullah apparently was greatly unpopular among the Arab nationalists because of his negative stand on the Syrian popular Druze Revolt between 1925 and

1927, and also owing to his amicable relations with the Zionists in Palestine.[22]

The other official contestants did not produce a real challenge to Faisal's candidature (i.e. Sharif Ali, the older brother of Faisal and the ex-King of Hijaz, King Fuad of Egypt and Abbas Hilmi, the ex-Kedive of Egypt). It should be emphasised that the success or failure of any unity project in the Fertile Crescent largely depended on the challenge of Ibn Saud. The relative normalisation of Faisal-Ibn Saud relations led the latter to display a flexible and a more moderate attitude towards the question of Fertile Crescent unity. Hence the latter was not an officially recognised candidate. Though the name of his son, Amir Faisal, was mentioned as a candidate, Ibn Saud himself seemed not to have taken much interest in the matter.[23] When Faisal eventually realised that he was the sole favourable candidate for the Syrian throne, he decided to canvass as much support as possible in order to assert his leadership in Syria. In August 1931 he went to Europe, ostensibly to get Iraq admitted to the League of Nations, but in reality he strenuously worked to achieve his personal ambitions. He met his Syrian associates in Paris (i.e. the Lebanese Druze Amir Shakib Arsalan, the Syrian Ihsan al-Jabiri, President and member, respectively of the Syrian-Palestinian delegation at Geneva, and also a Syrian nationalist leader associated with the republicans' Faris al-Khuri).[24]

In Paris, Faisal was addressed by the French officials as 'King of Iraq and Syria' and 'King of all the Arabs'.[25] Faisal returned to Baghdad fully satisfied with his apparently fruitful visit to Europe. This led to widespread rumours that Faisal's kingship over Syria and Iraq was indeed imminent. Therefore the Syrian nationalists, who had at their head Rustam Haidar, the man closest to Faisal, engineered a propaganda campaign among the Muslim Syrian population in support of the proposed unity. The initial success of the campaign was reflected in great public enthusiasm in favour of a monarchical system, and more so when the French High Commissioner decided to hold elections in 1931. On the eve of the elections in December, groups of royalists carrying pictures of Faisal held parades in the streets of Damascus.[26] Meanwhile Arabic newspapers in Iraq, Syria and Palestine published various articles to welcome the proposed unity. The short-lived high public enthusiasm for the scheme can be explained by the Syrians' strong desire to utilise Faisal's skilful ability to negotiate for their political emancipation with the two concerned Great Powers, France and Britain.

Meanwhile, most of the Syrian nationalists represented by the

National Bloc refused to dispense with their idealist Republican principle. This proved to be a serious obstacle to the proposed Iraqi-Syrian unity, particularly as the influence and the appeal of pro-Sharifian Syrian elements increasingly declined. Hence, when the National Bloc discussed the proposed scheme, it decided to reject it, and eventually to abandon it.

In Palestine, there was another serious obstacle to the proposed Iraqi-Syrian unity: 'so far as the Arabs in Palestine are concerned, they are too much occupied with their Jewish question to be really interested in any schemes for union'.[27] Furthermore, the situation continued to be politically unstable as a result of the failure to settle the Jewish question. Faisal's main intention to settle the Jewish question (as a preliminary matter for negotiating with the British for the emancipation of Palestine) through a plan of setting up an Arab confederation where Jews and Palestinians could settle peacefully never materialised.

Among the non-advocates of a strictly autonomous Lebanese political system was Riyad al-Sulh, a Lebanese advocate of Syrian unity, and later Prime Minister of Lebanon. Al-Sulh expressed his support for Faisal's unity scheme when he 'declared in Jaffa that Faisal was the leader of those working for the Arab cause and that when the Arab nations finally were working together, a King would be necessary as union was not attainable under a republic'.[28]

Finally, in Iraq (apart from the Sharifians and pro-Sharifian elements), the Iraqis in general felt that they themselves would be the losing side, while the Syrians would enjoy immense eco-political advantages from such a project. E.B. Main wrote in 1933:

> Iraq is no doubt richer (particularly with new potential oil reserves) than Syria, but the Syrians are more advanced than the Iraqis, and union would mean that the Syrians would simply move across to Baghdad and pick up the best jobs, returning in due time to their own pleasanter country. Such a prospect naturally does not commend itself to the Iraqis, who are looking for advancement themselves.[29]

The analysis of the Iraqi-Syrian scheme of unity would not be complete without an assessment of the role and the reaction of Britain and France.

Since the 1920s, a number of British officials had delivered various lectures in which they advocated not Iraqi-Syrian unity, but the formation of an unclearly defined union between Syria and Palestine (including at that time Transjordan). The proposal, for good economic reasons, gained favourable response among a number of British commercial and financial sectors. Their response was reflected in the *Near East* (a journal reflecting viewpoints on British commercial and imperial interests).[30] Eventually the same journal in 1927 accepted the inclusion of Iraq in the proposed unity. The British, who displayed sympathy with the project, thought of its political structure developing on federal lines. Thus Syria, Palestine and Transjordan were considered one natural unit, which ought to be linked with Iraq.[31] Though by 1931 the mechanism for the political settlement of problems was formulated, federal political unity presented considerable difficulties. Meanwhile, authors such as Pierre Rondot thought that by the 1920s the British had already given too much encouragement in the way of fulfilling Arab national aspirations.[32] But the plain fact was that Arab nationalism and Iraq's emancipation, if it had ever blossomed, was only to the extent that it served British interests (i.e. international 'imperial' communications and oil) *vis-à-vis* France and other 'Great Powers'. At the same time, Britain seemed quite anxious to maintain the *status quo* in the Arab East by not antagonising the French over the question of Iraqi-Syrian unity under Faisal's leadership.[33]

From the British point of view, Faisal's high optimism over the proposed unity scheme did not seem to be well founded. Thus, Faisal did not receive any official response from London to his previous request for advice on his future conduct over the question of Iraqi-Syrian unity. Instead, the British Ambassador was kept informed by British officials in London on their discussions to refuse the proposed unity. These discussions were only for Humphrey's personal information and guidance, and not for communication to Faisal or the Iraqi government. In October and November 1931, both the Standing Official Sub-Committee on Middle East Affairs and the Middle East Sub-Committee of the Committee of Imperial Defence formulated the decisions of refusal, which can be summarised as follows:

(1) that the most desirable outcome would be the Constitution of Syria as a republic with a Syrian as President;
(2) that for a single individual to hold the crowns of both Syria and Iraq would be most undesirable and would, in any case, be likely to prove unworkable;
(3) that any attempt by King Faisal to transfer his crown from Iraq to Syria would be contrary to British interests;
(4) that, should the crown of Syria be offered to ex-King Ali, no

grounds existed for opposing his candidature.[34]

Finally, it would be relevant to state briefly the French policy with regard to the questions of political independence and Arab unity. Their stand on these vital issues will not be fully known until the French documents on the concerned period be released. However, it is clear that French policy in relation to Syria and Lebanon had eventually, from 1936, followed a similar pattern to that of Britain with Iraq (i.e. treaty relationship). With regard to the verbal overtures made to Faisal in 1931, the French actually did not make any positive initiative or commitment for supporting Faisal's bid for leadership in the Fertile Crescent. The French soon realised the negative ramifications of encouraging Faisal to be the king of an Iraqi-Syrian unity, largely owing to his British connection. Thus 'Faysal with his British connections, and the more virile Iraqis with theirs, would be likely to dominate the Syrian portion of the new state, thereby replacing French influence by British.'[35]

Conclusion

Faisal played a distinct role in the Arab nationalist movement since the preparation of the Great Arab Popular Revolt in 1916, and until his last days as an effective ruler of Iraq.

His bitter early political as well as diplomatic experience with the two Great Powers, Britain and France, came to light at the Peace Conference in Paris in 1919, which culminated in his expulsion by the French Mandated authorities from Syria in 1920. His first Arab United Kingdom in Damascus collapsed, and with it his and his father's (Sharif Husain Ibn Ali of Hijaz) aspiration to achieve Arab unity under the Sharifian (Hashimites) suzerainty was delayed. Hence, Faisal's installation as the first Hashimite King of Iraq in 1921 made him more realistic in his approach for achieving his dynastic pan-Arab aspirations. Iraq's independence was a high priority in his struggle to achieve Arab independence and Arab unity, and for that he tended to marry his conception of Arab nationalism with a European-style *realpolitik*. Hence, Faisal perceived the 1930 Anglo-Iraqi Treaty as not only a solid indication that the country was on the verge of political emancipation, but that once again he would be able to pursue his dynastic aspirations in the Arab world. Between 1930 and 1933, Faisal's immediate operational objective was a federal Iraqi-Syrian unity as an essential step towards realising his cherished ideal of an Arab confederation under Hashimite suzerainty. But his scheme was not carefully articulated and, more seriously, it lacked sufficient popular support (apart from the pro-Sharifians and pro-royalist Iraqi and Syrian elements) in the countries of the Fertile Crescent. Furthermore, apart from the Arab interpersonal dynastic rivalries, Faisal's plan of unity was met with strenuous opposition by the two Great Powers, which eventually directed a fatal blow to his pan-Arab aspirations.

Notes

1. George Antonius, *The Arab Awakening* (London, Hamish Hamilton, 1938), pp. 157-8.
2. T.E. Lawrence, *Revolt in the Desert* (Garden City, N.Y., Publishing Company, 193?), p. 18.
3. Antonius, *Arab Awakening*, p. 292.
4. Ibid., pp. 293-4.
5. Zeine N. Zeine, *The Emergence of Arab Nationalism* (Beirut, Khayats, 1966), p. 151.
6. *The Political Awakening in the Middle East*, George Lenczowski (ed.) (Englewood Cliffs, N.J., Prentice-Hall 19??), p. 73.
7. Majid Khadduri, *Independent Iraq* second edition (London, Oxford University Press, 1960), p. 307.
8. Ibid.
9. Hans Kohn, *Western Civilisation in the Near East* (New York, Columbia University Press, 1936), pp. 277-8.
10. Khaldun S. Husry, 'King Faysal I and Arab Unity, 1930-33', *Journal of Contemporary History* Vol. 10, No. 2 (April 1975), p. 323.
11. Ibid., p. 326.
12. A. Kelidar, 'The Arabian Peninsula in Arab and Power Politics', *The Arabian Peninsula Society and Politics*, Derek Hopwood (ed.) (London, George Allen and Unwin, 1972), p. 149.
13. Husry, 'King Faysal I', p. 331.
14. Joseph J. Malone, *The Arab Lands of Western-Asia* (Englewood Cliffs, N.J., Prentice Hall, 1973), p. 85.
15. Harry C. Sinderson, *Ten Thousand and One Nights* (London, Hodder and Stoughton, 1973), pp. 121-2.
16. Clarence Ernest Dawn, 'The Project of Greater Syria', unpublished Ph.D. thesis, Department of Oriental Languages and Literatures, Ann Arbor, Michigan University, 1948, pp. 16-17.
17. Husry, 'King Faysal I', p. 324.
18. FO 371/16902/6840.
19. Husry, 'King Faysal I', p. 333.
20. FO 371/16854, Humphrys, Baghdad, 5 January 1933, cited in Husry 'King Faysal I', p. 332.
21. See, for more details, Nuri al-Said, *Arab Independence and Unity* (Baghdad, 1943).
22. Husry, 'King Faysal I', p. 327.
23. Ibid.
24. Dawn, 'Project of Greater Syria', p. 17.
25. Husry, 'King Faysal I', p. 326.
26. Dawn, 'Project of Greater Syria', p. 17.

27. E.B. Main: 'Iraq: A Note', *Journal of the Royal Central Asiatic Society,* XX (July 1933), p. 434.
28. Dawn, 'Project of Greater Syria', p. 18.
29. Main, 'Iraq: A Note', p. 434
30. Dawn, 'Project of Greater Syria', p. 31.
31. Ibid., p. 32.
32. Pierre Rondot, *The Changing Patterns of the Middle East 1919-1958,* trans. Mary Dilke (London, Chatto and Windus, 1961), p. 84.
33. Husry, 'King Faysal I', p. 333.
34. Ibid., p. 330.
35. Ibid., p. 331.

3 THE USE OF GERMAN AND BRITISH ARCHIVES IN THE STUDY OF THE MIDDLE EAST: THE IRAQI COUP D'ETAT OF 1936

H.H. Kopietz

I

To students of the Middle East the papers of the British public records have for a long time constituted an invaluable source. Since the late sixties, when the British government reduced the previous fifty-year rule to a mere thirty years, the study of the Middle East was transformed into a thriving industry as the historian and his colleagues obtained access to a huge range of materials going up to the 1940s. The records of the German archives have been examined however, to a much smaller extent, although they also go up to 1945. Other than students of diplomatic history, the Ottoman Empire, or specific aspects of the activities by the Third Reich[1] in the area, little attention has been paid to the materials, which, if used comparatively, could provide new perspectives and interpretations.

This pertains especially to the intelligence assessments by not only the political and military establishments, but by the large international organisations, who, like so many others, were trying to break, or at least substantially reduce, Anglo-French commercial monopolies. (This point will be dealt with below). As will be shown, these large corporations frequently kept their own political and economic research departments, the records of which obviously could shed important new light on the socio-economic transformations as well as the nature of the imperial economies.

Some would argue that the ready availability of the political records has seduced Middle East scholars to concentrate too much on the political aspects of the region's history. It cannot be denied that the diplomatic machinations and manoeuvrings between the involved powers are fascinating, but one does not have to subscribe to the materialist school to see that political history is largely dependent on the economic, geopolitical and strategic factors. It is for this reason that all possible sources should be consulted. Too many Ph.D. dissertations and monographs have exclusively relied on the Public Records Office, without proper evaluation of and comparisons to other European – not to speak of Middle Eastern – archives. That the latter are often inaccessible or difficult to use is of course recognised, but this in itself would seem to strengthen the argument.

The use of the German archives is hindered by several factors. The language barriers the most obvious. Perhaps more daunting is the problem of the archival organisation.[2] Notwithstanding its reputation for efficiency and organisation, the German bureaucracy, especially during the Third Reich, presents itself to researchers in the form of a Byzantine labyrinth. In contrast, the PRO is like a pleasant stroll through Kew Gardens. The German labyrinth can be explained in terms of German legalism, the vicissitudes of German history and the advent of the Nazi Party to power. Furthermore, most of the German records, in so far as they existed when the Allied forces captured them in 1945, subsequently travelled widely, ending up dispersed throughout Europe, the USA and the USSR. Today, however, the bulk of the archives are located in Bonn, Koblenz, Freiburg and Berlin. Other materials can be found in specialised research centres (such as Paris) as well as the important collections in the German Democratic Republic. Moreover, many of the papers can be found in publications of the series on *Documents on British Foreign Policy* or the *Documents on German Foreign Policy*. These, however, have to be used with great circumspection. While they are highly commendable and useful to the generalist and the diplomatic historian, they have relatively little use when employed for specialist studies, as they are more concerned with the larger and global political developments than with the political peripheries. Also, they often reflect the interests of the editorial committees and, as so often is the case, that memorandum seemingly insignificant to the generalist becomes highly significant to the specialist. This becomes especially important in the German case. It is for this reason that we have selected the *coup* of 1936, as it serves as a good example of how two divergent – and opposing – diplomatic missions recorded the event.

Before going into this, however, we shall deal more specifically with aspects of the German records, followed by a brief excursion into the nature of the British archives.

II

Historians, and their colleagues, still face a considerable task in the reconstruction of the historical forces which have shaped the recent Middle East. This task is made more difficult by currents of ideological considerations and philosophical and methodological differences, as well as the availability of sources. Perhaps more than any other geographical area of the world, historical studies are rent by factional and ideological disputes, personality and ethnic differences. Therefore it is suggested in this chapter that the careful utilisation of a greater variety of material might diminish these differences to some extent. However, until all the archives throughout Europe have been made available to the historian, definitive studies cannot be expected.

For political and other reasons, some European countries (France and Italy, for instance) still withhold many of their records from investigators. Other sources, such as those in Arabic, Hebrew, Turkish and even Farsi are becoming increasingly available. But we still have to await the full disclosure of Belgian, Dutch, French, Italian and, of course, Russian sources. These are not only relevant to the political historian, but especially to the socio-economic historian. Each of the above-mentioned countries had specific political, financial and strategic interests, and these records could further our understanding of not only the diplomatic machinations, but especially the imperial and colonial economies and their impact on the local political and economic structures. Moreover, many of the diplomatic and consular representatives serving in the Middle East had personal, if not economic, interests at stake, and their observations of both the local situation and the personalities can be useful. Company files, for instance, have not been extensively used by students of the Middle East, with a few exceptions, such as the important work by David S. Landes, *Bankers and Pashas.*[3]

The above argument is perhaps stating the obvious. A cursory review of the literature will show this unfortunate oversight in Middle East historical scholarship. Political history, while important on its own, is insufficient to explain the nature of political and social processes. And as we learn increasingly more about the nature of economic imperialism and its function in the development of Afro-Asia, it is these sources which become crucial. Moreover, as political interrelationships and commercial transactions are highly personalised – and not only in the Middle East – these archives shed important insights on the direction of political and economic changes.

Mussolini's government, for instance, used Italy's considerable presence in Egypt and its historical association with this country as a launching pad for Italian revisionism and cultural as well as territorial expansion. With an Italian presence of around 70,000 in 1935 and a close relationship between the Italian and Egyptian royal houses, this constituted a valuable starting-point. King Fuad had been a student before the First World War in Turin, as well as having been an officer in Rome. It was therefore not surprising that he and his son, King Farouk, should surround themselves with an Italian-based entourage, which included the Anglo-Italian financier Sir Robert Rollo and Ernesto Verucci Bey (the official royal architect and a suspected Italian secret agent). Austria, on the other hand, had been host to numerous members of the Ottoman and Arab élite (frequently ensconced in the Maria-Theresium Gymnasium in Vienna) before the First World War. During the inter-war years these graduates of the Habsburg Empire often retained close contacts with their erstwhile schoolmates, many of whom themselves had attained high political and commercial office. Thus, like the 'old boy network' of the Etonians, the Ottoman and Arab élite maintained, and in some cases still maintains, close and useful associations.

The economic historian can perhaps profit even more by analysing the trade Ministries' records of the many large corporations, such as Krupp, I.G. Farben, the railroad archives, etc. They contain large amounts of correspondence and financial records which detail on a daily basis their transactions and objectives.[4] Surely, their impressions of politicians and prominent businessmen cannot be dismissed? In some cases the nature of imperial economic competition becomes even humorous, as in the following example. When the Third Reich reinstated the German *Drang nach Osten,* trade and propaganda became the most conspicuous element of this policy, at least in the perception of the British and French interests. Thus, when I.G. Farben had developed a new serum against syphilis, a German contract with the Iraqi Health Ministry was stopped by the British Embassy. Or when the German industrial group Otto Wolff considered the development of iron-ore deposits in Egypt, the British Chancery considered this to be a threat to their own economic, and, potentially to their military interests and prevented the negotiations. Other archival material may produce even more startling information. The *Schutzstaffel* (SS), as the proclaimed guardian of Germany's national virtue, morality and security on a global scale, monitored Church and sectarian politics. Thus there exist memoranda on the Freemasons, the Jews and the Copts in Egypt, some of which are written by prominent academics or are translations of contemporary articles in other languages. A careful screening of these SS records may reveal other interesting material, as this Nazi institution also felt compelled to investigate the personal lives of prominent individuals.[5] The reason for this is self-evident: as the SS was considered the praetorian guard of the Third Reich, and thus responsible for the elimination or at least curtailment of any potential enemy of the state, these designated as such were subject to the scrutiny of the organisation. Thus it is not surprising to find departments which dealt with 'Kirchen, Sekten, Emigranten, Juden, Logen', 'Kommunismus und marxistische Gruppen', as well as 'Bekämpfung der Homosexualität und Abtreibung'. But while these archival materials may provide another angle and some comic relief to the historian, the more important material can be found in the German Foreign Office and related institutions.

As in most countries, the traditional institution responsible for the conduct of foreign, and the execution of political and diplomatic objectives, is the Foreign Office or its equivalent. But with the seizure of power by the NSDAP in 1933, the *Aussenamt* (AA) was challenged by competing party institutions, who regarded the AA either as incapable or ideologically untrustworthy of following the dictates of the party hierarchy.These competitive party institutions, often feeling themselves to be the true executives of the ideological line (which few really did understand) found themselves in constant conflict with each other.[6] During more normal times, relatively free of ideological and party impositions, the functions of the various bureaucracies were clearly delineated, and a certain amount of co-ordination existed between the various Ministries and departments. With the advent of the Nazi government, co-operation was seriously impaired as party functionaries moved in or parallel institutions were established. Moreover, their jurisdiction and responsibilities in many cases overlapped, causing further institutional clashes and tensions.

With regard to the Middle East, several new departments were created, either within the context of new Ministries or the re-organisation of existing ministries. To give an indication of the complexity of the available archives, a brief review of the most important departments dealing with the Middle East or Islamic affairs is in order.[7]

The Auswärtiges Amt (AA)

Until 1935, the *Orient Department* was largely responsible for Middle Eastern affairs, i.e. within Abteilung III; after the reorganisation of the AA in May 1936, the Orient department became part of Politische Abteilung VII; some departments were expanded, the most relevant being *Referat Deutschland.* Although ostensibly responsible for internal matters, the papers contain the discussions regarding the invitation lists to the annual *Reichsparteitag,* and a large number of sketches of Arab personalities, some of which include rather personal details.

The Aussenpolitische Amt (APA, headed by Alfred Rosenberg)

This organisation instituted several departments dealing with the Middle

East, such as *Kolonialvölker, Asien Süd-ost Probleme, Naher Osten* and *Orient* (which oddly included Egypt, Asia Minor and other areas as far as India). To the best of my knowledge these records, as far as they exist, have not been scrutinised. Individual records appear in other departments, such as the papers of the *Reichskanzelei* (located in Koblenz).

Auslandsorganisation der NSDAP (AO)

Ostensibly the AO was concerned with German expatriates, i.e. their politicisation within the guidelines of official ideology, and their political support for the Reich. In the course of time, however, the AO gained considerable influence in the formulation of foreign policy, and in some cases even controlled local diplomatic representatives. The organisation maintained its own *South-East European Department* which included the areas of the Balkans, Turkey, Persia, Arabia and Egypt, as well as Libya and Malta. An interesting aspect is that German expatriates constituted an asset to German foreign policy in that the party representatives constituted a controlling factor in the execution of foreign policy. Thus in the case of Iraq, the AO representative, Dr Jordan (also attached to the Iraqi Antiquities Department), in some cases actually had to approve the despatches of the German legation.[8]

In addition to these Ministries, other organisations dealt *inter alia* with aspects of the Middle East. Few of those have been used for research purposes of the area. The AO, for instance, had departments dealing with German youth movements, lecturer series, cultural activities (which in theory should have been part of the Ministry of Propaganda) and even the activities and role of German womanhood abroad. Moreover, the AO maintained separate sections on Palestine dealing mostly with the problem of *Haavara.* In other words, the German records as far as they concern the Middle East warrant a thorough re-examination, especially as most Ministries and departments overlap, and as they represent different political or ideological interests. Even the Deputy to the Führer, Rudolf Hess, maintained a separate Bureau for Foreign Policy, although in reality his powers were rather limited.[9]

The Ministry for Propaganda

This Ministry, headed by the Mephistophelean Dr Goebbels, had its own departments dealing with the Islamic world and the Middle East. One of the most significant offices, an adjunct to the Ministry, namely the Anti-Comintern Organisation, also headed by Dr Goebbels, surveyed political activity in south-east Europe, which included the Middle East.

The Schutzstaffel (SS)

The SS operated perhaps the most peculiar departments. Its major concern was the identification and isolation of anti-German and anti-Fascist elements, and as such reflected perhaps more than any other institution the ideological and political demeanour of the régime. Thus it established departments along thematic lines which could include practically all universal problems, as seen by the Nazi hierarchy. The agencies dealing with matters such as 'Communism and other Marxist Groups' or 'Churches, Sects, Emigrants, Jews and Masons' reveal interesting intelligence reports, which if used cautiously and in conjunction with British records, might throw some new light on particular movements or personalities in the Middle East. One should not underestimate their reports, as some of them were intelligently done, and some go into great detail, as the one dealing with the Freemasons in the Middle East has shown. One document, for instance, compiled by the security police, which dealt with the *Kirchenpolitische Lage in Aegypten,* constitutes a considerable effort on their part, and is by and large quite remarkable in its interpretation. Copies of this report were found in the AA, *Deutschland Abteilung.*

Other files which have not been utilised are those to be found in Reichs-Youth Leadership, the trade ministries, and the military institutions. More difficult to obtain are the records of the *Abwehr,* the Intelligence Service, which also maintained their own observations on the Middle East.[10]

The above outline suffices to indicate the complexity of the German records. In spite of the numerous studies on German foreign policy, little attention has been paid to the structural aspects, with the notable exception of Jacobsen's work. Itis this work, in conjunction with other reference works such as those by G. Kent, which can provide a fairly good guide through the maze of German archives. Yet there are several other pitfalls the student of Middle Eastern studies has to avoid.

Unlike the British system, in which each communication from the field staff would individually be docketed and minuted, along with the reply or instructions, the German files very often lack one or the other. On the other hand, it is possible to find elements of the correspondence in totally unrelated files. This was in part a reflection of the bureaucratic confusion, as well as personal insecurities. Despatches requiring policy decisions would be passed on to the superiors, such as the Secretaries of State, but seldom as high as the Führer himself. Only during the war did he take the majority of foreign policy decisions. It is therefore imperative that all files are consulted, since otherwise a large amount of material may be overlooked.

An example of political and ideological conflicts between the various institutions can be gleaned from the following example. Al-Nadi al-Arabi, a patriotic and in some senses ultra-nationalist pan-Arab club situated in Damascus, requested financial and military assistance from the German authorities. One of its leaders, Dr Imman, a German-trained dentist, had contacted the German Consul in Beirut, a Herr Seiler, who, as the official representative, should have contacted the AA via official channels. But probably knowing the cautious attitude of the AA, especially the attitude of the departmental head, Dr O. von Hentig, Seiler referred the matter to the local AO representative Geiger, who in turn issued letters of introduction. By the time Dr Imman travelled to Germany, Geiger, however, was the AO representative in Paris. From there, he referred the matter to a Herr Knothe in the Ministry of Propaganda, with perfunctory copies of the correspondence to Herr Dr von Hentig in the AA, the War Ministry and *Dienstelle Ribbentrop.*

The document shows several problems. No replies or any indication on the action taken are available, unless they are in the files of the Ministry of Propaganda, some of which are located in the German Democratic Republic. Moreover, this case indicates clearly how dispersed the records are, and how incomplete as a consequence the files in many cases are. The researcher therefore must investigate all possibly related files, even if they appear irrelevant. Obviously, the case also indicates the political struggles within and amongst the Ministries. That the Ministry of Propaganda should be contacted for military and financial support only emphasises its rapidly growing power. Equally important, at least for a time, was the APA, which repeatedly clashed with the AA. A case in point was the dispute over arms supply to and trade with Saudi Arabia, which the AA considered unwise but which the APA urged.

To summarise, therefore, we would argue that while many documents have been published in various collections, and while extensive microfilms of the records are available (in London, Washington, etc.) for the students of Middle Eastern history, they do not suffice. When the war ended and the records were captured they were rapidly photographed, mostly with an eye to the Nuremberg trials. Consequently much which did not appear relevant was overlooked. It is thus imperative that the originals are consulted. The latter are also much easier to read. Furthermore, it is imperative that the nature of the inter- and intra-institutional conflict is considered when evaluating the records. While this of course also applies to the British records, in the German case, due to the nature of the régime, this is considerably more critical.

Unlike the German records, the British archives are well organised and easy to use. Series FO 371 (general correspondence in the Foreign Office) is probably the most useful for the political historian, along with the records of the Cabinet, the Consular files, or the Private Correspondence. As in the German case, the economic and trade papers have not been extensively used. For Iraq, the intelligence summaries provided by the RAF station in Hinaida can be useful, but are frequently marred by considerable inaccuracies, and thus must be used with caution. There is, however, one frustrating element. For whatever reason, and in many cases this is inexplicable, many papers and whole files are withheld, often for long periods. In contrast, most German files are open to inspection, with the major exception of personnel records, although there exists a source of frustration as the present AA sits for long periods on some files.

Two final observations must be made before proceeding to the *coup* of 1936. Anyone who has used the British files will have encountered the frequent racial slurs by the diplomatic staff in the field as well as at home. By and large, and perhaps surprisingly, the German records are free of derogatory remarks. Perhaps the explanation is that, at least in the case of the Middle East, the diplomatic staff had, like so many other Germans, a romantic attachment to the peoples of the area. Another explanation could be that many of the German diplomats were well trained in the history of the areas, and many were fluent in the local languages. Although Dr Grobba, the Ambassador to Iraq, earned himself an unsavoury reputation, he was well trained, as was the aristocrat Dr O. von Hentig, who was a philologist in his own right.

The second observation is more in the nature of a reiterated plea. The economic papers, such as trade, commercial contracts, business records, etc., warrant the urgent attention of the historian. Masses of materials are available, and not only those within the diplomatic archives. The Chambers of Commerce throughout the Middle East, as well as in Europe, have hardly been touched, although they are easily available, even in the Middle East. Nor have the archives of companies been used. To given an indication of the wealth of materials available, the following records could be of great historical interest:[11]

I.G. Farben: Volkswirtschaftliche Abteilung, Turkey;
I.G. Farben: Volkswirtschaftliche Abteilung: the Economic Structure of French North Africa (Algeria, Tunisia, Morocco).

Similar reports, and in some cases studies, exist in Italy, Belgium, France and elsewhere. The Middle East historian can learn from his colleague, the African historian, who has made excellent use of such materials.

III

To the British diplomats in Iraq the *coup d'état* of 29 October 1936 came as a complete surprise. It was neither anticipated nor had there been any indication of serious political unrest within the ranks of the military. And this was in spite of the commonly expressed belief in the omnipotence of British political and military power in the country, and in spite of numerous political advisers, such as C.F. Edmonds in the Ministry of the Interior, and the large military presence in the country. Generally, and this applies to the 1930s throughout, British records on Iraq reflect considerable ignorance of local developments and poor political analysis, especially when they are compared to those covering Egypt and Palestine.[12]

In part this was undoubtedly due to the frequency of staff changes, and the little interest many, if not most, British diplomats had in Iraq. While Cairo, Alexandria and even Palestine (despite the inherent dangers to life and limb) offered fascination, not to speak of great and enjoyable amenities, Iraq to many was not much better – perhaps a little better – than being sent to Nigeria. Moreover, while the Iraqi government played host to several British Ambassadors within less than a decade, Egypt enjoyed the presence of Sir M. Lampson (later Lord Killearn) for over twelve years, providing him with ample opportunity to infiltrate the political and social scene and to establish a considerable power base. All this was absent in Iraq.

In contrast, the German Ambassador to Iraq, Dr Grobba, had been at his post since the late twenties. He was able to establish close friendships with leading personalities, especially with officers. Moreover, he seemed to be able to converse easily in Arabic, which always adds a touch of familiarity in the Middle East. His reports, therefore, show a range of information and a depth of analysis often absent in British reports. The Ambassador, moreover, was a shrewd politician, besides being personally ambitious. It was this which caused him readily to support the new German régime – in contrast to many of his diplomatic colleagues – after he had seen for himself during a leave the achievements of the Nazi Party. And perhaps it was this newly gained enthusiasm (which did not escape the notice of his British colleagues)[13] which prompted him to dramatise Iraqi pro-German sentiments, and to go beyond his diplomatic charge, as for instance promising German political or military aid without prior clearance from his superiors. All in all, the Third Reich could not have had a better representative and salesman for the new ideology.

By 1936, the year of the *coup*, this ideology had in political terms achieved considerable progress – at least in the eyes of the world. Germany had reoccupied the Rhineland; in July Hitler decided to intervene in the Spanish Civil War; Italy had completed her conquest of Abyssinia, causing the British government more than a passing anxiety attack. Partially as a consequence of these developments, Britain was forced to start negotiations with the Egyptian government again, resulting in the Anglo-Egyptian Treaty of that year. About the same time Great Britain started her rearmament policy, it became increasingly clear that a European war was almost a certainty. But a European war would by the logic of the alliance systems spill over into the Middle East, and it was therefore logical that Britain's allies (Iraq, Egypt, for instance) requested large amounts of arms. These London could not supply, causing not only embarrassment, but considerable conflict between the Foreign and War Offices.

Amidst international tension – if not chaos in Europe – during the summer of 1936, Arab requests for arms only added to British exacerbation, especially in view of the rapid events in Palestine. Any transfers of arms, especially to Iraq, could end up in Palestine, thus further endangering the already weak British military posture. London was caught in her own political machinations. It was thus a question of the 'two lesser evils'. A denial of arms to Iraq would alienate the Iraqi army, with the possibility of their seeking other arms supplies, especially from Italy and Germany.[14] British arms to Iraq, however, could undermine the British position. Britain did what it usually did in such cases: stall.

When Taha al-Hashimi arrived in London during September 1936, the crises between Great Britain and Iraq, and between the Foreign Office and the War Office, reached a climax. The latter told the General that they could not guarantee arms deliveries for at least two years. Consequently, the Iraqi Prime Minister, Taha's brother [15] Yahsin, ordered the General to return via Germany and Czechoslovakia in order to explore their ability to supply arms or the possibility of constructing arms industries in Iraq. Aware of this, the FO pressured the WO, and also requested urgent talks in the Cabinet. There it was agreed that Iraqi demands should be met, but the WO refused. In a strongly worded letter to the FO, General Haining of the WO wrote:

> The undeniable fact remains that we cannot get more that a pint out of a pint pot! . . . We have put the Iraqis on a 'pari-passu' basis with our own Army for stores we are making for ourselves and will see that a proportion of the earliest deliveries are allotted to them.[16]

Yet, the British arms industries were unable to deliver. A month later the first of several reports arrived indicating that Iraq was obtaining various light arms from Europe, including several hundred Bren light automatics, in addition to various other types.[17] By spring of the following year the situation deteriorated, as the requests were escalated to include aircraft and other heavy equipment.

To Britain, therefore, the greatest concern was Iraq's relations with Germany and Italy. That these two countries could conceivably supply arms, and thus further alienate the country from Great Britain, was more that just a nuisance. It carried the germs of great military and political dangers. British foreign policy, in view of the European situation and the rapidly growing Arab nationalist movements, was therefore increasingly on the defensive, at times even in a state of acute hysteria. And the local British personnel seem to have made matters only worse. Unable really to penetrate the Iraqi ruling elite, and taking political statements at face value, even in the mistaken belief that they had gained the trust of the Iraqi government, British diplomats were more often that not at a loss. Overly concentrating on the real or imagined threats to British interests by Germany or Italy (which in some instances was understandable, given the situation) the important political currents were wholly overlooked. Little attention was paid to the 'backstage' political developments. While frequent reports illustrated the various anti-British tendencies in educational institutions, or relayed accounts by hysterical schoolmistresses about pupils indulging in anti-British activities, little was said about the establishment of the important al-Alhali group, or the Nadi al-Muthanna. Practically nothing was said about the establishment of the Harakat al-Futtuwwa. Contrary to British concerns, the German Ambassador operated along different lines.

As far as it is possible to reconstruct, Dr Grobba's interests were orientated more to the development of personnel and unofficial ties to politicians and officers. From where the impetus came is difficult to ascertain. Presumably it was mutually beneficial. The army needed arms; the old officers trained before the war maintained certain affinities with the German culture and considered themselves as the 'Prussia of the East'. Germany served as the model in the eyes of many who were politically active. Moreover, the public of Iraq largely supported the Palestinian struggle, especially as more and more Palestinians as well as Syrians found refuge in Baghdad. It was these political currents which Dr Grobba astutely exploited, and reported. Thus it is not suprising that he supported those 'pan-Arab' tendencies, as they would serve Germany's interests in the long run. That his position engendered considerable controversy within German officialdom is not surprisng. But the Party was more inclined towards his views and it was from it that he obtained support.

Dr Grobba correctly stressed another aspect of Iraqi politics. He repeatedly reported the activities of the Ministries dealing with educational policies, and not only in connection with Germany's assistance programmes, but rather the implications they had for the growth of pan-Arab nationalism. In one particularly perceptive report he analyses in great detail the implication of the shift from dependence on British advisers to that of Syrian, Palestinian and Egyptian personnel. He noted a marked difference in the attitude of Egyptians, namely from one of 'cultural snobbery' to one of increasing identification with the goals of Arabism.[18]

These pan-Arab developments, of course, in so far as they were noted by British diplomats, were considered inimical to British interests. Therefore it was logical that the advocates of pan-Arabism would turn to the Germans and Italians for assistance, under whatever pretence. From the records of Dr Grobba, we know for instance that just prior to the *coup*, Hikmat Sulaiman, Bakr Sidi, Abd al-Latif Nuri, and Naji al-Asil were in close contact with him. And from the dispatches just after the event, a clear picture emerges not only about the events but also the personalities involved – which is certainly not the case if relying on the British records.

During the year preceding the *coup*, Germany's representatives had been very active. Baghdad appears to have been inundated with German propaganda, cultural as well as commercial. This did not escape the notice of the British, who recorded their concern by noting that several Ministries were turning to Germany for commercial contracts. A case in point was the secret Railway Agreement between Iraq and Great Britain.

In order to prevent a successful German bid for supplies to the recently nationalised Iraqi railway system, Britain had pressured the Yasin al-Hashimi government into agreeing to a secret deal which would grant British companies a monopoly. The Foreign Office realised very well that this could backfire. The Germans would not only 'wail' if they found out, but, as G. Rendel in the FO noted, 'We are bound to be got at, sooner or later, as, although Hikmat's paper was seized, everybody will soon know what was in it. He will see to that. He is thick with the Germans.'[19] Rendel was more correct than he could know. Hikmat had leaked the deal to Grobba and had also tried to publish it in *Sawt al-Ahali* and *al-Bayan*. Each time, however, the papers were banned, leaving Hikmat furious and driving him closer to Grobba. In August of 1936, he did manage to get one report out before the censors could move in. Grobba of course reported the incident to the AA, but for reasons of his own did not use it as a political device and instead refrained from commenting publicly. After the *coup,* however, he cited the incident as one of the causes for Hikmat's and Bakr Sidqi's seizure of power.

More worrying, however, than commercial and cultural inroads in Iraq were, as mentioned earlier, Germany's arms supply possibility. Both the British and German records reveal throughout 1936 feverish activity on all sides. The question, however, was, what were the real reasons for Iraq's sudden and large-scale requests for arms? We do know that the Iraqi armed forces were disgruntled with the government. We also know that several high-ranking politicians and officers had travelled to Europe and Britain. In the summer of 1936, especially, Bakr Sidqi was travelling widely. He visited Prague, and possibly Berlin. (Czechoslovakia was an important arms manufacturer whose specifications and standards conformed to those of Great Britain. Thus in some cases London permitted its allies to import arms from there.) Moreover, Bakr Sidqi was granted permission to enter Palestine, significantly coinciding with Fawzi Qawakji's organising a group of around a hundred volunteers to fight in Palestine.

According to the German Ambassador, General Abd al-Latif Nuri also had spent some time in Germany (1936), mainly for medical treatment, and he had returned as an ardent and enthusiastic friend of the Reich. Thus he was stated to be a guest of honour of the Führer at the annual Nuremberg party rallies.[20] Yusuf Izz al-Din Ibrahim, the Minister of Education, had spent some time in Germany as the guest of the government, as did Salih Jabr, a 'radical Shii', and Minister of Justice in the post-*coup* government.

Unlike the British officials, the German Ambassador therefore was in close contact with those involved in the *coup*. But was it an accident? Evidence would argue against such a conclusion. According to Grobba's daily, and even hourly, reports and his subsequent memoirs, it is evident that he was either very well informed, or possibly even involved. However, if there was an involvement, it was only in so far as he promised German arms and political support. This reasoning is based on the following information:

(1) Berlin, probably the APA, had promised arms to Iraq prior to the *coup*. Although there exist, to the best of my knowledge, no records about the earlier Iraqi-German negotiations about arms, immediately after the *coup* the Iraqi government requested, and received, several large arms shipments.

(2) Bakr Sidqy and Abd al-Latif Nuri had been in close touch with Dr Grobba throughout 1936; as was Hikmat Suleiman.

(3) On the evening of the *coup*, Dr Grobba attended a dinner given by Ra'uf Chadirchi which was also attended by Hikmat Suleiman!

(4) On the day of the *coup*, at 9 a.m., Dr Grobba cabled the AA that a successful *coup* had taken place, and that the new régime requested the population to follow the example 'of the Spanish nationalists', and that the population was to support the formation of a government following the lines of a national-socialist or Fascist model.

(5) On 1 November, Hikmat declared to Grobba and the Italian Minister that he 'held great sympathies for Germany' and that the *coup*'s government 'took its inspiration from the national socialist ideology'.[21]

From the day of the *coup* both Hikmat and Bakr saw Grobba practically daily. They sought his advice and his support, politically as well as militarily. It is not necessary to go into details of post-*coup* politics, which have been described by M. Khadduri and elsewhere, but it is noteworthy to mention the military role Germany played thereafter.

According to Dr Grobba, Bakr was determined to establish an independent Kurdistan. Perhaps for that reason he requested from Germany military assistance, as well as advice. Thus, in view of Britain's considerable military potential in the area, especially by virtue of its air force, he requested 18 anti-aircraft guns, worth at least 1 million Reichsmarks. Above that, the Iraqi government requested another 4 million Reichsmarks worth of arms. Rheinmetall Borsig in Berlin and Otto Wolff in Cologne were given the order. Furthermore, Bakr Sidqi requested a German military expert who duly arrived disguised as a geologist. Generalstabs-Oberst AD R. Heins planned for Bakr Sidqi Iraq's defence against a possible attack by Iran, as well as the establishment of a Kurdistan.[22]

Although the British legation suspected German-Iraqi collusion, they knew very little of the actual events. Thus, when the *coup* occurred, the British were more than startled, although the official report on the military did include the observation that the British Embassy in Baghdad was informed of unusual military activities at 15.15 p.m. on 28 October. British incomprehension lasted until January 1937. They could neither really understand what had happened, nor did they have a clear picture of the personalities involved. About Bakr Sidqi they stated: 'In a country where every kind of vice is rampant, he is a byword for debauchery.' Abd al-Latif Nuri they considered 'leaderless'. On Kamal Chadirchi and Yusuf Izzal-Din the FO had scant information.[23] When the FO requested information from the Air Ministry about Chadirchi they replied that 'he is a young man of extreme nationalist tendency and formerly editor of the chief nationalist newspaper'. The Cabinet, as a whole, was dismissed as 'men of straw'.

The most unsupported account was provided by C.J. Edmonds, adviser to the Ministry of the Interior. He believed that the *coup* was really a 'pre-emptive' exercise. Jaafar al-Askari, Edmonds claimed, had planned his own *coup,* against Yasin. The question remains: who knew more, the Germans or the British? It seems the Germans, at least from the records available.

Notes

1. H.A. Jacobsen, *Nationalsozialistische Aussenpolitik 1933-1938* (Frankfurt, 1968); L. Hirszowicz, *The Third Reich and the Arab East* (London, 1966); H. Tillmann, *Deutschlands Araberpolitik im Zweiten Weltkrieg* (Berlin, 1965); for the politics of the Third Reich in the Middle East the latter is undoubtedly the best study, if one discards the imposed rhetoric of the author, working in the German Democratic Republic.

2. The best and most readily available guide to the German archival materials on the AA is G.O. Kent's *Catalogue of Files and Microfilms of the German*

Foreign Ministry Archives 1920-1945, Vols. I-III, (Stanford, California, 1962-66). There are other guides available in the numerous archival centres within Germany, Washington and Moscow.

3. D.S. Landes, *Bankers and Pashas* (London, 1958); other works include those by R. Owen, C. Issawi and G. Cook.

4. Tillmann, *Arabpolitik,* pp. 451-2.

5. AA, Inland II A/B (Band 61/2) 1938; various intelligence services, for instance, had concluded that the prominent Fakhri al-Barudi, a Syrian Deputy and 'industrialist' was a homosexual, but should nevertheless be invited to the Nuremberg Rallies. AA/Abt. Inland/Referat Deutschland/Reichsparteitag Allgemeines/1938/82-09c.

6. See Jacobsen, *Aussenpolitik*, p. 64; Tillmann, *Araberpolitik, passim;* and Hirszowicz, *passim.*

7. Jacobsen, *Aussenpolitik,* pp. 623-764.

8. Politische Abteilung/Inneres/1938.

9. Jacobsen, *Aussenpolitik,* pp. 704-5.

10. L. Farago, *The Game of the Foxes* (London, 1971), pp. 661-8.

11. Tillman, *Araberpolitik,* pp. 451-2.

12. British representation in Syria was poor; although it was important to the Middle régimes, little attention was paid to the events in the country; only the information supplied by the French authorities was relayed. As such, the PRO has no useful information on Syria.

13. 'I have noticed a distinct difference in the German Minister since he returned last year from leave in the Vaterland [sic]. He was not, I believe, a Nazi before he left here . . .' (C. Bateman to FO, 3/9/1936. E 5818/375/93-FO 371/20006).

14. In theory, and according to the 1930 Anglo-Iraqi Treaty, purchases other than from Great Britain were illegal. But, as the staff of the FO observed, these clauses were vague, since anyone who conformed to the British specification was able to supply arms. The Minutes, 24/9/1936.E 5818/375/93-FO 371/20006.

15. C. Bateman to FO, 14/9/1936. E 5853/375/93-FO 371/20006.

16. General Haining (S.M.O. & I) to G. Rendel, 9/10/1936. E 6460/375/93-FO 371/20006.

17. See, for instance, E 6997/375/93-FO 371/20006, and E 6926/375/93-FO 371/20006.

18. AA/Pol.VII/Iraq Inneres/Grobba to AA/9/6/1936.

19. E. 5818 1375/19 – FO 371/20005.

20. AA/Abteilung II/Referat Deutschland&Einladungen zum Reichspartiei-tag, 1937/82-09.

21. This information is based on Grobba's *Männer und Mächte im Orient* (Göttingen, 1967), pp. 149-65 and AA files.

22. Grobba, pp. 157-9.

23. In fact, information on Iraqi politicians throughout the period was either erroneous or purposely misleading. E6796/1419/93-FO 371/20013.

4 FROM ELITE TO CLASS: THE TRANSFORMATION OF IRAQI POLITICAL LEADERSHIP

David Pool

The purpose of this chapter is to present an analysis of the pre-1958 political system in Iraq based on explanatory factors which are relevant to an understanding of the nature of similar pre-radical régimes in other Arab states and to an understanding of how and why such political systems were transformed.[1] In order to understand the qualitative nature of systemic change in the Arab states in the twentieth century, it is essential to move away from such concepts as 'traditional' and 'modern' and the rise of 'new men' or 'new social forces'. To explain how one kind of political system changed to another one requires the abstraction of those features which indicate the positive rather than residual attributes of that earlier system. Indeed some recent studies have attempted to do this,[2] with analytic and conceptual awareness.

An attempt will be made here, then, to select those general features of the pre-1958 political system in terms of a set of interrelated concepts which might be more generally applicable. The concepts suggested are: colonial rule and the creation of domestic political power, élite formation and political stratification, the relationship between those who control politics (those at the peak of the system of political stratification) and those who control wealth (those at the peak of the system of economic stratification). This latter relationship is important in that radical change, political, social, or economic, seems to be highly correlated with the concentration of economic and political power in the hands of the same individuals and families who share common class or strata position or, put another way, the more political institutions are operated in the political and economic interest of a particular defined social class, consisting of such individuals and families, the more fundamental the change. A point which requires some further amplification is that of 'the creation of domestic political power'.

The states formed by the mandatory powers in the Middle East involved the creation of a new centre from which power could be exercised and a new central focus for the segmental societies over which this new power was to be exercised: the tribal blocs, the provincial capitals, the regional market and trade centres. As a consequence, politics and the struggle for power, influence and status were particularly fluid and dynamic, no matter how temporary the new state was perceived to be. Furthermore, the fluidity was not simply a consequence of a power vacuum but a consequence of a social and economic vacuum necessarily occurring in a political community where the social economic and cultural bases of politics were not firmly rooted,[3] where politics and economics were localised, together with the introduction of a régime the major initial effect of which was systemic. Although tribal, village and urban rivalries persisted at the local level, a new centre responsible for and capable of allocating authority, power and wealth fundamentally reoriented the dynamic of politics in that not only did those who had power and wealth seek to resecure it, but those who sought such values were provided with new opportunities. The very fact that it was an alien colonial power which initially possessed the ultimate authority in such a fluid political framework clearly made a difference, even though that alien power worked in partnership with what was called an 'Arab Façade' of political institutions.

The major intention of this account, however, is to examine the process through which the vacuum was filled and the fundamental social, economic and political fluidity was transformed into a fluidity of personality conflicts and tensions on the surface of an entrenched socio-economic base. We shall see how the establishment of such an order transformed a political élite formed of disparate ruling groups of divergent former Ottoman army officers and tribal leaders into an élite based on class interests. There were two important factors involved here: the felt necessity by the colonial power for establishing a national élite and the colonial powers' perception of the social and political weight of the potential leaders existing at the beginning of the mandatory period.[4] Colonial policy, then, was a prime mover in the emergence of this class-based ruling élite which controlled the economic and political system until 1958. Let us then examine this process of state formation and the establishment of new state power concentrating on the two major wings of the Iraqi élite: the Sharifians and the tribal sheikhs, both of whom will be examined in the context of the process of their recruitment to positions of political power.

Amir Faisal and the Sharifians

The term Sharifian refers to those individuals who were associated with the Sharif of Mecca's revolt in the Hijaz against Ottoman Imperial rule and to those who were involved in the temporary administrations in

Syria and Jordan between the end of Ottoman rule and the beginnings of the Mandate system.

These men provided the backbone of the Arab revolt, or 'the revolt in the desert' as it is more romantically called, and of the somewhat less illustrious Arab administrations. The majority had been officers in the Ottoman armies, both regular and reserve, and had, in the confusion of war and military defeat, found their way to Hijaz and Syria at different times and by many assorted paths. Many of those who had been involved in the Hijazi beginnings had been captured by the British and had arrived in the Hijaz by way of prisoner-of-war camps in India. Although some had been members of anti-Ottoman organisations like al-Ahd, some had probably been reluctant heroes, initially in their struggle for Arabism, since 'India [i.e. the British government of India] handed them over with little courtesy – and handed over all available Arab prisoners without informing them of their destination or making a selection of the most responsive or most suitable.'[5] Some, like Yasin al-Hashimi, only joined the patriots after the complete withdrawal of the Ottoman armies from the Arab territories. Indeed this was the case with some of those who served with the Amir Faisal in the Arab administration in Syria.

The history of the Arab revolt itself has been related many times and has reached the level of myth and become the stuff of memorabilia and the cinema in the person of T.E. Lawrence, but where Lawrence later sought the obscurity of the rank and file the Iraqi Sharifians sought and attained the political limelight. Until a new generation of Iraqi officers extinguished their flame in 1958, they played a dominant role in Iraqi politics, through their possession of a wide array of political positions: ambassadorships, Ministerial offices, army officers, court officials, provincial governorships (see Table 4.1).[6]

That so many of these positions were held by former Ottoman officers was the result of a chain of circumstances going beyond their involvement with Faisal in the Hijaz and Arab administrations. Baghdad housed one of the few military preparatory schools in the Arab provinces of the Ottoman Empire and most of the Sharifian officers had had their introduction to military life through their attendance at this school, which provided the opportunity for social and political advancement unavailable to Ottoman Arabs elsewhere in the Empire. After three years at the school, those who passed their exams travelled to Istanbul to attend military college. The proportion of those passing on to the military college was not insubstantial: in 1903 there were seventy students in the party travelling to Istanbul, a figure which would

Table 4.1

Ja'far al-Askari:	Prime Minister; Cabinet Minister; Deputy; military officer; diplomat
Yasin al-Hashimi:	Prime Minister; Cabinet Minister; Provincial Governor; Deputy
Naji al-Suwaidi:	Prime Minister; Cabinet Minister; Deputy
Nuri al-Said:	Prime Minister; Cabinet Minister; central bureaucrat; Deputy; military officer; diplomat
Naji Shawkat:	Prime Minister; Cabinet Minister; central bureaucrat; Deputy; diplomat
Jamil Midfai:	Prime Minister; Cabinet Minister; Provincial Governor; court official; Deputy; diplomat
Ali Jawdat:	Prime Minister; Cabinet Minister; Provincial Governor; court official; Deputy
Tawfiq al-Suwaidi:	Prime Minister; Cabinet Minister; central bureaucrat; Deputy; diplomat
Jamil al-Rawi:	Cabinet Minister; Provincial Governor; Deputy
Jamil al-Wadi:	Cabinet Minister; Deputy; military officer
Rashid Khojah:	Cabinet Minister; Provincial Governor; court official; Deputy; central bureaucrat; diplomat
Abd al-Latif Nuri:	Cabinet Minister; Deputy; military officer
Sabih Najib:	Cabinet Minister; central bureaucrat; military officer
Ibrahim Kamal:	Cabinet Minister; Provincial Governor; central bureaucrat; court official; Deputy; diplomat
Sami Shawkat:	Cabinet Minister; central bureaucrat
Tahsin Ali:	Cabinet Minister; court official; Deputy; Provincial Governor
Tahsin al-Askari:	Cabinet Minister; Provincial Governor; central bureaucrat; Deputy
Ismail Namiq:	Cabinet Minister; Deputy; military officer
Hisam al-Din Juma:	Cabinet Minister; Provincial Governor; central bureaucrat; Deputy
Rustam Haidar:	Cabinet Minister; central bureaucrat; court official; Deputy
Nuri al-Qadi:	Cabinet Minister; central bureaucrat
Abd al-Hamid al-Shaliji:	Provincial Governor; central bureaucrat
Shakir al-Wadi:	Cabinet Minister; military officer; diplomat
Mahmud Adib:	Provincial Governor
Abdulla Dulaymi:	Provincial Governor

Rauf Kubaisi:	Provincial Governor; central bureaucrat
Said al-Midfai:	Provincial Governor
Mawlud Mukhlis:	Provincial Governor; Deputy
Arif Qaftan:	Provincial Governor; Deputy
Thabit Abd al-Nur:	central bureaucrat; Deputy
Khayri al-Hindawi:	central bureaucrat
Ibrahim Hilmi al-Umar:	central bureaucrat
Muhammad al-Hashimi:	court official
Fahmi al-Mudarris:	court official; bureaucrat
Tahsin al-Qadri:	court official; diplomat
Muhammad al-Bassam:	Deputy
Abd al-Ghafur al-Badri:	Deputy
Abd al-Latif al-Fallahi:	Deputy
Hamdi Sadr al-Din:	Deputy
Ali Ridha al-Askari:	Deputy; military officer
Tawfiq al-Hashimi:	Deputy
'Arif al-Suwaidi:	Deputy; Cabinet Minister
Khayr al-Din al-'Umari:	Deputy
Ahmad Kamal:	Deputy
Qasim Shukri:	military officer
Aziz Yamulki:	military officer
Ismail Haqqi al-Saffar:	central bureaucrat; military officer
Mahmud Sinawi:	central bureaucrat
Ibrahim Shahbandar:	court official
Bakr Sidqi:	military officer; diplomat
Ibrahim al-Rawi:	military officer; Diplomat

provide 10 per cent of the total number admitted to the college that year.[7]

For those who lived in the capital, attendance at the college was easier than for those who lived in the provinces. For Ali Jawdat, Sharifian and later Prime Minister, the journey from the northern province of Mosul was arduous: he travelled from Mosul by *Kalak* (a raft of inflated skins), and the trip took him eight days.[8] Ibrahim Rawi, who attained high military and diplomatic positions, recounts in his memoirs similar problems of distance and education. He was born in Ramadi, a town established by Midhat Pasha to encourage the settlement of the Upper Euphrates tribes, and had to transfer to Baghdad to attend military secondary school, for there were only two religious elementary schools and a state primary school at Ramadi.[9] For those without relatives in Baghdad, the difficulty of finishing at the school was compounded. Ali Jawdat comments in his memoirs that his friends from Mosul had to work during the day and attend the night school, whereas he was lucky in having relatives in Baghdad with whom he could stay, presumably at little or no cost. Most of the Sharifians, both civilian and military, did in fact come from Baghdad.

The general impression is that those who attended the military college in Istanbul came from poorer and less prominent families. Talib Mushtaq, the son of an Ottoman bureaucrat, confirms this impression:

> Istanbul was the Mecca ('ka'ba') of ambitious Iraqis, for whoever wanted an important position filled his bag with expensive presents and hurried to Istanbul, and whoever wanted advancement and promotion filled his pockets with tens of gold liras and went to Istanbul; and those wealthy families who wanted to give their sons a higher education sent them [these] . . . the majority of these attended the College of Law and the Mulkiye Shahana, the College of Political and Administrative Sciences as it is now called . . . as for poor families they made their sons attend the military school in Baghdad so that it might lead to their completing their higher studies in the Military College in Istanbul and graduate as officers in the Ottoman army.[10]

Ernest Dawn, in his pioneering study of the Syrian Arab nationalist movement, concluded that those with a military career came from more obscure, and thus probably lower, social backgrounds, since nine of the ten Syrian *al-Ahd* members were not included in biographical dictionaries, nor were any members of their families.[11] It would seem that what Dawn found for the Syrians holds true also for the Iraqi Sharifians with a military background.[12]

In many Middle Eastern societies, political co-operation (and in many cases, conflict) results from a shared upbringing, especially common neighbourhood, common schooling and common experiences.[13] In Iraq we also find those informal ties of shared schooling and experience underpinning later political rivalry and co-operation and simply providing a common knowledge of each other. A striking example of this latter feature is that Nuri al-Said, Taha al-Hashimi and Ali Jawdat, all of whom were to become Prime Ministers, were in the same secondary school class. Added to the shared experience of education, war and, for some, prisoner of war camp, were the social ties of friendship, marriage and brotherhood. Sets of brothers who were to become politically prominent were Sami and Naji Shawkat; Shakir and Jamil Wadi; Ali Rida, Tahsin and Jaafar al-Askari; and Jamil and Ibrahim al-Rawi. The three al-Askari brothers were related by marriage to Nuri al-Said and Ibrahim Kamal. Tahsin al-Qadri was related by marriage to Jamil al-Midfai, and Ismail Namiq was married to the sister of Abd al-Wahhab Mahmud, an Iraqi Cabinet Minister who was not a Sharifian but whose father had been (see Table 4.1 for their positions).

The great majority of those in the table had in fact fought with the sons of the Sharif of Mecca in Hijaz and Syria and the most prominent, militarily and diplomatically, held for a lengthier period of time a greater number of the top institutional positions. We are not concerned here with establishing the validity of their commitment to Arabism but to understanding the dynamic of their recruitment to positions of power, the significance of which lay not so much in their nationalist credentials as in their patronage connections with Faisal, son of the Sharif, commander of the Arab army and eventually King of Iraq. Their connection with the British officials who were later to play a determining role in the new Iraqi state was an important additional factor in their elevation, as we shall see.

In many ways these Sharifians were the core of the movement for Arab independence and a major political beneficiary of that struggle in post-Ottoman Iraq. From what social strata did they come? Were they, like the Syrians Ernest Dawn studied, the 'indigenous Arab elite', the Ottoman-Arab landowners, merchants, scholars and bureaucrats? Whereas Dawn found that not a single member of the early- or late-comers to the Syrian branch of the movement was from a 'lower-class' or 'humble' background, from the Iraqis seven were clearly of such an origin. The greater number of officers among the Iraqis clearly accounts for such a difference. As we can see from the table, 35 of the 51 whose education was discovered attended Istanbul military college. As Talib Mushtaq pointed out, many of those who attended the Baghdad military school were from the 'ambitious poor', while the other group which stands out is the fifteen educated in the Higher Educational Institutions. One might presume that they came from middle- and upper-level bureaucratic families[14] (see Table 4.2).

What the bureaucrats and officers had in common was that they were strata which began their public life at the centre. They were educated in governmen service. For example, Ali Jawdat's connections in and knowledge of an Arab Iraq were highly circumscribed. Travel outside Mosul, his birthplace, had been restricted to the journey to Baghdad for military schooling and the subsequent one to Istanbul for college. The remainder of his adult life had been spent in the Ottoman army and in the service of the Sharif of Mecca. The lack of involvement of large landowners and merchants in the Iraqi movement substantially differentiated them from their Syrian counterparts and resulted in a very different socio-economic domination.[15]

Under the Empire power and privilege had always been associated with state structures, like the bureaucracy, the army or the religious establishment. On the foundation of the new Iraq, the great majority of the Sharifians depended on the new state, as they had depended on the Empire, for their daily bread. Unlike the earlier generation of Ottoman officers, they were not assured of converting their position in the state apparatus into a position in society: the war had intervened, the Empire had been dissolved and they were still quite young. Unlike the tribal leaders discussed below, they had no 'natural' followers and no ready-made clientèle. In fact, their position resembled that of their leader, the Amir Faisal, in that it was one of total political dependency.

Faisal ibn Husain was born in the Hijaz into one of the leading Meccan families. He had never visited Iraq in his life although he had had some contact with leading Syrian Arabs who were involved in anti-Ottoman activities. Two sons of the Sharif Husain, Faisal and Abdullah, were prominent candidates for the position of head of state in the Arab territories occupied during the war. While Faisal was heading the Arab administration in Syria and there was a British military administration in Mesopotamia, he was enthusiastic in recommending his former comrades-in-arms to the British administration.

> There is now a large number of Baghdadi officers who have risked their lives and their futures, and those of their families in volunteering

> their services during the war, and at every period of the struggle they have served me loyally . . . to those who say it is impossible to constitute such a [national] government owing to the lack of trained men, I will say that until now not the slightest effort has been made to collect them for most of the highest posts in the Eastern Zone of the O.E.T. [Occupied Enemy Territory] are filled by Baghdadis today. Doubtless among the tribes a great deal of assistance will be necessary and the Baghdadis would all be only too glad to undertake it.[16]

At the time when Faisal wrote this he had every expectation that he would become King of Syria. Indeed, one year later he was elected King of Syria by the Syrian Congress in March 1920, and his brother Abdallah was elected King of Iraq by a separate meeting of Iraqis shortly after.[17]

Table 4.2

For 55 of the 66 members of the Iraqi élite there is some information

Average age in 1921:	31 (based on total of 32)
Education:	35 in Istanbul military college
	15 in Istanbul higher education
	1 Religious
	51
Occupation:	35 Officers
	4 Officials
	2 Journalists
	8 Lawyers
	49 total known
Birthplace:	19 Baghdad
	5 Mosul
	3 Syria
	5 Small towns (Upper Euphrates)
	2 Other
	34 Total
Father's occupation:	1 Military officer
	5 Official-landowners
	6 Small shopkeeper/artisan
	4 Tribal
	1 Merchant-landowner
	2 Religious
	19 Total

Events in Europe moved with their own dynamic: the French were awarded the mandate for Syria by the League of Nations. As a consequence, the Arab army, ill-organised and ill-equipped, was destroyed at Maysalun when it tried to prevent the French forces from moving from Lebanon into Syria. As a result of the French moves Faisal had become a king without a kingdom. He remained a favourite son of the British who, with their proclivity for monarchy, had a Mesopotamian kingdom without a king. British official thinking on the type of government suitable for Iraq was lucidly expressed by the influential H.W. Young.

> The ideal form of government for the particular races with which we have to deal in Mesopotamia and Syria at this present stage of development is, in my opinion, a benevolent patriarchate, which consists of and to a certain extent is dependent on public opinion, but which retains executive control.[18]

As to the specific patriarch, Abdallah was 'a sensualist, idle and lazy',[19] so Faisal was duly selected in London and then 'elected' by the British-nominated Iraqi Cabinet in Baghdad where they could, and did, make effective his earlier recommendation of those 'Baghdadi officers'.

A development parallel to the elevation of Faisal and one which worked similarly to the advantage of the Sharifians was that a handful of British officials who had been involved with the Hijaz revolt were to assume important official positions at the Colonial Office in London, and as Mandatory officials prior to independence in 1932, and as British Embassy staff in independent Iraq. Even though familiarity bred a degree of contempt, many of these officials were as zealous in the promotion of the men they had known as other British officials of Indian experience and bias were in opposing the return of the Sharifians.

Kinahan Cornwallis, who had served in Syria with Faisal, and who was later adviser to the Ministry of the Interior and in 1941 British Ambassador, wrote:

> The strength of the Baghdadi Military party, now chiefly resident in Syria, is perhaps not fully realised. Its members risked their futures and the lives of their followers for a very definite purpose when they joined the King of the Hijaz . . . they form the nucleus of a nationalist party which may give us infinite troubles in the future.
>
> I believe we shall have no difficulty in gaining them over if we adopt a generous policy. Men like Jafar and Nuri Pasha are not fools, and they realise that Mesopotamia cannot stand on its own at present.

> They like us and want us to help but only on the condition that we respect Arab ideals.[20]

Major H.W. Young, who had served in the Hijaz and Syria, and who was subsequently an adviser on Middle Eastern affairs at the Foreign Office and Acting High Commissioner for Iraq in the period immediately prior to independence, wrote a minute stating that 'there appears to be ample scope for employing the many Mesopotamian officers who served under Faysal.'[21] At a time when the Sharifians were engaged in clandestine subversion in Iraq against the British occupation, he wrote more strongly:

> It is lamentable that those very officers with whom Colonel Lawrence . . . and myself, among others, lived in the closest possible touch, and who looked to the British government as the mainstay of their revolt against the Turk, should be touring their own country in disguise with the object of obtaining signatures to anti-British manifestos. There is something wrong somewhere.[22]

Gertrude Bell, a protagonist of the Arab cause, a supporter of the Sharifian family and Oriental Secretary to Sir Percy Cox, first High Commissioner of the Mandate, expressed views very similar to those of Cornwallis and Young.

With these officials pushing Faisal and his followers, the only obstacle preventing his acceptance was his brother Abdallah who had been nominated by the Arab Congress in Damascus mentioned earlier. Busch, in his exhaustive account of the evolution of the contradictions, compromises and craftiness of British foreign policy between 1914 and 1921, states in a nutshell how 'Faysal's brotherly love was commendable but it was to a certain extent undermined by his willingness to discuss ther terms under which he would go to Iraq.[23] In the event Faisal accepted the nomination and his brother was given the Kingdom of Transjordan and both were confirmed in their positions at the Cairo conference of 1920. In the following year Faisal arrived in Iraq to a less than warm reception and without having made any terms. They were to be discussed after his coronation.

From the pivotal role of King, Faisal was able to secure the return of the Sharifians and their appointment to government office. Like him, they had little support in Iraq although most of them had been born there.[24] Most of them came from the Sunni Muslim triangle of Baghdad, Mosul and Rawa/Ana. The only connections which Faisal had with

Iraq were through the Sharifians and their roots were not deep. Few came from notable or leading families. Indeed, the urban notable families were rivals to Faisal and the Sharifians in the sense that prominent members of the Gaylani family from Baghdad, the Naqib family of Basra, and the Suwaidi family from Mosul were suggested as rulers.

The crucial factor in the building of a political career for Faisal was his connection with the British. Yet, as an outsider dependent on non-Muslim outsiders to legitimise his rule he needed the support of the different Iraqi communities and their leaders. Over and above the problem of building support from such heterogeneous, ethnic, sectarian, culturally and economic divergent groupings was the additional problem of the divergent attitudes to the British Mandate. At the same time as building general support and a network of clients among such socially and politically diverse segments and their leaders, Faisal could not afford to alienate the support and assistance of the British Mandate authorities, upon whose economic, political and military power the new monarchy depended for the budget to be balanced, the tribes to be subdued and kept subdued,[25] and, until 1930, for supporting Iraqi independence before the League of Nations.

The demands of domestic political support and external British support resulted in variations in Faisal's behaviour, depending on the audience.[26] The British attitude changed slowly from one of incomprehension to charges of moral weakness and 'love of intrigue' to veiled threats of deposition.[27] Clearly, the British lacked an understanding of the ambiguity involved in creating legitimacy, establishing political ascendancy and authority in Iraq over Iraqis, and the consequent deception, manipulation and political manoeuvrings. The Sharifians were an instrument of this political behaviour resultant from the weird dynamic of establishing a legitimate authority under the umbrella of a Mandatory power which many politically important Iraqis considered illegitimate.

The political ambiguities were a major element in the clientele-building which underpinned the efforts of Faisal and the Sharifians to gather followers from among multiple social, economic and political segments of Iraqi society. As Faisal had to create his independence out of a dependence on the British to emerge as an independent head of state, so the Sharifians had to create their independence from Faisal to emerge as independent politicians with clientèles and followers of their own.

The creation of such kinds of independent roles in a colonial context where for practical purposes overt opposition and conflict was not possible, necessarily involved deception, intrigue, manoeuvres and manipulation; in sum all the techniques of covert opposition and concealed conflict. Yet such modes of behaviour, frequently associated with the 'old régimes' of the Arab states, were merely the superficial behavioural aspect of politics in Iraq. Underlying this unstable individualist or 'politics of personalities' was the formation of a politico-economic alliance which provided the socio-political stability in the context of which the manoeuvres and manipulations took place, sealing the alliance between the Sharifians and the tribal sheikhs.

The Tribal Sheikhs

In much of the literature on political change, 'development' or 'modernisation', there is an image of the state as an active virile agent moving into and arousing the dormant parts of society. This is an image which is, at least, a distortion and, at best, one-sided, since the indigenous leaders of Iraqi society, the tribal sheikhs, were as concerned to penetrate the state and convert their tribal power into state power.

When the British came to Iraq, the largest tribal confederations had effectively been dissolved, although there were still large well armed tribes and powerful confederations like the Imarat Anazah, the Shammar Jarba and the Dulaym,[28] all of which had sheikhs like Ali Sulaiman and Ajil al-Yawar who were powerful in their tribes and powers in the land. Men like these, controlling the borders on the western boundaries, were natural allies or enemies of those who controlled the centre.

British tribal policy was one of consolidating the political and economic position of such sheikhs or creating and recreating positions of authority for sheikhs in tribes which had become fragmented or were in the process of fragmentation. The instruments of this policy were the British Political Officers (POs) and Assistant Political Officers (APOs), who had quite a degree of autonomy in the conduct of local affairs, within the context of the policy of 'indirect rule' or 'native administration'. The PO for Nasiriya, an important town in the Shii south, described his policy thus:

> I go straight for getting the power in each tribe into the hands of one man . . . It is a mistake to think that the Muntafic tribes cannot be brought back to the old system again. My tribal chain of responsibility is always the shaykh of the tribe, the rais al-firka [section head] and the rais al-hamula [clan head].[29]

It was a combination of convenience and economy. Ruling through structures which dominated large numbers meant that a widely spread and expensive bureaucratic and military presence could be dispensed with.[30] A further element in the policy of building up sheikhly authority seemed to be that of creating a provincial tribal squirearchy as a bulwark against the urban nationalist.[31] The tribal sheikh whose influence and authority were on the wane was not loath to appreciate this practice.

> In the working out of this policy [restoring power to the sheikh] we have had the active support of the shaykh himself who stands to carve out for himself, under the British government, a position steadily denied him by the Turks and infinitely greater than anything he has enjoyed for a very large number of years.[32]

One of the means of restoring the authority of the sheikh, in fact a continuation of the policy used by the Ottomans to encourage the sedentarisation of tribes, was that of directly associating the tribal leader with the administration. In some areas, all intermediaries between government and people were dispensed with and the sheikh became the only link in the local government chain.[33] For example, it was decided in the Amara district that there was no need to appoint *mudirs* and the sheikh was made responsible for the maintenance of security and the establishment of order and the collection of revenue within his territory. In this early period several sheikhs were appointed to administrative positions: Khayyun al-Ubayd, head sheikh of the Abudah tribe and later deputy in eight assemblies; Farhud al-Mughashghash; Abdullah Yasin, one of the largest landowners in Iraq by the 1950s and representative for Kut in all but one of Iraq's assemblies; Manshad al-Hubayb, six times deputy until succeeded by his son Mohammad al-Manshad. Early marked out by the British, these sheikhs were able to extend their local political power through their role as intermediaries between government and people.

Other techniques used for associating the sheikh with the administration and which had the consequence of strengthening sheikhly authority in the new state were: using the tribal leaders as entrepreneurs for tribal labour; as commanders of irregular military units consisting of their tribal followers; as revenue collectors, and through the direct donation of monetary subsidies. The policy of employing sheikhs and tribal followers directly had begun during the military campaign in the Hijaz and was extended to the battle for Mesopotamia.[34] Others, like Thamir Bey al-Saadun, 'a staunch supporter of the government [who] had faithfully carried out all the work of maintaining order in the Shamiya district' during the 1920 rebellion, received his reward in his appointment as Intelligence Officer in the desert at a salary of 2,000 rupees per month.[35]

Where the building of new irrigation canals resulted in bringing new agricultural lands into existence, the sheikh organised the tribal labour and was given authority to distribute the new lands. Sheikh Ali Sulaiman, paramount chief of the Dulaym, provided one thousand labourers for canal-digging and in return took charge of distributing 10,000 donums[36] of land among his tribe. Certain sheikhs were given exceptional economic privileges. Ajil al-Yawar and Mahrut al-Hadhdhal guarded the northern and southern routes to Syria, respectively. In return they were permitted to levy tolls.[37] Direct subsidies were substantial in the early Mandate period. In 1920 sheikhs in Dulaym province, both paramount and sectional, received £13,000, in the Muntafik £10,000 and in Diwaniyah £6,500.

At the local level there was an attempt to institutionalise the tribal leaders in local affairs. This 'gesture toward self-determination', as it was called by Lord Curzon, was the formation of Divisional Councils. The purpose of the councils was described by Arnold Wilson, Acting High Commissioner at the time, thus: 'To secure the full benefit of co-operation by tribal leaders and large landowners in the administration of these territories I am reviving forthwith . . . the institution of Divisional Councils.'[38] These councils were intended to be the training ground for those who would be represented in the National Assembly.[39] This intention was interesting, as an analysis of these councils shows that the great majority of members were tribal sheikhs. In Diwaniya, seven out of twelve were sheikhs; in Samawah, six out of seven; in Hilla ten out of fourteen.[40]

The legal framework which bolstered and encouraged the authority of the sheikh was the Tribal Disputes Regulation, issued as a proclamation by the British military authorities and confirmed by Royal Iradah in December 1924. The secretary to the British High Commissioner described the intent of the Regulation to Rustam Haidar, PPS to King Faisal:

> By means of this regulation an attempt has been made to reserve to tribal jurisdiction the decision of such cases as might, if referred to the courts, have resulted in decisions contrary to the ideals of justice as accepted by the tribes.[41]

'One of the most valuable legacies of the British regime', wrote Stephen Longrigg, authority on Iraqi history and former Political Officer. Yet the effect of the Regulation was not only the confirmation of tribal law as the law of the tribal land but of enhancing the jural role of the sheikh and thereby reinforcing his primacy, since tribal customary law was based on the arbitration role of the sheikh in any sectional dispute. The British High Commissioners were staunch defenders of this legacy to the tribes. In his Confidential Report for 1928, Sir Henry Dobbs noted how 'I have restrained successive cabinets from abrogating the Tribal Disputes Regulation.'

The most important buttress to the position of the tribal sheikh and the cement of the Sharifian-sheikh alliance was the ownership and control of land. The distinction between these two kinds of possession is important and is best analysed by returning to the period of the Tanzimat,[42] when Midhat Pasha, as Governor, attempted to alter the prevailing relationship between tribe and state and transform the role of the tribal leader. The implementation of the 1858 Ottoman land law, part of the Tanzimat reforms, aimed at extending the powers of the central authority and sapping the autonomy of the tribes and their leaders. Ottomanisation of the tribal leaders and sedentarisation of the tribe were the dual means toward this centralising aim, the former to be achieved through the dispatch of the sons of sheikhs to Istanbul for education and a taste for things *Osmanli* and the latter through offering title to large tracts of government land.

Ottomanisation, except in a few cases like that of Abd al-Muhsin Sa dun, was not successful, nor was sedentarisation, although it brought about greater effects in rural Iraq. The introduction of title deeds, *tapu sanads,* was alien to the Iraqi rural population for, in the main, land ownership was not based on formal legal rights but corporate tribal owernship and land use was ultimately a consequence of its ability to fight for it, defend it and come to temporary truces with predatory tribal neighbours. Under the British Mandate the tribes were very keen to have and hold titles to land, but in the last half of the nineteenth century the tribes were quite rightly suspicious of government and of its ways. As a consequence, urban notables, merchants and Ottoman officials bought up these *tapu sanads*, and not only in the tribal areas but also around the cities. The urban bourgeoisie of Ottoman Iraq was overwhelmingly Sunni, as was the Ottoman administration with whom the former had contact both socially and politically through family representation in the administration of both civil and religious affairs. They were ideally placed to capitalise on the availability of the lands.

Many of the larger tracts of land, the deeds of which were offered for sale, were in the Shii south, so that the expansion of the reformed Ottoman administration into the southern tribal areas was matched by the intrusion of Sunni landlords, both Ottoman and Arab. Adding to this potential economic and sectarian problem was the introduction of a formal system of title to land in tribal areas which were neither surveyed nor mapped. The result was that 'rich merchants and men of influence of all kinds obtained deeds for large tracts of agricultural land with boundaries and areas filled in pretty much at the discretion of the purchaser, regardless of the tribesmen.'[43]

It was believed that the intrusion of the urban bourgeoisie into areas which had previously been closed to them because of the strength of the tribes would be facilitated by the increased efforts of the Ottoman Empire to gain a stronger control over rural dissidents. Tribal strength and independence were not destroyed so easily and the new urban landowners were able to extract their share only where the tribes were weak, and normally the relative strength of tribe and administration varied with the distance from police post and garrison centre. Around Baghdad and Basra, for example, the *sanad* owners were able to extract their full share. In a town like Baquba (a town rich in date gardens and orange groves, populated by detribalised Arabs and commanding the road to Persia) economic, social and strategic features ensured that government control was constant and that the landowner received the fruit of his title deed. In Diwaniya and Hilla, on the Middle and Lower Euphrates, the tribes were very strong and the landlords were dependent not on striking up a working arrangement with the tribes but on the extractive powers of the Ottoman administration.[44] The variety was made more complex by the Sanniyah lands, which had been the property of Sultan Abd al-Hamid. These were large tracts of the most fertile lands in the provinces of Basra and Amara.[45] After the Young Turk revolution in 1908 and the subsequent removal of Abd al-Hamid, these lands reverted to the state, and thus, after the First World War, some of the most fertile and prosperous agricultural areas of Iraq were available.

When the British arrived they faced a situation where, first, landlords held title to land but where frequently the tribes were in full possession, and, second, where the state owned vast and fertile agricultural lands. British policy was initially based on the political expedient of alienating neither landowner nor sheikh, not recognising the then current situation by attempting to pressure the tribes to pay the landowner but imposing few sanctions against the recalcitrant tribal sheikh.

In practice the policy was argued in the *Revenue Circular:*

> I do not see how we can give them [the shaykhs in actual possession] any formal certificate of title, but I think we are justified, in cases where the Tapu tenant is not able to arrange cultivation . . . to give leases to the tribal shaykh . . . and require him, as part of these terms, to make such payment to the Tapu tenant as may be equitable.[46]

A different class of lands were those which belonged to the tribe as a whole and had never been alienated. Having to choose between a policy of giving individual cultivation rights to the peasant and one of leasing to tribal sheikhs, the British chose the latter, for the tribalised or non-tribalised peasant would be protected from the oppression of the sheikh 'by his mobility and relative scarcity'.[47] Given the habitual indebtedness of the peasant from one harvest to the next, this reliance on the market mechanism was highly myopic. The policy with regard to these lands again underlined the attempts to centralise tribal authority, no matter the degree of dissolution, under one sheikh. The 'improvements' laid out were:

(1) the fee should be determined on a reasonable basis;
(2) the lease should be in favour of a single sheikh;
(3) government should expressly retain power to secure fair treatment . . . for peasants.

This policy of temporarily leasing the vast amount of land available became a permanent feature of Iraqi politics. That the government decided on the price and the leaseholder was a strong weapon against individual tribal sheikhs under the British and during the independence period. Furthermore, it gave the central government an economic stick which had strong political implications in bargaining processes and gave the tribal sheikhs a permanent interest in the activities of central government.

Land was the major productive resource and the single source of wealth. Thus the economic stage was set for the building of the political alliance which was to dominate Iraqi politics until 1958. An alien monarch and a group of professional soldier-politicians without followers controlled the positions of central government through which resources were distributed. They had no natural followers like the tribal sheikhs, nor had they any power, status or wealth independent of the state. On the other hand, the tribal sheikhs were the accepted (or in some cases imposed) leaders of rural society. They possessed followers (many of whom were well armed),[48] wealth and prestige and had never been ready to be the instrumentalities of a central authority, Arab or Ottoman. While the sheikhs had a social, economic and political position to preserve, consolidate or expand, the Sharifians had a state position to expand. The two were largely complementary. Parliament and cabinet symbolised that complementarity: Cabinets were dominated by Sharifians and Parliaments by the sheikhs and rural land-owning interest so that these two institutions ensured the persistence of the great bargain: the stability of the dominance of sheikhs in the rural areas and the stability of the dominance of the Sharifians at the centre. The fluidity of political relationships between individual sheikhs and individual politicians, typical of a political system where clientele building was rampant, should not obscure the basic stability of the politico-economic alliance. Nor should the fact that in the post Second World War period there was a high number of non-Sharifians in Cabinets make the alliance less valid, for the basis of the alliance remained valid for the system as a whole.

Developments in the 1930s underwrote the system. During the 1930s Iraqi governments were increasingly in need of cash to finance educational expansion, economic projects and the expansion of the armed forces. Because the tribes were heavily armed and, subsequently, because of the unwritten alliance between the sheikhs and the politicians, increased taxation was not a financial option. The main resource held by the government was the power to dispose of state domains, which were sold and leased in larger and larger portions.[49] A further development was that the tribal sheikhs, in order to develop their lands, entered into partnerships with central politicians and urban merchants, facilitated by legislation proposed by the cabinet. Such land development was encouraged by the introduction of pump irrigation, which 'accelerated the process by converting tribal lands into privately owned holdings, increased the power of tribal shaykhs and gradually impoverished the peasant'.[50] The process by which land which had previously been communally owned began to be claimed by the pump-owner was facilitated by the 1932 Land Settlement Act whereby the pump-owner's actual ownership of the land was confirmed by the criterion of 'beneficial occupational use'. By this act many sheikhs were transformed into agricultural capitalists.[51]

This changing relationship of tribesman and sheikh to cultivator and landlord was legitimised by the 1933 Law Governing the Rights and Duties of Cultivators which 'largely had the effect of making the peasants serfs tied to the land and landlords'.[52] This Bill was proposed by the Minister of Finance, Yasin al-Hashimi, nationalist, Sharifian and by the early 1930s a large pump-owner.[53] The law laid down that a cultivator could only move from the land if he were free of debt. If he was indebted and the release from the landlord was not obtained, employment elsewhere was prohibited. Tribal and non-tribal cultivators were chronically in debt, for the Iraqi rural economy, like other peasant economies, was based on debt, usually incurred for seed against future crops. These, then, are two pieces of legislation proposed by Cabinet, passed by Parliament and promoting the interests of the land-owning sector of the alliance which included by this time not only sheikhs but Sharifians.

Some idea of the vast amounts of land distributed by the government and the resultant size of land-holdings is pertinent here.

Table 4.3

Mashara	Number of Agricultural Holdings
Under 4	24,270
4 – 20	25,849
20 – 100	41,905
100 – 600	27,555
600 – 1,000	1,847
1,000 – 2,000	1,702
2,000 – 5,000	1,221
5,000 – 10,000	424
10,000 – 20,000	168
Over 20,000	104

Source: Lord Salter, *The Development of Iraq, A Plan for Action* (Iraq Development Board, 1954), p. 190.

In the last category, over 20,000 mashara, were thirteen proprietors who owned between 50,000 and 100,000 and 21 who owned between 100,000 and 200,000.[54] In Amara province 5 per cent of landowners owned 69.7 per cent of the total cultivable area and in Basra 0.2 per cent owned 50.8 per cent.[55] The pages of the Iraqi government gazettes of the 1930s and 1940s give a good indication of the speed with which land was distributed and the size of the grants. To select one example at random, in December 1938 Muhammad Habib, paramount sheikh of the Rabia tribe and an earlier supporter of the British, received in *lazma* (freehold) six parcels of land totalling 75,291 masharas; in January 1939, four sons of Fahd al-Sadun received more than 70,000 masharas between them.[56]

The careers of Mohan al-Khayrallah and Yasin al-Hashimi provide good illustrations of the successful sheikh and Sharifian, respectively. Mohan was described in a British report in 1917 thus:

> Mohan is an exceptionally capable young man, and is managing the affairs of the al-Humaid admirably. One or two attempts were made by his uncles to get the power into their own hands, but the attempts ceased as soon as it became evident to all that Mohan was the man chosen by the government.[57]

Al-Khayrallah came from the Shuwylat section of the Humayd tribe and as late as 1927 leased his tribal lands from the Sadun family, one of the very few tribal families which had benefited from the Ottoman land policy. The Humayd were well armed, possessing about 3,000 rifles, a factor important in marking out its sheikh as a powerful provincial leader and facilitating his nomination to the Assembly where he represented the Muntafik province in ten out of the fourteen assemblies. With a powerful rural base and regular election as deputy he maximised his political position by switching his support from one central faction to another. By the 1950s his lands were estimated at one million masharas.[58] Other tribal leaders who illustrate the strong interrelationship between large landownership and constant occupancy of positions in the Assembly were: Naif and Muhsin Jaryan, father and son, of the Albu Sultan, who had four members of the family in eleven of the fourteen assemblies; Abdullah and Balasim Yasin, who owned half a million masharas and were in every elected Assembly.[59] Yasin al-Hashimi was a good example of Max Weber's dictum: 'the professional politician need not seek remuneration directly for his political work, whereas every politician without means must absolutely claim this'.[60] Although Weber was writing about the official payment of politicians, it applies equally to leading politicians working in a political environment of personnel instability who have no means independent of their occupancy of political office, parliamentary, Cabinet or bureaucratic. Al-Hashimi, like other Sharifians, utilised his political positions to gain wealth which allowed him to be less dependent on the vicissitudes of Baghdad political life. He came originally from an urban Baghdadi family of little means. His father was a *mukhtar* in the al-Barudiyya quarter of Baghdad. Al-Hashimi attended military school in Baghdad and then the military college in Istanbul. He was an early opponent of the British occupation, a leader of the opposition to the Anglo-Iraqi Treaty relationship, yet frequently held Cabinet office during the

Mandate. In fact he was a willing participant in the ambiguous politics of co-operation and opposition under the Mandate and a total participant in the Mandatory's operation of the spoils system, as illustrated in one High Commissioner's memorandum: 'I have always advocated the occasional "rotivationist" including of the able and scheming Yasin Pasha in the cabinet because only by this can he be prevented from becoming a Zaghlul'.[61] Though al-Hashimi was an instrument in the British policy of deradicalising the Iraqi opposition by drawing him into the web of place-seekers, he manipulated the system to strengthen his position and that of his followers. He used his Ministerial posts (the Ministry of Finance was his speciality) to enrich himself and his followers. When he was Minister of Communications and Works he granted a concession for an extensive land and irrigation scheme to a group including Thabit Abd al-Nur, a former Sharifian and political follower, and later invested in the concession himself.[62] In 1926, as Minister of Finance, he granted tax remissions and land grants to pump investors. By the mid-1930s he had become a large landowner and investor, possessing sixteen estates, each one of which was between 1,000 and 2,000 acres.[63] Through his policy of favouring the landowners through land grants, concessions, tax remissions and governmental positions, he built up a personal following, organised in the *Hizb al-Ikha*, and reinforced the role of the land-owning class in the political system.

Yasin al-Hashimi's career provides a good example of the way in which the personalistic politics of patronage contributed to the establishment of a political system dominated by landowners. Their policy preferences continually prevailed and consequently the private ownership of large tracts of land which were previously publicly or communally owed were encouraged. Although the dominance of the Sharifians at the centre was numerically watered down over the years, that initial structural complementarity of central politicos and provincial tribal sheikhs burgeoned into a fused systemic class interest of landowners. The power of the landowner, particularly the tribal element, ensured a stability of oppression and exploitation in the countryside and deprivation and squalor in the urban slums, creating conditions of radical opposition, not simply to the régime of monarchy, regency and the manipulation and factionalism of cabinet politicians, but to a system of rule based on class domination and exploitation. In Iraq this process of transformation of a ruling élite into ruling class created the social forces which were to bring the whole system down in 1958.

Notes

1. Most of the writing on Iraq has been of the descriptive historical type and as such has not attempted to explain or analyse. The works of S. Longrigg, *Iraq 1900-1950* (Oxford, 1953) and Majid Khadduri, *Independent Iraq*, 2nd edition (Oxford, 1960) do, however, provide excellent background for more analytic studies.

2. See especially John Waterbury, *Commander of the Faithful*, a behavioural attempt to define the qualitative nature of the functioning of the Moroccan political system, and El Baki Hermassi, *Leadership and National Development in North Africa* (Berkeley and Los Angeles, 1972), an excellent political sociology study of change in North Africa.

3. This situation was not simply one caused by Ottoman land policy which will be discussed below, but by the effect of culturally and socially hostile groups competing for power and privilege in a new system. The received wisdom on the role of the shii in the Ottoman state is one of isolationism, whereas the establishment of the Mandate saw a vigorous participation by shii of all social levels.

4. The 1920 insurrection in Iraq helped establish the strength of the tribal sheikhs in the minds of the British. See Amal Vinogradov, 'The 1920 Revolt in Iraq Reconsidered: The Role of Tribes in National Politics', *International Journal of Middle Eastern Studies*, Vol. 3 (1972), pp. 123-9.

5. B.C. Busch, *Britain, India and the Arabs 1914-1921* (California, 1971), p. 175. This is probably an exaggeration based on an examination of the British records. Ibrahim al-Rawi, who was a POW in India, states quite clearly that he and his comrades well knew where they were going, since an emissary of the Sharif was acting as translator and informing them of events in Arabia. Ibrahim al-Rawi, *Min al-Thawra al-Arabiyya al-Kubra Ila al Iraq at Hadith, Dhikrayat* (Beirut, 1969), p. 19.

6. See Phebe Marr, 'Iraq's Leadership Dilemma: A Study in Leadership Trends 1948-1968', *Middle East Journal*, Vol. 24 (Summer 1970), pp. 297-8 for statistics on political survival for the period 1948-58.

7. Ali Jawdat, *Dhikrayat 1900-1958* (Beirut, 1967), p. 18.

8. Ibid., p. 18.

9. Al-Rawi, *Min al-Thawra*, p. 9.

10. Talib Mushtaq, *Awraq Ayyami 1900-1958* (Beirut, 1968), p. 36, my translation.

11. Ernest Dawn, 'The Rise of Arabism in Syria', *Middle East Journal* (Spring 1962), Vol. 16, No. 2.

12. Dawn's general conclusion that the Syrian nationalists came from the 'indigenous Arab elite' contrasts with the evidence for Iraq.

13. Many studies have emphasised these factors, ranging from P.J. Vatikiotis' study of the ties binding the Egyptian Free Officers to M. Van Dusen's study of the emergence of the Ba'ath in Syria: P.J. Vatikiotis, *The Egyptian Army in Politics* (Bloomington, Indiana, 1961); M. Van Dusen, 'Political Integration and Regionalism in Syria', *Middle East Journal*, Vol. 26 (Summer 1972).

14. See J.S. Szyliowicz, 'Elite Recruitment in Turkey: the Role of the Mulkiye', *World Politics*, No. 3 (April 1971). Of those who attended this college between 1859 and 1907, 72 per cent were the sons of bureaucrats, the element corresponding partially to Dawn's 'indigenous Arab elite'.

15. There were, of course, some members of urban bourgeois families like Tawfiq al-Suwaidi, from a bureaucratic-land-owning family.

16. Faisal to Commander-in-Chief of the Indian Expeditionary Force. Report received 17 March 1919, p. 143, FO 371/4199.

17. See Jawdat, *Dhikrayat*, p. 89, and Tawfiq al-Suwaidi, *Mudhakkirati* (Beirut, 1919), p. 57.

18. Memorandum on the Future of Mesopotamia, H.W. Young, January 1919.

19. Minutes of a Meeting of the Eastern Committee of the War Cabinet, 27 November 1918, p. 13298 to 371/4148.

20. Confidential Report for Week Ending 19 September 1919, No. 134386, 27 September 1919, FO 371/4150. The individuals referred to are Nuri al-Said and Jaafar al-Askari, both of whom were many times Prime Minister.

21. Minute by H.W. Young, 24 June 1920, FO 371/5075.

22. Busch, *Britain, India and the Arabs,* p. 361.

23. Busch, ibid., p. 455.

24. Some, like Tahsin al-Qadri and Rustam Haidar, were Lebanese or Syrian.

25. Because of the wideness of parts of the country, the poor communications and the lack of an effective Iraqi army, the central government depended on the mobility of the Royal Air Force to curb the southern shii and northern Kurdish tribesmen.

26. He frequently depended on intermediaries like the Amir Zayd to convey messages to anti-British elements.

27. Interview with Faisal, in High Commissioner to Sec. of State for Colonies, 26 August 1922, p. 42829. L/PS/10 782.

28. The best source on the political economy of tribal Iraq is still John Batatu, 'Shaykh and Peasant in Iraq 1917-1958', unpublished Ph.D. dissertation (Harvard University, 1960). See also the useful *Iraq and the Persian Gulf,* Geographical Handbook series, Naval Intelligence (London, 1944). Two anthropologies of Iraqi tribes and tribal leaders are R.A. Fernea, *Shaykh and Effendi – Changing Patterns of Authority among the El-Shabana of Southern Iraq* (Cambridge, Mass., 1970) and S.M. Salim, *Marsh Dwellers of the Euphrates Delta* (London, 1962). The major reference work is Abbas al-Azzawi, *Tarikh Ashair al-Iraq*, 4 vols. (Baghdad, 1952-6).

29. The office of the PO, Nasiriya, to Deputy Civil Commissioner, Basra, 4 January 1918. Administrative Departmnte of the Basra Wilayat, No. 105/3 Iraqi Central Archives.

30. As the PO in Hilla noted: 'at present [1918] the tribe is the readiest medium to hand through which to carry on the administration of the district'. Reports of the Administration of the Occupied Territories: Mesopotamia, for 1918, p. 120. FO 371/4151.

31. This is an impression gained from reading the weekly and monthly diaries of political officers, memoirs and private papers.

32. Capt. A.H. Ditchburn, Administrative Report for the Muntafiq Division, Enclosure in S. for India to S. of S., FO 18 October 1920, E. 12851.

33. See Abd al-Jalil al-Zahir, *Al-Ashair al-Iraqiyya* (Dar Lubnan, Beirut, 1972).

34. See the correspondence in 'Co-operation with Fahad Beq ibn Hadhdhal', Confidential N. 883 to Chief Political Officer, 16 May 1917, Air 20/504.

35. *Reports of the Admin. . . . etc.* p. 375 FO 371/4151.

36. One donum = 0.6 acre.

37. Muhammed Fadhil al-Jamali, *The New Iraq, The Problem of Bedouin Education* (London, 1973), p. 43. and Intelligence Report No. 18, 1 August 1921, E. 10162 FO 371/6352.

38. Mesopotamia: Future Constitution. Cabinet B 317 p. 2023/19. Enclosure No. 2: Civil Commissioner, Baghdad, to Sec. of State for India, 10 November 1918 P. 60942 FO 371/4148.

39. See speech of Major Norbury in Monthly Reports of Political Officers for September 1919. 19 April 1920 FO 371/5072.

40. See Reports in FO 371/5071 to FO 371/5078.

41. Copy of Confidential Memorandum in Central Baghdad Archives.

42. The best analysis of land and the derivative socio-political relations is the dissertation, unfortunately published by John Batatu, 'Shaykh and Peasant in Iraq'.

43. 'Note on Land Policy' in *Revenue Circular* (Baghdad, 29 May 1919) Enclosure in India Office to Under-Secretary of State, Foreign Office, 10 September 1919, p. 127607 FO 371/4150.

44. This area was populated by the Fatla, the Bani Hasan and the Bani Huchaim, each of which had numerous well armed followers.

45. See Albertine Jwaideh, 'The Sanniyah Lands of Sultan Abd al-Hamid II in Iraq', *Arab and Islamic Studies in Honour of Sir Hamilton Gibb* (London, 19). Amara Province is of particular importance for there, and in Kut, sheikhly dominance and oppression reached their zenith.

46. 'Note on Land Policy'.

47. Ibid.

48. See Sir Aylmer Haldane, *The Insurrection in Mesopotamia 1920* (Edinburgh, 1920), Appendix VI for an estimate of the number of armed men in the tribal areas.

49. Abbas Alnasrawi, *Financing Economic Development in Iraq* (New York, 1967), pp. 129-30.

50. K. Langley, *The Industrialization of Iraq*. Harvard Middle Eastern Monographs (Cambridge, Mass., 1961), pp. 51-2.

51.In the 1930s capital investment in pumps was £5.5 million which, though not a large figure, contrasts with £1 million in industrial capital investments.

52. Ibid., p. 68.

53. See Phebe Marr, 'Yasin al-Hashimi: The Rise and Fall of a Nationalist', (unpublished Ph.D. dissertation (Harvard University, 1968), for an account of his career.

54. Alnasrawi, *Financing Economic Development*, p. 65.

55. Fuad Baali, *Relation of the People to the Land in Southern Iraq*, University of Florida Monographs (Gainesville, Flo., 1966), pp. 29-33.

56. *Mulhaq li Jarida al-Waqa, al-Iraqiyya* 26 December 1938, 23 January 1939, 30 January 1939. For detailed references to the distribution of land in the government gazettes, see Mohammad al-Suwari, *al-Iqta fi Liwa al-Kut (Feudalism in the Province of Kut)* (1958, no place of publication).

57. Appendix A to Nasiriya Report, *Administration Report Revenue Board* (Baghdad, Gov. Press, 1918), p. 393 FO 371/4150.

58. Doreen Warriner, *Land Reform and Development in the Middle East* (London, 1957), p. 142.

59. For details of the deputies see Abd al-Razzaq al-Hasani, *Tarikh al-Wizarat al-Iraqiyya;* Vol. I-IX (Saida, Lebanon, various dates). For land-ownership see Warriner, *Land Reform,* and FO, CO and Air files in Public Records Office.

60. Max Weber, 'Politics as a Vocation', H.H. Gerth and C. Wright Mills, *From Max Weber, Essays in Sociology* (London, 1948), p. 86.

61. Memorandum by Sir Henry Dobbs CO 730/40465/56 1927.

62. This was the Dyala Cotton Plantations Ltd (Asfar Concession). CO 730/108 Part I and II 40012.

63. Al-Hashimi was said never to have paid taxes. S.S.O. to ASI Hinaidi, 6 October 1931, 1/BD/23 70 A Air 23/382.

5 THE FORMATION OF THE IRAQI ARMY, 1921-33

Paul P.J. Hemphill

The Need for an Army

Politics in new states become pre-eminently a quest for order and stability. These are dependent upon established authority: the right to order certain actions, and the ability to secure their performance. There are two conditions: the acknowledged legitimacy of that authority, and its effective claim to a monopoly of force. In 1921, however, King Faisal was monarch, under British auspices, of a gloomy patrimony. His claim to the throne had been challenged by the Ottoman Establishment and also by the established Sunni families, the former being hostile to those who had deserted the Empire in its hour of trial, and the latter being resentful of Hashimite pretensions. Such was the extent of Faisal's support in Iraq that his election left many Iraqis debating whether the throne had come to him solely through the British, with the Provisional government submitting to their influence.[1] Once elected, his bane, and that of the Turks before him, was the disunity of his realm and the limits set to governmental authority by geographical and human diversity. Iraq had not been the product of any will to sovereignty on the part of its inhabitants. Its people were possessed of no consciousness of belonging to a political community. Beyond Baghdad lay tribal steppe and Kurdish mountain where, in the past, the writ of the authorities had rarely ventured unarmed, enclaves of diverse cultures having no ties of affection, loyalty and custom binding them to their new rulers.

The Sunni Arab 20 per cent was itself divided, as Faisal's candidacy had shown. Yet despite the antipathy displayed towards Faisal's 'Sharifian' entourage, who were seen as penniless parvenus and opportunists by the more established Ottomans, Sunni Arabs in general wished to maintain their traditional dominion over the non-Sunni and non-Arab communities. The Sharifians, too few to govern Iraq by themselves, were obliged to share power and the spoils of power with their adversaries.

The prospect of continued Sunni dominion was unwelcome to the Shiis, 50 per cent of the population, yet in the anomalous position of being an ostensibly oppressed majority. The Kurdish 20 per cent likewise had no wish to be part of the new state. At the Peace Conference, they had been promised independence, but the British were to be convinced that, for strategic reasons, Kurdistan should remain in Iraq. Sunnis and Shiis, the Kurds were asked to submerge their particularistic aspirations in a common Iraqi citizenship. Consensus was absent among the remaining 10 per cent also. Christian and Jew looked to Britain for protection whilst the Turcoman community in the north had hoped for the advent of a liberating Mustafa Kemal.

Consensus, the basis of a political community, was accordingly lacking, whereas the viability of the new state depended upon the effective integration of disparate and anti-national elements. Britain believed the stability and order conducive to this would be best achieved through its own well tried ideas and institutions, which were to be inculcated into all Iraqis by advice and guidance (indirect control) and the gradual devolution of authority and responsibility. The Mandate system as it was applied to Iraq was designed with this in view whilst maintaining British interests in the area. Strong rule and internal stability were essential to unity in the interests of the new king, his entourage, and the Mandatory. Stability and unity were prerequisites for progress and the criteria for admission to the League of Nations and, thereby, full independence.

But the bases of stability were tenuous, the legitimacy of authority uncertain, and consensus as to how and in whom this should be vested non-existent. The constitutional institutions established by the Organic Law were intended to create it. High Commissioner Cox endeavoured to legitimise Sharifian rule by creating the impression that power would be shared in such a way as to reflect Iraq's diversity. Theoretically, therefore, Majlis and Cabinet lists would reflect ethnic and sectarian differences. Equilibrium would be enhanced by personalised and reciprocal relations between politicians and patriarchs which would provide a valuable transmission belt between centre and periphery, thus strengthening state authority.

But at this early stage Iraq had no time to wait for the emergence of consensus and unity through the process of institution-building, threatened as it was by internal disintegration and external aggression – attacks by Turkish irregulars and Kurdish tribesmen and Wahhabi incursions in the west continued into the autumn of 1924, being curbed only by British forces. Faisal and the new rulers likewise could not wait. Only by rendering the young state viable could they ensure their political survival. The uncertainty of their positions and threats from within and without made a strong card essential in order that Iraq should survive whilst institutions took root and their control of them secured.

That card was an army capable of maintaining internal order, capable of dealing with spontaneous and separate disturbances, an army which could defend Iraq's sovereignty and integrity against external threat. The rulers must have observed with chagrin that whereas the 'people', factious and divided, could muster some 100,000 rifles, the Shii tribes being heavily armed, the kingdom depended for its existence upon British goodwill and British arms. Their sensibilities and prestige were offended by this dependent status. Moreover, their credibility in the eyes of their nationalist opponents was at stake, the latter being ever ready to accuse them of pandering to the British and of serving imperial interests. Although aware of the necessity of British support both in Iraq and in the League of Nations, they were compelled to emphasise their unwavering commitment to complete independence in order to counter nationalist criticism.

They felt acutely therefore the need for an army of sufficient numbers and firepower to guarantee independence, for only with this could Iraq ever attempt to dispense with British assistance. Moreover, wishing to be seen as undisputed representatives of the nation, the king and his politicians had to have the backing of a strong army which was also seen as such; only then could it serve as the ultimate coercive sanction in ensuring unity and upholding their authority. They wanted, therefore, a strong army both as a symbol and defender of national integrity, and as a bulwark for their own authority.

Yet their perception of the need for an army went deeper than this. The national army envisaged for Iraq did not have a tradition of national identity or any association with the established authority to fall back on. Both had first to be created. Given their desire to mould the state and its institutions in their own image, and the necessity of unity in order to achieve this, it was essential that the army should be given an identity which would be acceptable to its soldiers and the people from among whom they were drawn, an identity compatible with their own idea of nation. It was conceived therefore as the creator of unity, the crucible of the nation, and the carrier of its virtues and its goals.

That the idea which they sought to impress upon all Iraqis, regardless of race and faith, was essentially an Arab one was to be expected with the Sunni Arabs' desire for dominance. That this idea was particularly an Arabist one was also to be expected, given the background of the politicians who sought to expand the army and the men chosen to command it. That the army should be seen as the instrument for fostering the idea was similarly predictable, in so far as the majority of the politicians themselves were men of Ottoman military background and aware of the efficacy of the military as a socialising institution.

The origins and nature of their Arabism, including the development of Arab nationalism after the Turkish Revolution of 1908, fall beyond the scope of this chapter. It must suffice to stress the importance of the Arab officers in this process. The effect of Arab nationalism upon Ottoman Mesopotamia had been only marginal. Its people had long been isolated from the Levantine heart of Arabism, an isolation strengthened by the centristic orientation of Arab officials, and the centralising zeal of the state. It was in Istanbul that Iraqis first became acquainted with Arabism, having left the confines of their provincial backwater. Of these, the officers constituted the overwhelming majority, playing a vital role in the development of Arab consciousness before the First World War, and an instrumental part in the Arab Revolt of 1916. Like the Young Turks, Arab officers became the vanguard of their particularism, modelling themselves upon the Young Turks as a 'Young Arab' antithesis to the Unionists and the policy of Turkification.

During the war, these officers used martial means for national ends, and not to install military régimes. But it was natural that they should play a prominent role in the politics of the kingdom of Iraq, imposing their nationalism upon the new state. Under the Empire, the military profession had been particularly attractive to families of modest means, especially the middle and lower levels of salaried officialdom, in so far as a military education was free. The state, obliged to provide for the education of the sons of its officials, encouraged them to select what it considered the most economical and useful of options: This class of minor functionaries was more numerous in Iraq than in other Arab provinces. It had long been an impoverished land in comparison to the mercantile Levant and the cosmopolitan capital, and offered fewer opportunities for the ambitious. Iraq therefore had more than its share of commissioned officers, whilst the numbers of cadets outnumbered students in civil institutions.[2] These were factors of considerable importance when in 1921 officers constituted the largest pool of educated persons amongst a backward and divided populace. There was a dearth of administrators, officers and politicians, whilst the veterans of the Arab armies had education, experience and revolutionary respectability to their credit. Large number entered politics and the public service, their revolt being a meal-ticket to position and, they hoped, prosperity. Nine of fourteen premiers between 1922 and 1932 were ex-Ottoman officers (including Nuri al-Said, Jaafar al-Askari, and Yasin al-Hashimi), as were thirty-two of fifty-six possible Cabinet Ministers. Of these, Jamil Madfai and Ali Jawdat became premiers after independence.

These soldiers-turned-politicians traded in their uniforms for the intrigue and manoeuvring of Iraqi politics. Aware of the praetorian past of the army of which they had been members, it was inconceivable to them that the Iraqi army should involve itself in politics as it had done. Rather, it had to be the loyal and obedient servant of state power. But the national ethic which they espoused, the martial spirit of Arab (and within it, Iraqi) nationalism, was a vital element in the consolidation of Sunni rule – a fact which their Sunni adversaries realised and accepted. Together, as rulers and would-be rulers, they sought to create a nation with an Arab identity by identifying with the Arab revolt, and by inculcating Iraqi youth with the ideas behind it. The army, seen as a school for citizenship, became accordingly as much as Arab army as an Iraqi one.

This inculcation of national feeling and its martial tenor began with the educational system. As Director-General of Education between 1923 and 1927, Sati al-Husri, the Syrian ideologue of Arabism, sought to establish a coherent and controlled national ideology throughout the school system. His aim was to disseminate pan-Arabism and to assimilate diverse elements into a homogenous whole and, regardless of the feelings of Shiis and Kurds, 'to spread faith in the unity of the Arab nation, and to disseminate consciousness of its past glories', to combat the enemies of 'Uruba, to teach, to awaken, and to discipline. His history syllabus in particular was designed to impart knowledge of the fatherland and the nation's past. It led up to the study of the Risorgimento and German unity, with analogies and prefigurations of Iraq as the Arab Piedmont or Prussia.[3] As an adjunct of civil education, he emphasised military training as a means of instilling national sentiments, and regarded national service as important as compulsory education.

Husri and those who appointed him saw the army as a vital socialising agent within the framework of their Arabism. And indeed, what could be better than an army drawn from all classes of society for moulding the prototype Iraqi, taking the individual, atomised and steeped in traditional prejudices, from his restricted milieu, and reshaping him? The community of the barracks and the battlefield, the military schools and the officers' mess would make Iraqis out of peasants, nomads and townsmen alike, of Sunni and Shii, of Arabs and Kurds. Arguing for conscription in 1928, al-Husri wrote of the soldier:

> He lives with a group of the sons of the country, who are drawn from different towns and who hold various beliefs and positions. He lives with them, subject to a system in which they are all included without exception. He works for a purpose which is loftier than all of these, for a purpose which ensures the life of the fatherland and the welfare of the nation. Military life makes him feel clearly the existence of nation and fatherland. He learns the sacrifice of blood and self in the cause of the nation and fatherland.[4]

Sami Shawkat, Husri's spiritual successor, although a more extreme advocate of Arabness, observed later that 'experience has proved that the best school for the moulding of the character is the army and military discipline, which makes a man of the individual through his courage, his patriotism, and his consciousness of everything.'[5]

The ideal of the soldier at his best was little removed from the perfect citizen, embracing a tradition far older than the nation it now upheld. This tradition was inherent in Sunni Islam which had long ago endowed its armies with the prestige and authority of an institution meriting divine blessing, the military profession coming to be regarded as identical with the fulfilment of a religious duty. The martial ethos of the Arab and Islamic past incorporated the ideal masculine temperament and the stoic virtues by which men ought to be measured, virtues respected by Arabs and Muslims over the centuries.

The tradition persisted, despite its degeneration during the Caliphal and Ottoman period, to be incorporated in the reformed Ottoman army after 1828, and transposed on Iraq by the men of that army.

Such was the urgency that inspired its creation, and the martial background of its founders, that the Iraqi army was put on a pedestal whilst virtually still on paper and given an image to which politicians, nationalists and ideologues, anxious for identity and independence and apprehensive of aggression, strove to give substance. The media accordingly responded, often confusing intent with actual realisation:

> The people crowded on to the streets to see their beloved soldiers, the protectors of the country. We were struck by the patriotic expression on the faces of the sons of the country when they saw our brave soldiers.
>
> We wish every success for our soldiers and hope that Iraq will soon have a strong army so that the country may gain complete independence and true freedom.[6]

The need for an army found expression therefore in a form far less mundane and far more emotive than the political interests of Iraq's rulers, important as these were. As Hasani stressed, in words still used by Iraqi politicians and soldiers, 'The army is the shield of the nation, and without it, neither a king nor a kingdom can stand erect.'[7]

Whitehall, however, attributed ulterior motives to the politicians' desires, Nuri in particular arousing British suspicions, officials doubtlessly being aware of the past. One wrote that Nuri was 'ready to produce the most fantastic schemes of military dominion', desiring 'a large army to enable him to make a coup d'état in favour of King Faysal, and to declare him as an absolute monarch, as both the king and Nuri chafe constantly against constitutional restraints'[8] and an Acting High Commissioner observed that 'Nuri, the imp of mischief, is obsessed with the dream of an absolute monarchy founded upon a praetorian army of which himself is the chief.'[9] Iraqi and British designs were consequently at odds with each other.

The British Design

Britain, as Mandatory, shared the Iraqis' desire for an army but questioned both their motives (see above) and the practicality of their demands. On one hand, the British policy was a response to the demands of British taxpayers for a cut-back in military expenditure in Iraq. On the other, Britain could not afford an Iraqi outburst such as that suppressed in 1920. Moreover, an army capable of upholding governmental authority and of maintaining internal order was considered a prerequisite for the stability which would ensure British interests. It was decided at the Cairo Conference of 1921, therefore, that defence should be jointly undertaken, the Iraqis providing an army which would be supplemented by the Royal Air Force and the British-officered and predominantly Assyrian Levies. Initially, the British favoured separate forces. British officials considered a national army so wasteful that it should virtually be dispensed with, and wished to concentrate on the RAF and the Levies, which were demonstrably more efficient. Such would have been anomalous in a prospectively independent Iraq, and accordingly it was recognised that the Levies could be but a stop-gap measure, their tasks being assumed in time by the national army. The Treaty of 1923 stated therefore that Iraq would ultimately be responsible for defence, and whilst British assistance would be progressively reduced, Iraq would expand its forces to a degree commensurate with her needs and resources, allocating no less than 25 per cent of her revenues for this purpose.

It was for Britain, however, to decide what those needs were and how Iraq's finances would be spent to meet them, the new army's training and armament being Britain's responsibility, and its operations restricted by an obligation of joint-consultation. In the semantics of the Mandate system, such assistance and advice were tantamount to control. High Commissioner Dobbs believed that consultation and a formal intimation that British support could not be expected would forestall unilateral military action on Iraq's part. He also stressed the danger of rushing things, a defeat inflicted upon a large Iraqi force by a recalcitrant tribe, for example, possibly precipitating a general tribal rising and thereby a dangerous situation for British forces. He recommended that Iraq, government and army alike, be put into 'swaddling clothes' until Britain finally withdrew. He did not visualise the possibility of Iraq alone ever being able to defend herself against external aggression, and favoured a limited role. He declared in the spring of 1925 that '9,000 good ground troops would keep internal order as an appendage to a sufficient mercenary air-force.'[10]

The controversies which ensued from such an outlook were to dominate the Mandate period and were to shape the attitudes of officers and civilians alike towards the British connection on one hand and the role of the army on the other. Although the first Askari Cabinet and all succeeding Ministries expressed in their programmes the desire for a strong army to defend Iraq's integrity, whilst Iraq lacked finances and also independence, it was dependent upon Britain for its defence. Such being the case, Britain could choose the means whereby Iraqi and British interests would be defended.

The attitude of the Residency was well known in Baghdad political circles, and resented. Figures of between 15,000 and 20,000 were more to the Iraqis' liking. Yasin, as premier in April 1925, took exception to Dobbs' ideas on two main grounds:

> First, that what was most badly needed for the Iraqi Army was rapid expansion, which could only be got by conscription, and secondly, that the Iraqi people would believe the scheme to be a plan for putting their army under British control.[11]

The pro-conscription lobby gained an important ally in the British Inspector-General, Major-General Daly, who proposed a wider military commitment on Iraq's part: some 19,000 troops, including an air force and the reduced Levies. He argued, counter to Dobbs, for a 'definite role', observing that an army confined to the maintenance of internal order

> ceases in any real sense to be an army at all, and is unlikely to obtain even a moderate degree of military efficiency . . . It would lack the inspiration that a national spirit alone can give, and would merely degenerate into a species of police-force or gendarmerie.[12]

His argument for adequate forces hinged primarily on the question of morale and its debilitation through dependance upon a foreign power. Iraq, he stressed, 'must bear her part . . . if such a part is not before the eyes of her army, that army will be emasculated at birth, and will become an unnecessary burden upon the state.'

Iraqis could not avoid a suspicion that Britain had no wish to see Iraq with a strong army – that their army was to be merely an arm of the imperial forces. For almost a decade, Britain was seen as obstructing the growth of the army, restricting its expansion and its role. This belief lingered, Salah al-Din al-Sabbagh writing many years later that the army was not intended by Britain to be a national army – an Iraqi army, yes, but not an Arab army; rather, an army controlled by Britain to be used against its own countrymen and not against the imperialists. It was not in Britain's interest, he asserted, that the people should rally around a strong army; Britain did not fear its weapons so much as she feared the solidarity of the people with the army under the flag of Arabism.[13]

British opposition was readily apparent when in June 1927, Jaafar al-Askari introduced a conscription Bill, telling the Majlis that 'the importance of national armies to active nations cannot be concealed. The national army in each country symbolizes its life and guards its independence . . .' Iraq, clinging to its existence, and aspiring to independence, its borders long and undefended, and surrounded by strong neighbours (Iran and Turkey), needed a conscript army. Iraq should not have to depend upon outside support, nor could it take full responsibility for its defence unless its numbers were increased.[14] Whitehall maintained, however, that Iraq could neither afford nor raise such a force. Britain doubted furthermore whether conscription could be enforced; the tribes which had resisted it under the Ottomans would doubtless resist it still, causing such widespread risings, and requiring such forces, that it would cost much more than the savings it might theoretically make possible. Moreover, British military opinion doubted the value of imposing service upon reluctant recruits, time and money being squandered in training them into parodies of soldiers with no inclination towards military life.

The Shii agitation and the tribal unrest which greeted the introduction of the Bill were in British eyes a foretaste of what could happen. Extreme nationalists protested against compelling patriotic youths to join an army largely controlled by the British. The Shii al-Nahda Party claimed that the Sunnis desired a conscript army for the domination of the Shii, and particularly the Shii tribes. The sheikhs interpreted conscription as a plan to destroy their tribal authority. But although this unrest and Britain's refusal to co-operate led to the withdrawal of the Bill, followed soon afterwards by the resignations of both the Cabinet and Daly, succeeding Cabinets persisted in their demands, keeping alive the issues of conscription and the army's future role.

Whitehall maintained its opinion that conscription was unwise and that British forces would not assist its application until it was shown to be acceptable to the people in general. Britain retained therefore an unpublicised yet effective veto. By 1929, the army was considered by British observers to be organised, ready and equipped to deal with raids from across the border and internal order, *backed by the RAF.*[15] It was apparent that it was not considered fit for a wider role. During negotiations for the Treaty of 1930, which was to regulate Anglo-Iraqi relations after independence, Britain was guided by the Air Ministry's opinion that the defence of Iraq must, ought and could be maintained from the air, the air force acting as a powerful and unobtrusive deterrent against aggression and internal disorder.

The army's numbers grew gradually, therefore, from 3,500 in 1922 to 7,000 in 1927, reaching some 11,500 at independence. The officer corps increased proportionately, one officer to about 24 men. The restraints exercised, or rather imposed, is illustrated by the fact that the army doubled in size between 1932 and 1936, an expansion due largely to the introduction of national service, at long last, in 1934. The officer corps failed, however, to keep pace despite an unprecedented intake into the Military college (established in 1924).

Britain's doubts regarding expansion were motivated to a considerable degree by the arguments outlined above, namely: an army suited to Iraq's needs and resources, as the British saw them, and the need to keep a weather-eye upon threats to internal order. Hence came Dobbs's warning against rushing things, and his doubts as to the wisdom of enforcing conscription upon an unwilling populace, and the reality that the deterrent effect of British warplanes had done more to discipline restive tribesmen and rebellious Kurds than the government and its forces. But a third factor also contributed to British thinking, in so far as the quality of an army is determined by its officers, and on these, the British military mission harboured many reservations.

The Iraqi Officer Corps

In April 1921, there were some 600 ex-Ottoman officers on the pension list, including some 400 recently returned from Damscus; this was far more than could be employed for some considerable time. About 190 Sharifian officers clamoured for immediate employment, but the likelihood of satisfying the demands of the redundant officers, Sharifian and Ottoman alike, was remote. Jaafar al-Askari, as Minister of Defence, had to provide for his former comrades-in-arms who could be expected to be more faithful to the Arab government than those who had not joined the Arab army after 1916. But there was the remainder to consider. There were the Arabists who did not desert, men like Yasin al-Hashimi, whose quarrel had been with the Unionists and not with the Empire. These had joined their fellows only after the fall of Damascus, regarding the Allies and not the Turks as the Arabs' true enemies. Yasin's brother, Taha al-Hashimi (a future Chief of Staff and premier), and the future leaders of the 'Golden Square', Sabbagh and Fahmi Said, were perhaps typical of these. Then there were loyal Ottomans who had returned from Anatolia after 1918, unenthusiastic about what many former servants of the Ottoman state regarded as unwanted statehood. Amin al-Umari, prominent in Iraqi politics after 1937, was one of these. Finally, there were those who had no Arab inclinations whatsoever and therefore no reason for defection: Kurdish officers such as Husain Fawzi and Nur al-Din Mahmud (who were later to become Chiefs of Staff). These could not be ignored, particularly the ex-Ottoman officers of all persuasions who, returning to unemployment and destitution after 1918, played active parts in the revolt of 1920, many providing the tribal insurgents with advice and weapons.

The British had no time for the political criteria Jaafar would have liked to employ, and impressed upon the government the need to make full use of the abundant material available, although with the possible exception of Arab officers known to have participated in the Iraqi revolt and those who had opposed the Allies in Syria. Of the 600 aforementioned officers, therefore, 250 were commissioned by royal decree in 1922 after taking a training course. The numbers eventually absorbed were much greater. These ex-Ottoman officers had now to be weaned of past professional ways and trained to a new doctrine and a new system.

Although progress was made, the Staff College being established in 1927, the Iraqis were being sent to senior officers' courses in India and England (among them, Bakr Sidqi). The British military mission had a poor opinion of the army's Ottoman inheritance. The tactical knowledge and power of command of senior officers was seen to be weak; throughout the inter-war period, the military mission consistently derided their Turkish way of doing things and their old-fashioned military ideas. There was a need, the Administrative Report for 1926 observed, 'for better-educated men, better able to teach what they have learned'.[16]

Possibly exasperated with the task of retraining old soldiers, the British put their faith in an indigenous officer corps, created in their own martial image, as the future commanders of an army which would be organised, trained and equipped on British lines. Britain possibly expected no effectiveness on the part of the Iraqi army until this new generation had reached positions of command. It was not until 1927, however, that the first cadets passed out of the Iraqi military college, the officer corps being therefore almost exclusively composed of men of ex-Ottoman training and background. The officer corps was to double in size between 1922 and 1936, and the number of ex-Ottomans decreased, through retirement and dismissal, from 70 per cent in 1927 to about 50 per cent in 1932, and an estimated 15 per cent in 1936.[17] But those who remained rose to the highest ranks, holding effective control of combative units, and exerting a powerful influence upon impressionable juniors.

Britain had high hopes for the young officers. The military college was established as far as possible on the Sandhurst model, accepting students from secondary schools and the law school. As secondary education was neither universal nor free, and therefore confined to those who could afford it, cadets were drawn from comparatively well-to-do urban families and those with connections.[18] Places were reserved for the sons and relatives of tribal sheikhs – contingent with the state's policy of bringing the tribal patriarchs into the political system – who received a separate education suited to their lower educational standard. But the urban officers were to remain in the majority: in 1928, only 25 per cent of officers were of tribal origin as compared to 75 per cent of the infantry rank and file.

As the Ottoman 'Rushdiyya' system of free elementary military education was not revived, and the number of places offered far fewer than those of the 'Adadiyyat-al-Askariyya' (the Ottoman equivalent), the military profession ceased to be a refuge to the impecunious, as it had often been in the past. The numbers accepted for military education were considerably less than under the Ottomans, reflecting the limited demands of the state, which, in turn, enabled recruitment to be more selective. In 1914 there were 700 students in three Rushdiyyas, and 500 at the Adadiyya,[19] but between 1927 and 1934, a mere 240 cadets passed through the Iraqi military college. The first batch of cadets gazetted in 1927 totalled 50, and between 1928 and 1934 the annual output averaged only 28. Only after independence did the pattern change, as it did with the expansion of the army proper, the annual intake increasing to meet the demands of a rapidly growing force. In 1935, 73 graduated, and in 1936, 120.[20] This expansion necessitated extending the recruiting of officer material to social strata hitherto neglected: the promising sons of poorer families who were able to enter secondary school on government scholarships.

But prior to independence the cadets were largely drawn from families and backgrounds not incompatible with the British model of the 'Gentleman Cadet' worthy and capable of Sandhurst curricula: an all-round military education fitting them to take their place in the army as instructors and leaders and, as officers, 'possessed of a high morale, a great sense of duty, and in fact to be in every respect physically and mentally fit to hold a commission . . . both in peace and war'.[21]

Yet, despite the inculcation of British ideas and ideals, which implied a functionally circumscribed and professionally preoccupied army, and constant intercourse between Iraqi and British officers in the classrooms and in the field (the polo field included), the strategy of creating officers in the British mould did not proceed according to plan. The officers were fertile ground for the martial and nationalistic spirit, praised by the politicians and pedagogues, which appealed to their national and religious sensitivities.

In so far as Iraqi politics and society were essentially personality-orientated adn bound to a considerable extent by patronage and interpersonal ties, there could be no institutional autonomy, whether in the military, administrative or political spheres. The narrowness of the social strata from which officers, officials and political activists alike were drawn brought the officers into society and into contact with like-minded men of different callings. Officers who had served in the Ottoman and Arab armies continued to mix with former comrades-in-arms who had left the colours. Cadets and junior officers, to whom teachers and instructors had conveyed the ideas of their elders, remained in touch with school friends and family acquaintances who had selected civilian careers. The common background and continued contact between officers and civilians therefore facilitated the transmission of ideas and attitudes between the civil and the military sectors. The officer corps could be no more immune to the pressures prevailing in the polity than any other individuals or groups. The army was therefore no isolated and self-sufficient force, but reflected instead the society of which it was a part, and also the influences and aspirations operating wihin that society.

Accordingly, as Iraqis, the officers rankled at the restraints imposed by the British upon the state. With their civilian contemporaries, they resented the duality of responsibility which the nationalists were to term 'al-Wad' al-Shadh', the perplexing predicament which gave an outward appearance of self-rule whilst preserving the essence of British control over state and army alike.[22] As soldiers, they had their own professional perspective which saw Britain restricting the growth of the army and displaying little confidence in its capabilities. In his memoirs, Ibrahim Rawi, a veteran of the Ottoman and Hijaz armies, expresses the resentment which prevailed mongsta officers of all ranks, and commends Bakr Sidqi for his obstructive attitude towards British officers.[23] He recalls how the British military mission was 'al-Kul fil al-Kul', how no promotions or retirements could be made, how no equipment could be purchased or distributed without its prior consent or approval. Sabbagh wrote of how the British had opposed the expansion of the army in various ways in order to perpetuate their control.[24]

Moreover, the officers' nationalist feelings were offended by the dependent status of Iraq and its army. Mahmud Durra, gazetted in 1930, recalls how one of his instructors, an ex-Ottoman officer, fostered his Arabism and anti-imperialism, and how outside influences sharpened the cadets' awareness. It is certain that even before entering the military college, he and his peers had been imbued with the nationalism of teachers like Talib Mushtaq, who, in his memoirs, stresses that he lost no opportunity to acquaint his pupils with the cause of Arabism and the independence struggle. The influence of Sati al-Husri is apparent in Durra's recollection of how

> our souls were filled with pride for our history and its glories, compelling us towards the achievement of miracles in our homeland. Captivated by the dream (of Wahida) we awakened to see in the Iraqi army, the Arab Prussia, the force able to realize our dreams of establishing a great Arab state which would restore to the Arab nation its past glories and forgotten civilization.[25]

Durrah and his comrades saw how Mustafa Kemal and Reza Shah Pahlevi had freed their nations from foreign control. Their teachers convinced them that military participation in politics was a national duty, whilst Durrah felt that in default of the politicians, a military leader would emerge to liberate Iraq. It is clear from his account that when Dr Sami Shawkat delivered his notorious speech to a gathering of Baghdad students and teachers in the autumn of 1933, he was preaching largely to the converted. His speech, 'Sina'at al-Mawt', was, in effect, a tribute to martial nations, an expression of admiration for the achievements of states which had freed themselves from imperialism. The caudillo strain had apparently leapt the Atlantic in the guise of a militant nationalism which equated national resurgence with the guiding hand of strong leaders, backed by patriotic armies who promised true independence, progress, and prosperity. Accordingly, Shawkat declared:

> We hear and read that there is no political independence without economic independence, and no independence without learning . . . Yet Egypt and India, although rich and culturally advanced, are not yet independent states, whereas Afghanistan, where life is still in the Fourteenth Century, Saudi Arabia, where people live on dates and camel-milk, and pursue no modern studies, and the Yemen, without any wealth, are independent.

More important than wealth and learning, upholding the honour of nations, and preventing their enslavement, is strength. Riches without strength produces only clamour and tears from the weak and scorn from the strong. This strength, Shawkat declared, lay in the perfection of the 'Art of Death', in iron and fire:

> If Mustafa Kemal did not have forty thousand soldiers trained in the Art of Death . . . would we have seen Turkey restore the glories of Sultan Selim in the Twentieth Century? If Pahlevi had not a thousand officers who had perfected this holy art, would we have seen the restoration of the glories of Darius? And had not Mussolini tens of thousands of Black-Shirts skilled in the profession of death, he would not have been able to place the crown of the Roman Emperors upon Victor Emmanuel.

The lesson was a simple one. The youths of Iraq had to train as soldiers; Iraq had to have, in a short time, half a million soldiers and hundreds of aircraft. The end result was likewise clear: 'Riches and knowledge would be within our grasp; we would take from them what we wished after we are powerful, as demanded by our great history.'[26]

Sabbagh, Fahmi Said and other young officers who had served in Damascus had no need to be tutored in the importance of the Art of Death or in the mechanics of imperialism. They had witnessed at first hand the fall of Damascus, 'the cradle of Arabism and the source of the national struggle', to superior French forces, and to them, the perfidy of imperialism was baltantly clear.

Sabbagh's memoirs reflect the hyperbole common to many muthakarat, and also the bitterness of the predicament in which he wrote, being on the run from allied vengeance after the débâcle of May 1941. But his ideas were not far removed from those of his contemporaries and juniors, whilst providing a deeper insight into the attitude of the officer corps towards the British than that provided by Durra. He expressed his nationalism simply and intransigently: he was a Muslim, and Islam was opposed to infidel rule; he was an Arab, and Arabism rejected foreign armies on Arab soil: he was a soldier, and soldiers were not to be guided by foreigners.[27] One could not be more precise than this.

To his mind, and to those of many Muslims, there was something basically anti-Islam in imperialism. The historical struggle between Christendom and Islam had never really ended, but was being fought on different battlefields and with different weapons.[28] To Sabbagh, the imperail 'mission civilatrice' was but as extension of the Crusades. British interests favoured the divison of the Arab lands, and with France, Italy and Spain, Britain sought to preserve this division through continued European rule. British prejudice and British motives were apparent, he asserts, in the favour shown to non-Muslim minorities: the Jews in Palestine and the Assyrians in Iraq. He could well have added the bias of the French towards the heterodox Alawis and Druze in Syria.

According to Sabbagh, Britain's attitude was particularly evident with regard to the Iraqi army. The apparent friendliness of British officers was but a part of the deceit of imperialism, resembling the courtesy of a supreme commander towards his subordinates, or worse, the benevolence of an imperialist master towards his slaves.[29] Just as official British policy conspired to emasculate the army, so the deceit of British officers was designed to sap the Arabs' strength and pride, to 'eliminate our firm principles, and to kill our national feelings'. This perception of an imperialist plot inspired Sabbagh to allege that British intelligence agents worked among the tribes and minorities – people anti-pathetic towards the state and its Arab mission – fomenting revolts which would drain the army's strength, and distract it from its Arabist role by confining it to the maintenance of internal security (Dobbs's limited role).

Like Durra (and Shawkat), Sabbagh saw in other states what was absent in Iraq. Attending Atatürk's funeral in 1939,

> I saw signs of progress which amazed me . . . a social revolution in education and economics, and in cultural and spiritual affairs. I saw the pride of the Turks in their fatherland, pride in their nationalism, their self-reliance and their independence.

His thoughts turned to Iran, which he believed had much in common with the new Turkey. The independence of such states he wrote, was as strong as Iraq's was spurious. He observed how Iraq crawled whilst they ran because they were free to choose their own way: no one controlling them, free to arm as they pleased and as geographical and strategic considerations dictated.[30]

Sabbagh wrote these words over a decade after Iraq's admission to the League of Nations, but they were particularly applicable during the Mandate years and, demonstrating the affinity of ideas between soldiers and civilians, echoed the feelings of the nationalists with regard to the Treaty of 1930 which paved the way to independence. The treaty guaranteed a continued British presence in Iraq, Faisal and Nuri conceding this in order to secure a treaty and independence as soon as possible. Sabbagh was to describe it derisively as 'The Anglo-Nuri Treaty'.[31] The air-bases and continued British influence stipulated by the treaty naturally aggravated the nationalistic and professional feelings of the officers, their resentment being compounded by Iraq's obligation to provide all manner of assistance to make the British stay comfortable. Accordingly, they found common cause with the nationalist politicians who denounced the treaty as giving pseudo-independence, the continued presence of the British military mission being but the reverse side of the imperialist coin.

The political and ideological climate, therefore, shaped the officers' political awareness and also their perception of the role of the army in politics and society. Far from having created a docile and apolitical officer cadre, British 'advice and guidance' had engendered in the officers a national consciousness not inconsistent with the political élite's idea of nation. The officers saw the army, as its founders had intended, as the symbol and defender of that nation. Indeed, their understanding of that role was to develop to a degree unlooked for and unwanted by either the Mandatory or the Iraqi government in so far as it was to render them highly susceptible to politicisation and, ultimately, to intervention.

Accordingly, from the point of view of organisational structure and also from that of the ethos of the officer corps, the formation of the Iraqi army was to all ostensible purposes completed by 1932. Iraq now possessed the army which the politicians had desired, albeit one smaller than that which they had considered necessary. It was, nevertheless, a well trained and well equipped force of some 11,500 men, commanded by conscientious officers who had received the best military education Britain could provide, short of sending them all to Sandhurst and Camberley. Moreover, Britain having acknowledged with independence Iraq's right to look after its domestic affairs, the government was now free to expand this army and to use it as it wished.

Yet, for all the nationalistic fervour of its younger officers, and for all the talk of Iraq as the Arab Prussia, the army lacked an identity as an efficient and self-confident force in which the nation it was held to represent could rightly be proud. The Iraqis had in effect constructed a roof without walls in so far as the army had failed to establish itself in the image with which it had been provided by its creators and eulogists. For years the British had controlled its activities, whilst its poor performance against Kurdish insurgents had served to strengthen British doubts as to its effectiveness. It was not to its credit that in late 1930 the authorities had to request British support in order to deal with Sheikh Mahmud, or that in early 1932 Iraqi forces were routed by Kurdish tribesmen led by Mulla Mustafa Barazani, and were only saved from disaster by the Royal Air Force. Such events, far from justifying earlier expectations, had meant that the army and its officers had acquired the makings of an inferiority complex which British disparagement did not help to dispel.

Having embraced their ascribed role, the officers needed to vindicate it. The civilian politicians were just as anxious that they should do so. Having in the past presented the army as the symbol of national independence and strength, they had no wish to have to eat their words. The opportunity arose in a 'crisis' which was engineered to a considerable extent by an assertive government and an exasperated army. The Assyrian Affair was a test for the unity of Iraq, the independence of its government, and the prowess of its army. It was indeed a watershed which established the army as a factor in state affairs, representing on the one hand a triumph for the traditional martial spirit and, on the other, an overdue release from the British dictum.

The Assyrian Watershed

To Iraqi politicians, the Assyrians were a standing affront to all that the newly independent kingdom stood for, perpetuating Iraq's disunity, and inviting continued British interference. This Christian minority, foisted upon Iraq by the Mandatory, was unwilling to assimilate, and the Iraqis were not over-eager to dissuade them. Iraqi accounts reflect a sense of exasperation with a strange people of a strange faith, who persisted in regarding themselves as British protégés, and who were openly contemptuous of independence. The Iraqi army was not immune to anti-Assyrian feeling and likewise saw them as an insult to unity and independence. In addition, the soldiers considered them to be an insult to their own self-esteem, racial and sectarian prejudices combining with professional considerations.

Iraqi officers had long nurtured a grudge against Assyrians in general, and the Assyrian Levies in particular. They resented this basically imperial force, and it was intolerable that British officers serving with the Levies were wont to disparage the national army whilst praising the prowess and *esprit* of force under direct British command. Yet the reality that 4,000 Assyrians had passed through the Levies by 1933, and were still in possession of their rifles, was a factor which induced Arab fears of their martial prowess. Iraqis in general, whilst resenting the affinity of the British towards this loyal and favoured minority, had come to accept the Assyrians' assessment of themselves as true: that one Assyrian soldier was worth three Arab soldiers.

When, during the summer of 1933, political circles became increasingly impatient with the obstructiveness of the Mar Shimun, the Assyrians' spiritual leader, a military solution was contemplated. The politicians found the army an attentive listener, the officers being eager to repair their tarnished reputation and to salvage their credibility as a fighting force. The wishes of the government that the Assyrian problem be eradicated altogether lost nothing in their execution by Colonel Bakr Sidqi, who became a conscientious instrument engaged upon a task which may have been very congenial for himself and his men. Accordingly, when finally sent north to deal with potential insurgency, the officers were promising credulous Ministers liquidation of the Assyrian problem in five minutes.

The Assyrian operations took somewhat longer than this, and Bakr's handling of them demanded little, if any, military skill. But the mood in Iraq was one of exultation, as the one minor skirmish became a victory in the Iraqis' relieved imaginations. Whitehall watched in horror as a pursuit degenerated into a pogrom, concluding that the army had run amok. But the Iraqis were jubilant; the troops returned to Mosul to triumphal arches; in Baghdad they were greeted with flowers and perfumes, with singing and cheering. Bakr's name and fame were widespread, commended by the government, Taha al-Hashimi, the Chief of Staff, and Crown Prince Ghazi. Far from being disciplined for their excesses, as British officials demanded, he and other officers were promoted for their part in the victory.

To British officials in Iraq and London, Bakr was the villain of the piece, but even the British military mission had a good word for him. General Headlam, Acting Inspector-General that summer, reported that

> Bekr Sidqi . . . showed himself to be a leader of determination, energy and foresight . . . I have no doubt that the influence of his presence inspired his troops and raised the morale of all ranks . . . The government and people have good reason to be thankful to Colonel Bekr Sidqi and his force.[32]

The successful conclusion of the Assyrian operations had important ramifications for state and army alike. The *Endlösung* may have been ineptly handled by the government and ruthlessly executed by the army, but the end result had been worth attaining. A troublesome minority had been erased, and a thorn in the side of Iraqi unity had been removed. Moreover, the British dictum was shown to have been broken. In Baghdad, the politicians had ignored British demands for caution and moderation, whilst in the field Bakr and his officers had successfully evaded British supervision through the simple expedient of excluding British officers from the zone of operations. British reticence was transformed into reluctant acquiescence, the proposal for an international enquiry having been firmly rejected as a derogation of sovereignty. For Iraqis, the 'crisis' was a significant *coup* for the forces of unity and nationalism, and a warning to all those who did not wish to be citizens.

It was also a demonstration of both the need and the worth of a strong army, a factor of considerable importance to politicians who had long sought to instil in Iraqis a respect for the national army and a belief in its necessity. This had been one of the missing ingredients in the formation of the Iraqi army, and the soldiers' achievement in August 1933 provided it. In the wake of the suppression of the Assyrians, the rush on recruiting offices everywhere was unprecedented, and the significance of this was not lost upon the advocates of conscription. They now wished to exploit the victory by expanding the army amidst a euphoria which made national service not only possible, but even attractive. In a speech delivered in Mosul, Rashid Ali expressed not regret or repentance, as Britain would have wished, but pride. Addressing soldiers and civilians, he presented a demagogic argument for conscription, in which he reflected his colleagues' long-felt desire for an army possessed of emotive symbolism as the source of sovereignty, unity and strength. For years they had argued in the face of British obstruction and popular indifference and now they were able to provide the proof. The true Iraqi citizen had to feel as they and the officers had felt, that unity would be achieved and maintained through the strength nad inspiration of a strong army. The Mosul speech is worth quoting at length in so far as it defined the role of the army from the politicians' perspective:

> You no doubt now appreciate the country's need for a regular force to build up a strong foundation for our existence. I find in the present a suitable opportunity to arouse in your noble souls a feeling of the urgent need for such a force to build up a strong foundation. By this, I mean an army, yes, an army. (Loud applause and cheers for the army, the king and the government) Yes, the army should be strengthened in order that it should protect our honour. Service in the army should be made general and compulsory. This is necessary if we are to safeguard our honour, in defense of which, the whole nation has risen up as one man. Everyone of us should share in the honour of performing this sacred duty in order to fulfill the saying: 'If you wish to be honoured, be strong.'[33]

For the army itself, the crisis was just as significant. It had found the identity which it had sought, and had expunged an inferiority complex imposed upon it by the British and by its own failures. The final ingredient in the formation of the Iraqi army was added when, in August 1933, that army hit headlines of glory and popular acclaim. After years in the shadow of the Mandate, it was presented in the saviour role as the epitomy of the national ethic and the harbinger of national unity and progress. The populace and the army accepted this grand role with a casualness verging on carelessness as Iraq's first military hero and personality – in a political system dominated by personalities – rode in triumph through the streets of Baghdad. The 'man on horseback', or rather the man in the command car, had arrived, lecturing an impressionable public on the army's innate yet only recently publicised manifest destiny:

'Your display of the noble Arab character', Bakr told the Moslawis,

> and your enthusiasm in honouring the Iraqi Army, which has disciplined the rebel Assyrians, and your great welcome to it in appreciation of the small duty which it has performed, has brought back to mind those immortal episodes of true patriotism, the noble deeds in which the people of Mosul were prominent under the most trying and difficult of times, when the sword of occupation was upon our becks. Thanks to you, added to admiration and esteem, thanks which I offer as a pledge of what the army is about to perform *in the future, in accomplishment of the great duty which the army has felt, and is still feeling, that it must be prepared to perform. Therefore let us, with Army and Nation, await that day.*[34]

Notes

1. See Abd al-Rahman al-Bazzaz, *Muhadhirat 'an Al-'Iraq* (*Lectures on Iraq*), (Cairo, 1954) pp. 51-6.
2. Abd al-Razzaq al-Hilali, *The History of Education in Iraq in Ottoman Times* (Baghdad, 1959) p. 165 and pp. 249-52.
3. Sati al-Husri, My Iraqi Memoires pp. 10 and 20.
4. Quoted by W.L. Cleveland in *The Making of an Arab Nationalist* (New Jersey, 1971), p. 167.
5. Sami Shawkat, *'Hadhihi Ahdafuna' (These are our aims).* (Baghdad, 1939), p. 7.
6. *Al-Istaqlal* 13/9/23. Colonial Office 730/9010.
7. Abd al-Razzaq al-Hasani, *Tarikh al-Wizarat al-'Iraqiyyal (History of Iraqi Cabinets),* Vol. 3, p. 81.
8. Foreign Office, 371/E3768/86/65:28/7/1927.
9. Situation Report to 27/9/1927:FO 371-E4471/86/65.
10. Minute dated 26/4/1925: CO 730/82/24432.
11. Despatch, High Commissioner, Baghdad to S/S Colonies 16/4/1925: CO 730/74/19004.
12. Proposed Reorganization of the Iraqi Army, p. 168, to Air Ministry, 29/9/1926: FO 371–E6261/112/65.
13. Salah al-Din al-Sabbagh, *Fursan Al-Urubah fi Al-'Iraq (The Knights of Arabism in Iraq)* (Damascus, 1956), p. 43.
14. Hasani, *Tarikh al-Wizarat*, Vol. 2, p. 22.
15. *Report to the Council of the League of Nations on the Administration of Iraq for 1928* (London, HMSO, 1929), pp. 100-1.
16. *Report to the League for 1926,* p. 103.
17. See *Iraq Government Gazette,* 1927-36.
18. See P. Sluglett, *Britian in Iraq, 1914-1932* (London, 1976), Ch. 8.
19. Hilali, *History of Education.*
20. *Government Gazette,* 1927-36.
21. Syllabus of the Royal Military College, Sandhurst, for 1921, p. 3.

22. See F.W. Ireland, *Iraq, a Study in Political Development,* pp. 367-9.
23. Ibrahim Rawi, *From the Arab Revolt to Modern Iraq: My Memoires* (Beirut, 1969), pp. 150, 151, 161, and 163.
24. See note 13.
25. Mahmud Durrah, *Al-Harb Al-Iraqiyyah Al-Britaniyyah (The British-Iraqi War of 1941* (Beirut, 1969), p. 14.
26. Shawkat, *Hadhihi Ahdafuna,* pp. 1-3.
27. Sabbagh, *Fursan Al-Urubah,* p. 30.
28. See Peter Mansfield, *The Arabs* (London, 1977) for a British view of a prejudice which has 'gone deep into our subconsciousness'.
29. Sabbagh, *Fursan Al-Urubah,* p. 58.
30. Ibid., pp. 60-1.
31. Ibid., p. 37.
32. Extract from a report on 'the part played by the Iraqi Army in the suppression of the Assyrian rebellion in Northern Iraq', Baghdad 12/9/1933: FO 371/ E5367/7/93.
33. 30/8/1933: E5585/7/93.
34. Stafford, *The Tragedy of the Assyrians* (London, 1935), p. 204.

6 INTERNAL MIGRATION IN IRAQ

Atheel Al-Jomard

This chapter investigates the determinants of internal migration in Iraq, and is divided into two parts.[1] The first part investigates the determinants of interregional migration, which is basically of the rural-urban type, by using the census data of 1947, 1957 and 1965, from which two periods were considered, 1947-57 and 1957-65. The second part investigates the determinants of rural-urban migration by using a sample survey data conducted by the author in the rural areas of Ninevah and Babylon regions in the northern and central part of the country, during 1974/5.

1. The Determinants of Interregional Migration

A list of the potential structural variables was drawn up which included all the variables that would be reasonably expected to explain the movements which occurred during each of the two periods of 1947-57 and 1957-65, on which data can be found. The list included sixteen variables for the first period and eighteen variables for the second. These variables were chosen from the rural and urban areas of the regions of origin and destination.

The estimated relationships are of the following forms:

(1) For the period 1947-57 MIJ/Pi,MIJ =
f (Li,Lj,Ki,Kj,Dij,Ui,Uj,Ri,Rj,Gi,Gj,Ci,Cj,Si,Sj,Yij, random errors);

(2) For the period 1957-65
MIJ/Pi,MIJ = f(Li,Lj,Ki,Kj,Dij,Ui,Uj,Ri,Rj,Ti,Tj,Ci,Cj,Qi,Qj,Si,Sj,Yij, random errors);

where: i(j) = refer to the region gaining (losing) migrants;

Li(Lj) = the ratio of the literate people (males and females who can read and write) in the urban areas of region i(j);
Ki(Kj) = the average expected wage rate in the modern urban sector. Alternatively, the average wage rate was also used;
Ui(Uj) = the urban population of region i(j);
Ri(Rj) = the rural population of region i(j);
Gi(Gj) = the concentration ratio (Gini Index) of land holdings in region i(j);

Ti(Tj) = the annual rate of land redistribution to cultivators which took place after 1958, in region i(j) divided by the number of the rural population in the region;
Ci(Cj) = the annually cultivated land in region i(j) divided by the number of people depending on agriculture in region i(j);
Qi(Qj) = the ration of literate people (males and females who can read and write) in the rural areas of region i(j) to the rural population of region i(j);
Si(Sj) = the ratio of the people born in region i(j) and enumerated in region j(i) to the number of people born and living in region i(j), calculated at the beginning of the period;
Dij = the distance in kilometres between the major regional urban centres;
Yij = the contiguity dummy variable;
Mij = net migration between region i and region j;
Pi = the population of the gaining region.

With a view to determining the algebraic form of the migration function, the double-logarithmic form gave the best fit in terms of R^2, F test and t test. The following forms of the explanatory variables were tried, considering the urbanisation variable (U) for illustration:

$$Uij = (ui/Uj)^{a1} \qquad (i)$$
$$Uij = (ui\text{-}Uj)^{a2} \qquad (ii)$$
$$Uij = Ui^{a3} \qquad (iii)$$

It should be pointed out that: form (i) hypothesises that migrants respond to relative differences in the variables. This specification implies that net migration has identical elasticity with respect to the origin and destination values of any variable 'homogeneity restriction'; form (ii) implies that migrants respond to absolute rather than relative differences in the variables, and the homogeneity restriction is also imposed as in the previous form; form (iii) hypothesises that net migration may have different elasticity with respect to the origin and destination values of any variable. The different forms of the function and the variables were also tried at the regional level with thirteen observations for each region. Only the results of the logarithmic function of form (i) for the country as a whole with Mij as a dependent variable are displayed in this paper, for they show more consistency with the theory and higher statistical significance.

2. The Determinants of Rural-Urban Migration

Two samples of about 5 per cent of the villages of each Ninevah and Babylon regions were drawn randomly, using the lists available in the population census as well as the information provided by the relevant government departments in Mosul and Hilla, the provincial capitals of Ninevah and Babylon regions respectively. The samples included 70 villages in Ninevah and 40 villages in Babylon. The villages that were considered inaccessible to the survey team were replaced by others. Eight villages in Ninevah and three villages in Babylon were considered inaccessible.

The questionnaire forms collected information on certain economic, demographic and social variables from a sample of the people who are still residing in the villages, which provide the data required for the regression analysis which is necessary to estimate the migration function. They also collected similar data on the migrants who left these villages, which is necessary to carry out the discriminant analysis between the migrants and the non-migrants.

The variables considered in the rural-urban migration model are listed below.

Dependent Variables (Migration Variables)

Y_1 = total migrants as per cent of total population;
Y_2 = total migrants in absolute numbers.

Independent Variables

1. Income Variables in ID

X_{11} (X_1) = income *per capita* in the village
X_{12} = income per household in the village
X_{13} = income *per capita* for adult population in the village
X_{14} = average income per adult per household in the village

2. Age and Six Variables

X_{21} = the ratio of the males whose ages are over 15 years to the total population
X_{22} = the ratio of the males whose ages are 15-35 years to the total population
X_{23} (X_2) = the ratio of the males whose ages are 15-35 years to the total male population

3. Marital Status Variables

X_{31} = the ratio of the married males to the total number of males

X_{32} (X_3) = the ratio of the married males whose age is 15-35 years to the total number of males in this age group

4. Education Variables

X_{41} = crude literacy ratio

X_{42} = literacy ratio for males

X_{43} (X_4) = literacy ratio for males whose age is 15 years and over

5. Household Variables

X_{51} (X_5) = the average size of the household in the village

6. Accessibility Variables

X_{61} = per cent of village population visisted a major urban centre in the last month

X_{62} = the distance from the main road

X_{63} (X_6) = a dummy variable to indicate whether a village is within one kilometre from the main road or not.

The Variables Considered in the Discriminant Analysis

In the attempt to identify the main characteristics of the rural individual which are associated with the propensity to migrate, the following variables are considered:

D_1 = the annual income *per capita* in the household

D_{12} = the annual income per adult in the household

D_2 = the sex of the individual

D_3 = the age of the individual given in years

D_4 = the educational attainment of the individual given in completed years of education

D_5 = the marital status of the individual

D_6 = the size of the household to which the individual belongs

D_7 = the ratio of the members who visited a major urban in the last three months to the total members of the household.

The test was carried out on two sub-samples of individuals which were taken randomly from the two major samples.

Conclusion

1. The Interregional Migration

The regression results revealed that the economic variables in the urban areas, namely the expected wage rate and the average wage rate variables, had insignificant effect on migration in both periods. With respect to this result the following reservations must be considered.

(1) The average wage rate is calculated from data on the manufacturing industries, so in regions where the industries which employ a large proportion of the qualified manpower, and therefore pay comparatively higher wages, are located, like the oil industries in Baghdad, Karkuk and Basra, the average wage rate will be over-estimated, particularly for the rural migrants who stand a little chance of getting a job in such industries.

(2) The regional average wage rates were not deflated by regional price indexes due to inadequate data, and therefore the real wage rates in large cities like Baghdad, Mosul and Basra may have been over-estimated.

(3) Two different estimates of the job opportunity index based on Todaro's definitions are used in this study. The first definition assumes that the employment turnover in the industrial sector is negligible and the second definition assumes that the employment turnover is complete. Both definitions assume that the time horizon considered by the migrant to obtain a job in the industrial sector is one year and that the selection of the employees is random. Both of the estimates yielded equally insignificant results. While it is our contention that the employment turnover in the industrial sector of Iraq is low, there are no data to qualify this hypothesis. The randomness of the selection procedure is also arguable, and the extent to which this source of bias exists is rather difficult to determine.

It is worth pointing out that the reasons stated above, which could have contributed to the insignificant results of the wage variables, could have equally existed in other studies in which these variables were found highly significant. It is more likely that the insignificant results of the industrial wage variables are due to the exceptionally poor economic conditions in the villages which exacerbated the pressure that the rural push forces exerted on rural migrants, who represent a great bulk of the interregional migrants, and forced them to be content with simple jobs in the service sector with a wage rate considerably less than that in the industrial sector.

The urban education variable is found insignificant in both periods. However, the multicolliniarity between this variable and the urbanisation variable, which is found to be 0.72 and 0.75 in the first and the second periods respectively, may have contributed to this result.

The urbanisation variable is found significant in both periods. The size of the urban centre reflects to a certain degree all the non-economic factors as well as indicating the employment opportunities in the service sector where jobs would be satisfactory to the rural migrants.

The distance variable is found significant with the correct negative sign in both periods. When the distance was replaced with the contiguity dummy variable, the correlation coefficient increased from 0.49 to 0.55 in the first period and from 0.31 to 0.40 in the second period, and the dummy variable was significant.

The multiple correlation coefficients for the two periods were rather low. The reasons may be the limited number of explanatory variables inserted in the model on which the data are available, the inaccuracy of the data we used, the aggregate form of the migration variable, etc. However, many other migration studies which used cross-section data have obtained similar results.

The rural factor are shown to have had more influence on interregional migration than the urban factors in both periods. Floods, soil salinity and fluctuations in weather conditions were serious factors which lowered the productivity of the land and the income *per capita* in the rural areas. Until 1958, the landlords always managed to take a large share of the output and charge high rates of interest to keep the cultivators at the subsistence level and tied to the land. The housing, health and diet conditions were also desperate. In most cases the only barriers to migration were the laws that disallow migration, particularly those of 1932 and 1938 and the direct force exercised by the landlords. Nevertheless, large numbers left the villages despite the risks they encountered, which varied from being returned home by force of law to the expulsion of members of the family and relatives of the migrants, who could not leave the village, by the landlord after confiscating their livestock and properties.

After the revolution of 1958 and the enactment of the agrarian reform law, the power of the landlords diminished and the laws enacted before 1958 which tied the cultivators to the land were abolished. At the same time promises were given that the expropriation of large land holdings and the redistribution process would be completed soon, and that agrarian co-operatives would be formed to organise the cultivation and marketing activities and replace the previous links the cultivators had with the landlords and their agents. The cultivators welcomed the new policy and waited for the promises to come true. In the meantime, they had to resist blackmail by the landlords, the bureaucracy in the government offices handling the application of the new law, and the uncertainty of the future. The political instability, the delay in the application of the new law and the disturbed social order in the rural areas made the cultivators sceptical about the future and the migration waves started again, this time more freely, for the risks the migrants used to face before did not exist any more. Furthermore, the promises given by the government to the residents of the shanty towns in the outskirts of the cities, and particularly Baghdad, in the early 1960s, were equally appealing to the potential migrants in the rural areas.

The dominance of the rural push factor in the migrants' decision function were clearly revealed in the results of a survey conducted in 1957 by D. Phillips in four parts of Baghdad city where migrants were living. When they were asked why they had left their place of birth the common answers were such as 'we did not have enough to eat,' 'hunger', 'oppression by the landlord', 'dispute with the landlord over the size of our share', 'we could not get enough water for our crops', 'our land was flooded and the crop died.' The results also reflected the insignificance of the job opportunities and the wage rate in the industrial sector on migration. Only 12.8 per cent of the migrants were employed in the manufacturing industries while about 75 per cent were taking simple jobs in construction as hod-carriers and builders of mud huts and in the service sector as guards, porters, servants and unskilled office-workers who were employed in large numbers, especially by the government, and some of the migrants were working as vendors of milk products, vegetables, cigarettes and sweets. Most of these occupations were in fact disguised unemployment, but they still provided income which was considerably higher than that which the migrants used to receive in the rural areas. About 40 per cent of the families received annual income of about ID 90, 17 per cent received ID 150 and the top 18 per cent received about ID 200 or more. Eighty per cent of the families believed their total incomes, in cash and kind, to be higher than in the rural areas, 75 per cent believed their present housing to be better and 90 per cent believed their present diet to be better. In general, the migrants were satisfied with the income they received from rather unproductive jobs. Jobs in the industrial sector, which provides comparatively higher income, were not urgently sought after by the migrants, and their availability was not an important factor in the migrants' decision function when they left the rural areas. In thise case, the equilibrating mechanism of the job opportunity index in the industrial sector, as proposed by Todaro, would be ineffective and the equilibrium employment rate of migration may be much higher than that estimated by Todaro-type models. Migration from the rural areas towards the large urban centres will continue as long as the expected income of the migrant in urban centres is higher than that in the rural area, irrespective of the type of job obtained. With the subsistence income and poor standard of living prevailing in the rural areas, the effective policy to control migration seems to be that which concentrates on improving the welfare conditions in the rural areas. The policies which aimed at solving the migration problem by subsidising the migrants and replacing the shanty towns around the cities with brick houses, yet failing to make considerable improvements in the rural areas, as those pursued in the early 1960s, had only been self-defeating and produced more migration.

2. The Rural-Urban Migration

(a) At the Village Level. The six variables employed in the migration function have explained about 86 per cent of the changes in the migration rate in Ninevah region and about 80 per cent in Babylon. When the variables in each of the regions are classified according to their explanatory power, it may be observed that the education variable comes among the most important three variables. The income variable seems to be less important in Ninevah region, where it comes fifth in terms of its contribution to R^2 than in Babylon region where it comes second. The income variable in each of the two regions has the expected negative coefficient, but it is not less significant in Ninevah region than in Babylon region. This may be explained by the argument that since the rural population of Babylon has more access to the large market of Baghdad the money income in the rural areas of Babylon has proportionally increased and therefore became a better indicator for the real income than it is in Ninevah region. The age variable has the expected positive coefficient in each of the two regions and it is significant. The education variable is not significant in the two regions, which may be due to an equal distribution of educational services among different rural localities. The marital status variable is only significant in Ninevah while the household variable is significant in Babylon. The accessibility variable should be treated with reservation because of its ambiguous definition.

(b) At the Individual Level. The seven variables employed in the discriminant analysis yielded rather satisfactory results. They explained about 60 per cent of the difference between migrants and non-migrants in Ninevah region and about 70 per cent in the Babylon region. The success rates of discrimination were 90 per cent and 92 per cent in Ninevah and Babylon respectively. The income and the age variables had negative coefficients in each of the two regions. Whether the migration decision with regard to income is based on the rural-urban income differential or the expected differential (which is Todaro's hypothesis), the propensity to migrate would change inversely with the rural income. As to the age variable, the migration propensity of the younger people may be higher because their present discounted value of the income differentials is higher. The sex variable has the expected positive coefficient in the two regions, for the male in the rural society of Iraq, as is the case in most Middle Eastern countries, tends to be the decision-maker in the family, and the job opportunities in the urban areas open to a male migrant are greater than those open to a female migrant. The education variable has the expected positive coefficient in the two regions, for educated and skilled migrants stand better chances than the uneducated and unskilled migrants and also face higher income differentials. The marital status variable has the expected positive coefficient. The single potential migrant is more of a risk-taker than the married one, and the cost of movement of a single person is less than that of a family. The household size variable has the expected positive sign, for a large household can afford the departure of some of its members without severely reducing the household's rural income. The urban accessibility variable had the expected positive coefficient in both regions.

The order of the variables in terms of their discriminative power has some similarity in the two regions. The age and the household variables are within the first three important variables in each of the two regions while the rural income variable is unexpectedly within the last two unimportant variables.

The general conclusion that may be drawn from these results is that the rural determinants are reasonably successful in explaining rural-urban migration in Iraq, and the migration policies which may aim at influencing the rural variables are expected to produce satisfactory results in terms of controlling rural-urban migration and reducing urban unemployment.

RESULTS

1. The Interregional Migration

Regression Results, 1947-57

Variables	Coefficients	(t) values.
Ao	2.313	4.00***
Ui/Uj	0.60	3.89***
Gi/Gj	-2.573	1.85**
Si/Sj	0.305	3.28***
Yij	0.886	6.71***

R^2 = 0.55
DF = 86

Regression Results, 1957-65

Variables	Coefficients	(t) values
Ao	2.569	3.71***
Ui/Uj	0.348	1.66**
Ti/Tj	0.203	1.42*
Ci/Cj	0.284	1.83**
Qi/Qj	-0.673	1.29*
Si/Sj	0.541	3.07***
Yij	0.827	5.10***

R^2 = 0.40
DF = 86

2. The Rural-Urban Migration

(a) At the Village Level

Regression Results NINEVAH

Variables	Coefficients	(t) values
Ao	-0.569	8.89***
X_1	-0.192	1.98**
X_2	1.146	7.70***
X_3	-0.161	2.17***
X_4	0.102	1.05
X_5	0.118	1.13
X_6	0.101	5.0***

R^2 = 0.855
DF = 63

Regression Results BABYLON

Variables	Coefficients	(t) values
Ao	- 0.636	10.26***
X_1	- 0.209	1.75**
X_2	0.795	2.93***
X_3	0.074	0.47
X_4	0.209	1.33
X_5	0.210	1.91**
X_6	0.100	3.70***

R^2 = 0.798
DF = 33

(b) At the Individual Level

Discrimination Results NINEVAH

Variables according to their discriminative power		Coefficients of discriminant function
D_3	Age	- 0.040
D_4	Education	0.123
D_6	Household size	0.156
D_7	Visits to urban centre	2.340
D_2	Sex	0.086
D_1	Income	- 0.025
D_5	Marital Status	0.055

R^2 = 0.602
DF = 192
SR = 90%

Discrimination Results BABYLON

Variables according to their Discriminative power		Coefficients of discriminant function
D_3	Age	-0.025
D_6	Household Size	0.295
D_2	Sex	0.106
D_7	Visits to urban centre	3.658
D_4	Education	0.107
D_5	Marital Status	0.060
D	Income	-0.027

R^2 = 0.736
DF = 32
SR = 92%

DF = degrees of freedom
* = the coefficient is significant at the 10% level.
** = the coefficient is significant at the 5% level.
*** = the coefficient is significant at the 1% level.
SR = success rate

Notes

1. I would like to thank my supervisor, Professor E. Penrose, of SOAS, London University, for her advice and discussions concerning the material in this paper. I would also like to thank Mr C.P. Chalmers of Birckbeck College, London University, for his help in the computer work. The responsibility for remaining errors is mine.

7 THE DISTRIBUTION OF INCOME IN IRAQ, 1971

Shakir M. Issa

The object of this paper on income distribution in Iraq is to present and analyse the personal income distribution in the country as a whole as well as that of urban and rural areas in 1971. The main purpose of this paper is to compute a measurement of overall inequality as well as dealing with geographical areas by assessing inequality between urban and rural areas.

Income distribution in Iraq has not been studied previously due to the limitation imposed by the absence of adequate statistical data and the inadequacy of the data that have been available. The subject is of considerable importance, since income distribution is a vital consideration in linking the production and consumption sides of the economy. On the one hand, the functional distribution of income reflects the shares of the factors of production and on the other, the propensity to save and consume will vary at different levels of income.

This paper will cover first, the sources and nature of the data used, and second, the definition of income adopted. The later sections will deal with the overall distribution of income in the country as a whole, the differences in income distribution between urban and rural areas, and lastly a comparison with selected oil-producing countries.

1. Source of Statistical Data

The data used in this paper is from the household budget survey of 1971, compiled by the Central Statistical Organisation. The survey is based on a statistical systematic cluster multistage model. The household was considered as 'an individual or a group of individuals who participate in providing food and other necessities of life and share a common budget'. The sample was taken on the basis of one and a half percentage per 1,000 of total households situated in the rural areas. The proportion was two per 1,000 in the urban areas. The number of households in the sample amounted to 1,000 and 1,600 households in the rural and urban areas respectively. As the survey was conducted in three stages, only the first and second stages (June and December 1971) covered the entire population sample, while the third stage (March 1972) was restricted to only 40 per cent of the population sample. It is for this reason, among others, that only the first and second stages are emphasised in the analysis.

The size distribution of personal income is on an annual basis, and is obtained by scaling up by six the monthly household incomes in both June and December of 1971.

2. The Concept of Income

The definition of personal income which was used for this distribution is 'the money income of all kinds of earner before any deduction of taxes, income in kind, produced and consumed by households mainly in the rural areas, imputed rent in the urban areas and pensions, gifts and charities in cash and in kind'.

In this paper we will refer to two types of income: the cash income as the money income, and adjusted income, which means the addition of imputed rent and income in kind to cash income.

The relation of the concept of income as used here to that adopted in the national accounts is as follows:

Gross domestic product at market prices
less (-) factor incomes from the rest of the world (net)
less (-) indirect taxes (net)
less (-) provisions for the consumption of fixed capital
less (-) [savings of Enterprises and Direct Taxes on Enterprises + government property income]
less (-) pensions, gifts and charities
plus (+) current transfers from the government and abroad
= personal income

In comparison with the definition used in this study, the above approach has some differences which are identified below:

(1) Some of the items included in the definition, such as pensions, are obviously not income, in the sense that they do not result from economic activity. However, according to the household budget survey, they ought to be included. The other items are gifts, charities, etc., whether from relatives, friends or from any other source. These are transfer payments and appear on the expenditure side of the households who made them – but they represent income to the recipient. In the survey these gifts and such-like were not very significant.

(2) The other item which needs clarification is the allowance set aside

for the consumption of fixed capital (i.e. depreciation) from the incomes accruing to those self-employed in both agriculture and non-agriculture. This was not deducted from the incomes of those self-employed in agriculture. Similarly, no deductions were made for depreciation from the incomes of the self-employed in the non-agricultural sector, which includes small traders, or those owning small businesses. Possibly some allowance for depreciation was made for those households in the high-income bracket engaged in manufacturing, but unfortunately the survey was not explicit on this point.

(3) The property income which comprises rent for the houses (or land) rented to others, as well as the imputed rent for owner-occupied houses, has been recorded on the basis of a gross rent concept and no allowances have been made for maintenance or repairing.

With the above considerations in mind we have arrived at the concept of 'gross personal income' which, including current transfers to the household, is the definition adopted in this study.

3. Distribution of Income by Households

The distribution of income in 1971 among all the households covered by the survey in Iraq is on an annual basis, scaling up by six the monthly household incomes of both June and December 1971.

Since the sampling fraction differs in the urban areas from that in the rural areas, it was necessary to weight the results of both areas to ensure their correct representation when extracting aggregates for the country as a whole.

The household, both in its role as producer and consumer, was the unit commonly used as an important measure of the inequality of income distribution. However, the debate continues as to whether it is the household or the individual that should be regarded as the basic unit for assessing income distribution.

The sample includes 2,600 households (1,600 in the urban and 1,000 in the rural areas) weighted in proportions 1:1.38 respectively in Table 7.1. The table presents the income distribution in the country as a whole, and classifies the households according to 14 income groups for both cash incomes and adjusted income.

The table highlights some important points. The first is a greater disparity between the top and bottom brackets for adjusted income as against cash incomes. These were only 0.7 per cent of total households earning ID72 per annum in 1971, while at the higher level 7.6 per cent of households had incomes of nearly ID1,750 per annum.

The size of households at the bottom of the distribution is likely to be very small. The households comprise mainly the landless, unskilled workers, those employed on smallholdings, and those in rural-urban non-agricultural enterprises.

The difference in income between the top and bottom income brackets was approximately in the ratio of 23.5:1 of cash income and 25:1 of the adjusted income.

The second point is that most households are concentrated in the centre of the distribution. For cash incomes, nearly half of the income units are found in the income groups ID200-499, and nearly 60 per cent in the income groups ID200-599 of the adjusted income. This is illustrated by the frequency distribution in Figure 7.1, which shows the number of income recipients in each income group. In this distribution, the figures are standardised so that they correspond to income groups of the same length. This sort of presentation is useful, but it does not do full justice to the tails of the distribution. To the left it is possible to find households with negative income, while to the right of the distribution it could progress towards the highest level of household income in the country.

The income group ID300 to ID399 includes the highest number of income units in both cash and adjusted income. The frequency distribution shows clearly that there are more income units in the lower cash income groups than in the adjusted income group. In addition, the most common frequency is around ID200 for cash income and around ID300 for adjusted income. In both of these cases, the incomes were not much below the national average, which is ID468 in the former and ID577 in the latter. Broadly speaking, those households lying below these averages accounted for 76.3 per cent in the cash income. This percentage is lower in the adjusted income, where it is 67.2 per cent, i.e. households earning income below the national average income when the adjustment takes place.

However, with the average size of household for the country as a whole being 7.1 persons, the estimated average *per capita* personal income is ID81.3. In comparison with the *per capita* personal income estimated by the National Accounts (CSO) which was ID78.3 in 1971, our estimation is higher by 3.6 per cent. This discrepancy is explained by the different definitions used.

Reference should be made also to an alternative way of presenting and interpreting the data of the overall distribution of income. This is shown in Table 7.2, where all households are divided into equal groups,

Table 7.1: Distribution of Income in Iraq, 1971

Income Groups	CASH INCOME				ADJUSTED INCOME			
Income Groups (ID per year)	Number of Income units (Household)	Average Incomes (ID per year)	Percentage of Total		Number of Income units (Households)	Average Incomes (ID per year)	Percentage of Total	
			Income units	Income			Income units	Income
1 – 99	113	71.8	3.8	0.6	20	69.5	0.7	0.1
100 – 149	223	124.3	7.5	2.0	71	126.7	2.4	0.5
150 – 199	324	176.2	11.0	4.1	163	175.8	5.5	1.7
200 – 249	312	224.3	10.6	5.1	245	224.8	8.8	3.2
250 – 299	267	273.0	9.1	5.3	259	272.8	7.7	4.2
300 – 399	481	345.0	16.4	12.1	510	348.8	17.4	10.5
400 – 499	322	449.0	11.0	10.5	411	451.0	14.0	10.9
500 – 599	204	548.8	6.9	8.1	298	547.1	10.1	9.6
600 – 699	143	641.5	4.9	6.7	219	643.2	7.5	8.3
700 – 799	126	749.1	4.3	6.9	162	751.4	5.5	7.2
800 – 899	84	851.9	2.9	5.2	111	846.3	3.8	5.6
900 – 999	67	947.3	2.3	4.6	97	946.9	3.3	5.4
1,000 – 1,249	114	1,110.8	3.9	9.2	149	1,111.4	5.1	9.7
1,250 and over	160	1,690.7	5.4	19.6	224	1,747.8	7.6	23.1
Total	**2,940**	**468.1**	**100.0**	**100.0**	**2,939**	**576.9**	**100.0**	**100.0**

each containing 10 per cent of all households. These groups range from those households with the lowest incomes to those with the highest incomes. It seems that as the difference between the cash and the adjusted income distribution related to adding the income in kind and imputed rent to the latter, results in adjusted income are more equally distributed. The highest 10 per cent of households have cash incomes about 13.7 times of the lowest 10 per cent of households, declining to only 9.9 times in the adjusted income.

Nevertheless, the top 50 per cent of the households get 77.0 per cent of the total cash income and 74.4 per cent of the total adjusted income. This means that they get 3.4 times the cash income of the lowest 50 per cent of the household and 2.9 times the adjusted income of the lowest 50 per cent of households. The characteristics of these distributions and their differences can also be observed from Figure 7.2 in which Lorenz curves for the cash and adjusted income have been plotted. The further the curve deviates from the diagonal, the more unequal is the income distribution. The conventional index of inequality is the Gini coefficient. This is the area between the diagonal and the Lorenz curve, as a fraction of the total area below the diagonal. The index varies from zero, showing perfect equality, to unity, showing absolute inequality. The cash income Gini coefficient is 0.4035, while for the adjusted income it is 0.3615.

4. Distribution of Income by Individuals

In this context a great deal has been made of the differences between the income distribution of individuals (see Table 7.3) and that of households. Comparing both distributions, the results suggest that the distribution of individuals is more equal. The lowest 10 per cent of individuals get nearly twice as much cash or adjusted income as that received by the lowest 10 per cent of households. On the other hand, the highest 10 per cent of individuals had an income lower than the top 10 per cent of households by 15.5 per cent of adjusted income and 16.2 per cent of cash income.

The Gini concentration ratio shows less inequality in the income distribution of individuals; the ratio is 0.3188 for the cash income and 0.2645 for the adjusted income. This greater equality in the distribution is a consequence of the variation of household size with income level. As we mentioned, the average size of household for Iraq was 7.1 individuals per household, the average size of household for the lowest three income groups was 4.2, 5.0 and 5.8 individuals, while the average size of household of the top of the three income groups was 9.0, 9.1

Figure 7.1: Frequency Distribution of Income in Iraq, 1971

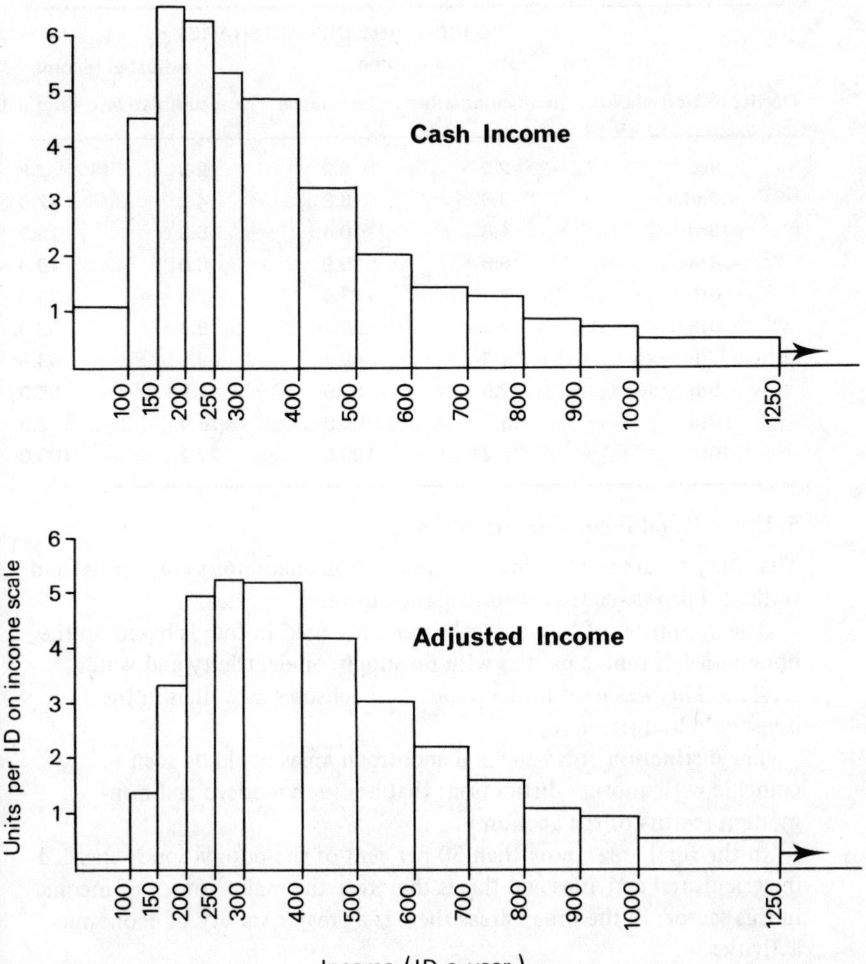

Source: Table 7.1.

and 8.9 individuals per household.

Table 7.2: Iraq, Percentage Income Shares of Deciles of Households, 1971

	PERCENTAGE INCOME SHARES			
	Cash Income		Adjusted Income	
Deciles of Households	Non-cumulative	Cumulative	Non-cumulative	Cumulative
1st	2.2	2.2	2.8	2.8
2nd	3.6	5.8	4.2	7.0
3rd	4.6	10.4	5.3	12.3
4th	5.5	15.9	6.0	18.3
5th	7.1	23.0	7.3	25.6
6th	7.7	30.7	8.3	33.9
7th	9.7	40.4	9.9	43.8
8th	12.5	52.9	12.1	55.9
9th	16.9	69.8	16.4	72.3
10th	30.2	100.0	27.7	100.0

5. Urban-Rural Income Distribution

The study of urban-rural income distribution encounters conceptual and statistical problems that require clarification.

The definition of 'rural areas' commonly used in Iraq is based on the boundaries of municipalities with no supply of electricity and water services. This was used in the population censuses as well as in the household budget surveys.

The distinction between rural and urban areas could be seen to coincide with another distinction: that between modern and non-modern sectors of the economy.

In the rural areas more than 80 per cent of the population is engaged in agricultural activities and this is therefore the major source of income in this sector. In the urban areas there is a greater variety of economic activities.

Before carrying a straightforward country-wide comparison, however, it is necessary to make several qualifications:

(1) In the rural areas most household incomes represent not just an individual's earnings, but the return to the labour of all family members. The return, however, is not simply a return to labour, but also to the land and capital used in agricultural production (mixed income).

Figure 7.2: Lorenz Curve of Income, Iraq, 1971

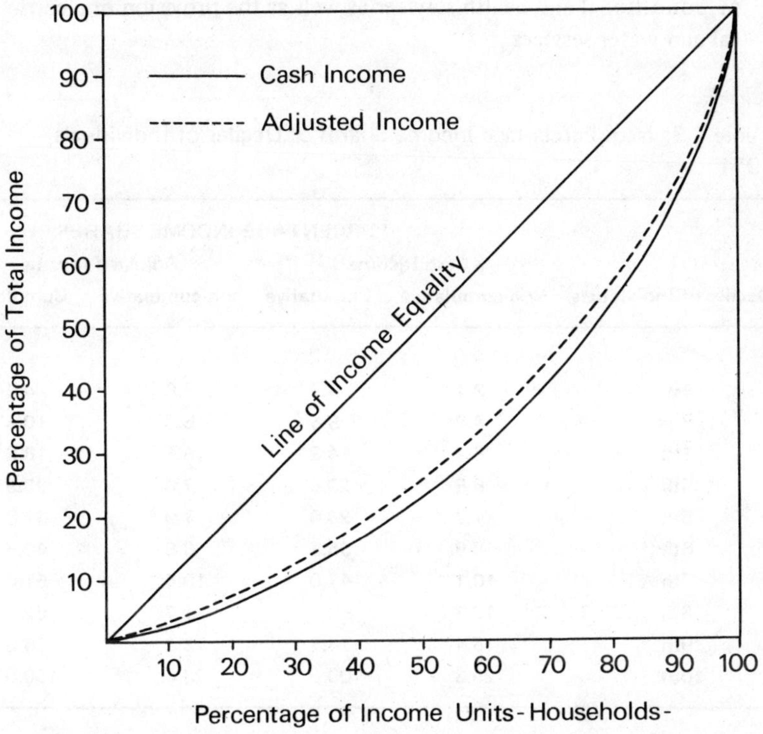

Generally this is not the case in the urban areas, except in those limited number of cases where the household is self-employed.

(2) the nature of agricultural production subjects rural households to significant seasonal and year-by-year income fluctuations. Urban household income, on the other hand, is subject to no such fluctuations.

(3) Most rural households are able to provide part of their food needs from their own production. This is seldom the situation in urban areas, and where it does occur it is, on the whole, of little significance.

(4) There exists a large apparent difference in the cost of living between urban and rural areas. The higher cost of living in the urban areas is partly the result of the cost of housing. The cost of food is also higher in the urban areas. Reference must be made also to the

differences in style of living: differences in, and unequal distribution of, educational and health services as well as the provision of electrical and water services.

Table 7.3: Iraq: Percentage Income Shares of Deciles of Individuals, 1971

	PERCENTAGE INCOME SHARES			
	Cash Income		Adjusted Income	
Deciles of Individuals	Non-cumulative	Cumulative	non-cumulative	Cumulative
1st	3.7	3.7	4.6	4.6
2nd	4.8	8.5	5.8	10.4
3rd	5.7	14.2	6.5	16.9
4th	6.6	20.8	7.0	23.9
5th	7.2	28.0	7.9	31.8
6th	8.9	36.9	8.8	40.6
7th	10.1	47.0	10.4	51.0
8th	12.3	59.3	11.7	62.7
9th	15.4	74.7	13.9	76.6
10th	25.3	100.0	23.4	100.0

Table 7.4: Iraq: Percentage Income Shares of Deciles of Urban-Rural Households, 1971

	PERCENTAGE ADJUSTED INCOME SHARES			
	Urban Income		Rural Income	
Deciles of Households	Non-cumulative	Cumulative	Non-cumulative	Cumulati
1st	2.8	2.8	3.0	3.0
2nd	4.0	6.8	4.3	7.3
3rd	5.3	12.1	5.3	12.6
4th	5.6	17.7	6.8	19.4
5th	6.9	24.6	7.3	26.7
6th	8.5	33.1	8.8	35.5
7th	9.7	42.8	10.2	45.7
8th	12.6	55.4	12.1	57.8
9th	16.5	71.9	15.8	73.6
10th	28.1	100.0	26.4	100.0

The first point to note in the urban-rural distribution of income is the obvious differences in average income. The average cash income of an urban household is 1.5 times that of a rural household, or 1.2 times higher for the adjusted income in urban over rural incomes.

The average income of the top 50 per cent of urban households is 3.1 times that of the bottom 50 per cent: the rural ratio is only 2.7:1. Thus, even though the bottom 50 per cent of urban households get 26.7 per cent the former is, on average, better off than the latter. It is clear, therefore, that a considerable inequality of income distribution prevails.

However, out of total adjusted income in the rural areas, only 7.3 per cent goes to the lowest 20 per cent of households, while the top 20 per cent receive 42.2 per cent. In the urban areas the top 20 per cent receive (44.6 per cent) higher income than in the rural areas, while the lowest 20 per cent receive (6.8 per cent) less than the share of rural income, which goes to the lowest 20 per cent of rural households.

In comparing the inequality of income distribution through the Gini concentration ratio, we found that this ratio was 0.3683 for the urban areas and 0.3417 for the rural areas, implying that the incomes are distributed more equally in the rural areas.

6. Comparison of Iraqi Income Distribution with other Countries

The inequality in income in any country can be assessed in comparison with that of other countries. There is, however, no agreement about the kind of comparison which can be made. Differences in economic structure and the state of economic development affect such a comparison. There are, moreover, further difficulties that must be borne in mind: whether data is comprehensive or from a sample survey; for urban or rural areas, or for the country as a whole, the differences in types of income and the nature of income-earners.

There are, nevertheless, various means of describing in numerical terms the distribution of income and the inequality it contains. Table 7.5 shows only two measures used to carry out such a comparison. First, there is the ratio of concentration which gives in a single figure the estimation of the overall inequality, and second, the calculation of the income shares of both the lowest 20 per cent of households and that of the top 20 per cent. The selection of the countries involved in this comparison was possible only because there existed statistical data within which there was, to some extent, a similar coverage and definition to that of data used in Iraq. These countries were also oil-producing.

These estimates for the Gini ratio of concentration show the inequality to be greater than that in Iraq for most of the other countries. This is most obvious in Iran, Libya and Indonesia. The other way is to look at the income distribution structure itself, the share of total income received by the lowest and highest 20 per cent of households. Though the share of the lowest 20 per cent is low everywhere, the differences in absolute income levels should be kept in mind. At the other end of the distribution scale, for those in the top 20 per cent of households, though their share is higher than the lower 20 per cent by 6.3 times in Iraq, it is 15.6 times higher in Mexico, 11.4 times higher in Iran.

Table 7.5: Gini Ratio and Income Shares: Iraq and other Countries

Country		Gini Ratio	Income Shares of Lowest 20 per cent	Income Shares of Top 20 per cent
Mexico: 1968[1]		0.3292	3.6	56.0
Iraq: 1971[2]	(a)	0.3615	7.0	44.1
	(b)	0.3683	6.8	44.6
	(c)	0.3417	7.3	42.2
Indonesia: 1969[3]	(a)	0.3867	7.5	48.2
	(b)	0.4062	7.5	41.9
Libya: 1969[4]	(a)	0.4053	5.8	46.8
	(b)	0.4240	5.0	49.4
Iran: 1971[5]		0.4969	4.0	45.8

Source: Regarding figures for other countries than Iraq, the calculations of these ratio and shares was made on the statistical data published by: UN ILO, *Household Income and Expenditure Statistics, No. 2, 1960-1972, Africa, Asia, Latin America* (Geneva, 1974): (1) Mexico: P. 164, whole country; (2) Iraq: (a) whole country; (b) urban areas; (c) rural areas. (3) Indonesia p. 87, urban households of (a) Jakarta and (b) Bandung. (4) Libya: p. 9, urban households of (a) Tripoli and (b) Benghazi. (5) Iran: p. 88, whole country, urban areas.

8 IRAQ: PROBLEMS OF REGIONAL DEVELOPMENT

Keith McLachlan

1. Introduction

Iraq has experienced generally accelerating, if fluctuating, social and economic change over a period of more than two decades. Much of this change has been made possible by augmenting oil revenues, with particular effect since 1955. The style and direction of economic development, it may be argued, has been largely inimical to the welfare of those provinces on the periphery and has done little to benefit other provinces outside Baghdad and Basra. While the outlying districts have suffered from failures in the policies implemented by successive central governments, it is equally apparent that governments have found intractable problems in stimulating development in the regions. Not a few of such difficulties derive from the essentially poor resource bases of many of the Iraqi Governorates.

The conventional view of Iraq is that 'Iraq is underdeveloped in the exact literal sense. Its society is primitive and disintegrating; and its environment is only now being brought under control . . . and the environment remained uncontrolled because capital was lacking.'[1] There is increasing evidence to suggest that assumptions of very considerable untapped potential for agricultural expansion in Iraq are untenable and that the accepted view of the country and especially the appreciation of the areas outside the four southern provinces should be altered to take account of actual experience over the past years when Iraq has, by most standards, had access to appreciable capital.

It is possible that 'Iraq is truly the gift of its rivers'[2] was historically valid. At the present time it is more important that all the country's major surface water sources rise outside the national borders in states where exploitation of water for hydro-electric power, urban water-supply and irrigation purposes includes intensive use of rivers feeding the Mesopotamian area of Iraq. Dams on the Euphrates have been built in Turkey in the Keban dam and in Syria in the Tebaka dam. Turkish plans call for at least two more Euphrates dams while Syria has scope for greater use of Euphrates waters though probably not in the immediate future. In Iran many small dams have been constructed across streams running west from the Zagros range and small but locally important volumes of water that formerly fed Iraqi districts have been diverted for use in Iran. In aggregate Iraq has lost its former control over disposal of the waters of its river systems and in years of poor precipitation in the upper catchment areas Iraq will, as the downstream riparian state, be most at risk. In the 1974/5 crop year, which was also a poor year of flow in the Euphrates, the irrigated area of the Euphrates valley in Iraq was reduced by some 4 per cent, since the country received only the residue of flow after offtake by the upstream states.

If the volume of the Iraqi water resource from its rivers must be called into question, it is appropriate to examine the soils situation too. Throughout the riverine tracts of the country the predominant soil type is silty calcareous loam, normally classified as fertile and with good tillage characteristics. The area is interspersed, however, with saline zones affected either by bad natural drainage or by saline and alkaline conditions brought on by irrigation practices of an inappropriate kind, particularly associated with inadequate drainage. The precarious balance between irrigation water quality, height of water table and soil fertility in the climatic conditions of the Mesopotamian plain is indicated clearly by the large sums now being expended by the state on flushing agricultural areas that have been under intensive cultivation for only short periods of time, as at Amara and Dujaila.[3] Extremely poor crop yields would tend to confirm the conclusion that the irrigated areas of the Tigris-Euphrates are by no means prolific agricultural areas.[4] Problems affecting land ownership and tenancy before 1958[5] and confusion arising from the frequently changing and generally inefficiently administered agrarian reform since that time[6] have been exacerbating factors on rather than the causes of low agricultural productivity. If this analysis is accepted, the problems that the governments of Iraq have experienced in improving levels of agricultural production are readily explained. Equally, the slow rate of development spending achieved in the agricultural sector (Table 8.1) and the poor response in areas where expenditure has been made may be seen as much the result of objective technical constraints as failures in government policies.

Yet the Tigris-Euphrates lowland, especially in its southern reaches, has traditionally been the most populated and intensively cultivated area of the country despite the problems outlined above. The peripheral regions, including the western and southern deserts and the mountains of the north, are even less well endowed with resources of water and soil than Mesopotamia. While the mountains of the north receive appreciable snow and rainfall amounts, the desert lies in the irrigated zone with generally negligible rainfall amounts. Small areas are being developed in the desert zone through provision of water for irrigation from deep wells though this territory is in many ways a nomadic livestock preserve and contributes only modestly to national production. Specialist cultivation of early fruit and vegetables is possible in the desert once irrigation water is available, though there are no signs that such a level of sophisticated agriculture is emerging at the present time.

Table 8.1: Proposed and Actual Expenditure by the Development Plan in Agriculture 1973/4 and 1974/5 (thousand Iraqi dinars)

	1973/4	1974/5
Annual plan expenditure-estimate	310,000	1,169,000
Annual plan expenditure-actual	243,985	565,511
Actual as % estimate	79	48
Agricultural expenditure-estimate	65,000	190,000
Agricultural expenditure-actual	37,786	77,757
Actual as % estimate	58	41

Source: *Annual Abstract of Statistics 1975,* Ministry of Planning, Iraq.

The highland areas of the north and north-west at first sight appear to have great prospects for agricultural development. Rainfall is generally above 30 inches (760 mm) and in higher altitudes rises to more than 50 inches (1,275 mm). At the same time, precipitation is more reliable. Unfortunately the upper river valleys are narrow and the plateaux of rough topography or of limited surface area. Prolonged destruction of the forest and scrub cover of the mountains by grazing herds, by clearance for cultivation and by charcoal-burners has brought in its train erosion, soil loss and a severe deterioration in the potential of the area. Ten years of warfare and the destruction brought in its wake will scarcely have helped stem the degradation of the area. Thermal constraints on the length of the growing season and difficulties of transport add other dimensions to the physical problems affecting agriculture in the northern area.

Geography has, therefore, been relatively unkind to Iraq. Inheritance of political frontiers that leave the country's vital sources of surface water supply in the hands of neighbouring and not necessarily friendly states has increasingly aggravated the burden of physical constraints on development of agriculture. The same national borders have added further human dimensions to the problems of the regions in so far as perceptible cleavages exist between Sunni and Shii, and Arab and Kurdish Iraq, discussed elsewhere in this book. The pattern of diversity is well emphasised by geographers writing on Iraq.[7,8] What needs to be made absolutely clear is that the spectrum of physical areas contains only small proportions of rich, stable and productive land and very high proportions of varieties of marginal, degraded and uncultivated cultivatable land (Table 8.2). What is more, the surface area of productive land is diminishing as a result of over-optimistic attempts at irrigation on the extensive margin, while the volume of water resources available for irrigation is being reduced both by use of river waters outside Iraq and by use of water for urban water-supply and industry within Iraq.

Table 8.2: Iraq: Land Use (square kilometres)

Total area	438,446
Arable	75,364
Pasture	230,000
Woodland	51,000
Fruit and vine	1,280

Source: estimates from various sources, including 1953 census and W.B. Fisher.

Table 8.3: Surface Water Resources of Iraq (milliards cubic metres/year)

Year	R. Euphrates	R. Tigris
1970	27.99	30.45
1971	30.04	24.47
1972	30.43	37.85
1973	15.27	26.78
1974	9.02	30.06
1975	9.42	26.10

Source: *Annual Abstract of Statistics.*

Table 8.3 shows official Iraqi estimates of trends in surface water flow in the Rivers Tigris and Euphrates for the period 1970-5.

2. Development Plans and the Regions

Promises of close government attention to the development of the regions have been included within most Iraqi economic plans. In fact, it is difficult to isolate measures within any of the published plans that are specifically designed to foster regional development other than those prepared for the Kurdish area. Allocations within the plan have been at the national level and by sector. Indeed, there is a case for believing that funds have been allotted on a project-oriented basis even within the sectors, a feature that has produced a distinct bias to the regional pattern of investment activities, as will be shown later.

Financial allocations to the Kurdistan Autonomous Area have in recent years been separately presented in the annual investment programmes. In 1974/5, for which full figures are available, ID 123 million was earmarked for Kurdistan, of which ID 32 million was for agriculture, ID 11 million for industry, ID 27 million for transport and communications, ID 16 million for construction, ID 7 million for the Northern Region Development Authority and ID 30 million as emergency relief. It is altogether unclear how much of the allocation was actually disbursed, and even less clear how much was spent on creating improved conditions for the inhabitants of the northern region against expenditures on military and quasi-military structures, strategic roads and the implementation of land reform.

Since the development plans have lacked either specific allocations for regional development or a coherent plan for the regions, the provinces have been affected by development activity under the plans coincidentally with the sectoral investments. Regional development has become a function of the strength of the sector most widely represented in any given province: that is, the geographical pattern of developments in Iraq is determined by the accidents of geology and political choices expressed through the sectoral allocations of the development plans.

Industry apparently holds a favoured position within the development objectives of the Baath government. During the 1976-80 plan period it is projected that the rate of growth in manufacturing industry will rise to 32.9 per cent within a target for the economy as a whole of 16.8 per cent. Yet industry is located firmly in the major urban centres and especially in the Baghdad region, where no less than 50 per cent of industrial employment is reported. Basra, too, has a strong position with 25 per cent of industrial workers. Outside these centres, industry created under the development plans has been small-scale and largely cosmetic, at best catering for local requirements of the construction industry or for processing perishable foodstuffs.

Concentration of the country's main industrial plants in Baghdad and Basra regions is entirely supported by economic logic. These are, after all, the areas in which the large-scale resources of power and water are available, in which the skilled cadres are to be found and demand to remain, and in which the major markets reside. For Iraqi planners the situation is made the more difficult as a result of the poor development of traditional industries in the country's smaller towns and cities. Other than Baghdad, Iraq has virtually no established craft centres for carpets, metal-work, jewellery, pottery or leather-work which might act as foundations for the creation of modern industry and as intermediate establishments bridging, albeit imperfectly, the gap between capital and province, modern industry and traditional agriculture.

The pattern of investment in the oil industry has, at first sight, shown a bias towards provincial areas in so far as oilfields and their related operational facilities are located around the Kirkuk, Mosul and Basra areas. Maintenance of production units, well-head equipment, water-injection plant and pipelines demands very small numbers of personnel and the impact of the production side of the oil industry has only aided the development of technical and administrative organisations in the main centres servicing the oilfields, and even they are of small size.

Pipeline export facilities have generated a small and often negligible degree of employment in the areas through which they pass. The marine export terminals have fared better and Fao and Khor al Amayah within the Basra area have seen important expansion of storage oil-handling and marine-service employment. Iraq's export refineries will also be constructed at Zubair, adding to the large aggregate weight of oil industry activities there. Elsewhere in Iraq, the location of individual refineries and other oil-industry installations is generally insufficient to make an appreciable mark on the local economy. The fact is that the oil industry, despite its apparent wide geographical network in the country, has further enhanced the economic strength of the major urban centres and has tended to benefit both Baghdad as the administrative centre and Basra as the operational centre to the exclusion of the provinces.

Yet the outstanding achievements of Iraqi industrialisation have been achieved with industry essentially based on the petroleum sector. Petrochemicals are emerging as the principal area of state investment. The major projects completed or in hand within the Ministry of Planning projects' list include the Basra petrochemical complexes One and Two, the Basra fertiliser plants One, Two and Three, expansion of the Mishraq sulphur plant and creation of the Akashat and al-Qaim chemical complex. Smaller-scale developments are planned for Samarra, Khalis and Samawa. The timing and pace of construction of the petrochemical industry have been erratic, with projects adopted or postponed depending on the availability of finance for the plan, though this industry has been a more successful competitor for funds than all others with the sole exception of the oil industry itself. By far the greatest bulk of investment in petrochemicals will be directed to Basra governorate and specifically to the Basra-Zubair zone. Growth of the al-Quaim chemical complex will entail the construction of a new town and a degree of genuine regional industrial development, in sharp contrast to other plants which, by size or employment structure, will have only limited effect on the areas in which they are planted. The pattern of investment in the petrochemical industry will, therefore, tend to reinforce the imbalances between the country's central axis through the riverine belt Basra to Baghdad and the outlying districts.

A similar situation arises with respect to other significant areas of industrial investment. Among the metallurgical and light industries projects included within the plan, a group lying second only to petrochemicals in order of funds allocated, virtually every major scheme will be located in Basra-Zubair area. The Khur al-Zubair steelworks and its associated sponge iron plants are the most pertinent example of the strengthening of the existing population centres, while the new Iraqi aluminium industry, other than the Nasseriyah aluminium processing plant, is also located in Basra. Indeed, very few industries in this section will be set up at sites far from Basra or Baghdad.

A poor rate of growth in agriculture has, with the sole exception of the Kurdish area, been the most profound factor in the widening of the economic gap between urban and rural areas in the period since 1958. The failures in agriculture experienced by successive governments have stemmed not least from the intractable nature of the Iraqi environment and the constant underestimation of the physical constraints on agriculture in all regions of the country. Events have been worsened by frequent changes of policy towards agriculture and by a chronic inability of the administrations responsible for agriculture to claim and disburse the financial allocations made within the various plans for economic development.

The scale of actual expenditure on agriculture has only represented slightly more than half the allocations made for plan periods as shown in Table 8.4. This contrasts with an 84 per cent ratio between allocations and disbursements for industry and 60 per cent for buildings and services in the 1970/1 to 1974/5 plan period. In that same period almost twice as much was actually disbursed on industry as on agriculture, which is a relative position typical of the plans since 1958. Yet it is estimated that some 50 per cent or more of the population is engaged in agriculture against approximately 6 per cent in industry.

Table 8.4: Allocations and Disbursements of the National Economic Plans to Agriculture, 1960-75 (million Iraqi dinars)

Years	Allocations	Disbursements	Disbursements as per cent of Allocations
1960 and 1961 (b)	43.9	18.2	41
1962/3 and and 1963/4 (c)	58.5	10.8	18
1965/6 to 1969/70 (d)	173.5	54.4	31
1970/1 to 1974/5 (e)	413.0	208.2	50

Source: *Annual Abstract of Statistics.*
Notes: a. Including irrigation. b. Provisional Economic Plan. c. Detailed Economic Plan. d. Total projected expenditure for this plan was put at ID 142.0 million. e. 1974! 5 disbursements are estimated only and should be lower according to the Central Bank of Iraq, thereby reducing disbursements as a proportion of allocations to below 50 per cent.

Planning for agriculture has been impeded considerably by frequent changes in government policy. Both agrarian structure and irrigation strategy have been adversely affected in this manner. Even where new policies have had much-improved concepts and greater measures of funding associated with them, they have been adopted regardless of the ability of the administrative infrastructure to cope with their implementation. Political changes in Baghdad have invariably meant important changes in the personnel involved in the planning and administration of the agricultural sector, with the result that officials in the countryside have been made isolated from the decision-makers and ineffective even in the application of the most elementary services to the farming community.

The spread of insecurity in rural Iraq has unhappily long antecedents. Tribal disputes over territory, antagonism between nomadic and settled groups, the depredations of tax-gatherers and reliance on primitive irrigation systems, often badly maintained, have been long-standing impediments in the way of improvement of agriculture. A 1932 law sponsored by the British authorities sought to register title to all land but effectively led to the registration of large tracts of agricultural land in the names of tribal chiefs and the deprivation of the mass of people from their former communal rights to usufruct. Following the 1958 revolution a land reform law was enacted decreeing the redistribution of agricultural land. A ceiling of 250 hectares of irrigated or 500 hectares of rain-fed land was applied throughout the country (though not implemented in Kurdistan until very recent times). Expropriation of land from the former large landowners was pressed ahead more rapidly than the state had ability to redistribute to peasant farmers. As late as the end of 1975 government statistics showed that 1.27 million hectares were on temporary lease from the government to farmers. This contrasts with 2.58 million hectares sequestrated under Law 30 of 1958 and Law 117 of 1970. The agrarian reform law has been frequently modified since its original enactment bringing in its train uncertainty and insecurity.

Mismanagement of the agrarian reform would on its own have sufficed to disrupt the development of Iraqi agriculture. Unfortunately, it went hand in hand with neglect of the co-operative system designed to underpin the small farmers benefiting from the reform. Essays in state farming, collectives and agro-industries have induced further doubts over the future in the minds of the remaining farming community and have damaged the long-term prospects for agricultural recovery on the traditional cultivated lands. By 1975 there were 1,653 agricultural co-operatives controlling 4 million hectares, 72 collectives with 134,000 hectares, and nine integrated state farms with approximately 100,000 hectares.

Government interventions into agriculture have succeeded in paralysing spontaneous developments by the rural community without providing consistent policies and the human and physical infrastructure to make the agricultural plan function. Rural incomes have remained low, especially outside the intensively irrigated areas of the Tigris and Euphrates valley (see Chapter 7 of this volume). There is no better commentary on the economic and social depression affecting rural society and agricultural activities in Iraq than the rate of rural-urban drift.[9] Lawless makes the point that '[Rural migration] is perhaps the major socio-economic problem facing the government.'[10] Iraq certainly has compounded its problems with agriculture by creating a scarcity of labour in rural areas to the degree that 'voluntary labour' drives have been run to ensure that crops have been harvested. By the end of the 1976-80 plan period, there will be only 4.1 million in rural areas against 9.1 million persons in urban areas.

A paradox facing the economic planners in Iraq, and one that has never been resolved, is the apparent potential for intensive irrigated agriculture throughout much of the riverine zone and the thesis that a tightly administered hydraulic system has historically been the key to the wealth of civilisation arising in Mesopotamia yet a present-day agriculture which exhibits all the characteristics of extensive cultivation even on terrain that is served by irrigation works. Erratic though generally augmenting flows of rural population to the towns since the First World War, together with other political problems noted above, have meant that extensive farming remains the rule in all but a few rice-growing areas. It is estimated that some 5.75 million hectares are under cultivation, encompassing some 2.53 million hectares actually planted in any year, 2.79 million hectares under fallow in any year and only 128,000 hectares in fruit trees and vines and 51,750 hectares of woodland. No less than 230,000 hectares are classified as managed pasture while the vast bulk of the country is uncultivated desert, range and mountain. Most reliable estimates suggest that some 6 million hectares lie in the irrigated zone and some 4.5 million hectares in the rain-fed zone. The two major rivers on average service some 1.25 million hectares for irrigation (0.75 million from the Euphrates and 0.50 million hectares from the Tigris).

Despite low rural population densities and extremely limited use of existing irrigated areas, Iraqi plans for agricultural development have, with effect from 1951/2, concentrated on the provision of hydraulic works on the river systems. In part the hand of the planners was forced by geographical realities of the riverine area. Water levels in the Euphrates south of Ramadi and in the Tigris south of Baghdad are, especially during the annual flood, at greater altitude than the surrounding land as a result of the build-up of the large volumes of silt carried by the rivers and their tributaries. Given the flat topography of the Mesopotamian Plain and the tendency of the rivers to change their course, the construction of earth retaining embankments has been necessary to keep the water flow within existing channels. Failure to maintain the embankments can lead to severe flooding over wide areas with a consequent loss of agricultural land and inundation of towns and villages. There is in consequence an economic imperative for the planners to allocate funds for the improvement of embankments as natural conditions lead to rising levels of the courses of the rivers.

In Iraq hydraulic works have multiple functions. Arising from the inescapable need to constrain the rivers within their courses, the governments of Iraq have sought to construct river control works to spread the load of spring floods over longer periods and to divert flood waters where least damage would be done. At the same time, attempts have been made to regulate the flow into and out of storage areas and canal systems. Finally, there have been a number of works designed to store water to extend the irrigated cropping season. It is notable in the last twenty years that multi-purpose hydraulic structures have been adopted by the planning authorities and inaugurated with only the river control, hydro-electric and diversion functions operational. Provision of irrigation canals and land reclamation has lagged far behind schedule on most major schemes. Indeed, the balance between completion of dams, barrages and regulators as against storage reservoirs suggests a continuing preoccupation with river control rather than a positive approach to the spread of irrigation services (Table 8.5), even though overt policy of the state is for rapid expansion of irrigation.

A second, and by no means inconsiderable, pressure on the government for development of irrigation lies in the nature of the rainfall régime. Highly episodic natural precipitation within Iraq and fluctuating snowfalls in the regions of the upper watersheds of the Rivers Tigris and Euphrates cause appreciable variations in the availability of adequate moisture for cropping and therefore sharp changes in production and yields of agricultural crops. This is reflected both in unstable levels of personal income in farming and in variable contributions by agriculture to GDP. Iraq is experiencing increasing difficulty in feeding its population from domestic resources and in years of poor rainfall or low flood levels in the rivers the position is exacerbated. In 1974 Iraq imported animal products and foodstuffs valued at ID 184.34 million, or some 26.3 per cent of all imports. In the better rainfall year of 1975 foodstuffs and animal products worth ID 192.47 million or 15.5 per cent of all imports. Planning for development has implied, at least at the bureaucratic level, a requirement to stabilise output through extension of irrigation to dry-land areas in addition to reclamation at the extensive margin. Official targets have been ambitious but have rarely been met. Extension of irrigation facilities to 437,500 hectares is planned for the 1976-80 period, with large-scale schemes for the Mosul, Kirkuk and Lower Khalis areas, though at best these projects will only be begun in the 1976-80 period with completion, especially of the irrigation component, scheduled for the longer term.

The fascination of hydraulic engineering to both planners and politicians has in no way been constrained by reports as early as 1955 that engineering of the river systems was of little benefit to those engaged in agriculture unless problems of marketing, credit, security and social welfare were also attended to.[11] Government statistics blur the distinction between allocations and expenditure affecting the agricultural and irrigation programmes, though the irrigation budget has normally run at some 25 per cent of total allocations to agriculture. On the basis of projects begun it would appear likely that irrigation received a much larger part of funds actually disbursed under the plan than all other agricultural services.

Table 8.5: Major Hydraulic Works in Iraq

1. Dams, Barrages and regulators
Hindiyya barrage
Diyala dam
Kut barrage
al-Majarra regulator
Dibban regulator
Warrar regulator
Ramadi barrage
Samarra barrage
Dukan dam
Darbandi Khan dam
al-Gharraf regulator
Tharthar regulator
2. Water reservoirs
Darbandi Khan reservoir
Dökan reservoir
Tharthar reservoir
Habbaniya lake
Abu Dibbis depression

Source: *Annual Abstract of Statistics.*

The very nature of the irrigation projects implemented in the river valleys has meant that relatively small and geographically discrete areas have benefited. Development, too, has tended to be concentrated around the River Tigris and its tributaries entering from the north. The Euphrates, by contrast, with more difficult management problems and greater unreliability of flow, has been less the object of irrigation schemes and the areas in its vicinity have been less rapidly and thoroughly developed, thus inducing a further dimension to regional disparities in income.

It is important to take into account the loss of irrigated lands in any consideration of trends in land reclamation and the pressures on the government to allocate funds to irrigation engineering. At the most modest official estimate, some 25,000 to 30,000 hectares are lost each year through the effects of salinity and alkalinity on irrigated lands. In practice this means that at least one new irrigation project of the size of Kirkuk irrigation scheme must be commissioned every four years (the Kirkuk project will cost some ID 200 million) simply to keep pace with the rate of loss of established irrigated land. While it is true that the haste with which many irrigation developments have been begun and brought into production has militated against proper provision of drainage works and training of farmers in appropriate techniques of irrigation, it is also generally not appreciated that the very systems of irrigation practised in much of the riverine area in combination with the precarious balance between height of water table and the nature of the soils inevitably lead to rapid and widespread problems of salinity and alkalinity. Such problems increase costs of cultivation and reduce the proftability of farming and substantially contribute to depressed living standards in rural areas.

The planning of agricultural development, which might be expected to be the most readily available and effective vehicle for promoting rural improvements, for offsetting the worst effects of growing disadvantage for the farmer *vis-à-vis* the urban worker, and for reducing the dis-equilibrium between the pace and scale of development of the riverine axis between Baghdad and Basra and that experienced elsewhere in the country, has, in fact, had quite the reverse result. Over all, financial allocations to agriculture have been high but actual expenditure low. Vast sums have been and are continuing to be spent on engineering works on the great river systems apparently under the head of agricultural investment. But much of the benefit accruing from river control has only an incidental impact on agriculture since follow-up works in irrigation have come forward slowly or have been tacitly abandoned to an unspecified future. Where irrigation development has taken place it has been patchy in incidence and success. It is officially claimed that Iraq has the potential, utilising existing facilities and those to be created during the 1976-80 plan period, to irrigate as much as 4.5 million hectares on a perennial basis.[12] Current government estimates indicate, however, that water use in cultivation has changed little since the early 1950s (Table 8.6). Government statistics, though often conflicting, point to a present-day cultivated area under irrigation of approximately 11.6-12.0 million mesharas or 2.9 million to 3.0 million hectares, varying year by year. It is interesting to speculate where the labour force could be found to service perennial irrigation on 4.5 million hectares since absolute rural population is stable to declining and cannot currently handle peak season labour demand on the largely single cropped area of 2.9 million hectares.

Table 8.6: Irrigation Areas by Type (hectares)

Rain-fed	2,752,062
Flow irrigation	1,685,236
Pump irrigation	1,119,526
Water-wheel irrigation	56,143
Others (mainly flood irrigation)	51,382
Total rain-fed and irrigated	5,664,349
Total irrigated	2,912,287

Source: Lord Salter, *The development of Iraq* (London, 1955).

In summary, it can be said that the lack of regional planning or even the preparation of plans for the regions, the only possible exception being Kurdistan, has left the provincial areas of the south-west and north-east as economically declining backwaters. Project orientation of the plan has favoured oil, petrochemicals and manufacturing industry. The employment creation elements of and the main investments in these sectors have been overwhelmingly concentrated in the riverine axis running through the oases of the Tigris-Euphrates lowland. Severe constraints of the physical environment have induced chronic pre-occupation of governments with engineering projects on the great rivers but with at best geographically limited and short-term results for agriculture in general and irrigated agriculture in particular.

Prospects for rural and agricultural development within the current plan period and beyond induce little optimism for the future. While it is feasible to foresee much more intensive and profitable cropping of the irrigated areas of Mesopotamia, this could be achieved only with a total revolution in irrigation system, in technological level of cultivation, in agrarian structure, and in administrative infrastructure. A new approach to agricultural change in the provinces would also demand wide-reaching changes in government policy and probably the abandonment of the most valued political objective of the present régime for the agricultural sector – the extension of socialist organisations in rural areas to bring as much as 85 per cent of farmland under state-controlled co-operatives and collectives. It would seem more than likely that areas outside the Baghdad-Basra axis and its immediate environs will remain predominantly agricultural, but that promises of serious financial and technical aid to that sector will, as in the past, be mainly unkept. Considerable and continuing oil wealth accruing through crude oil and other exports has so far and will remain the real cornerstone of the Iraqi economy and obviate the need for a sound and coherent long-term policy for agricultural improvement in the face of a difficult and deteriorating water-supply situation allied to a fertile but fragile soil endowment.

It will doubtless be convenient for politicians in Iraq to believe that the retarded state of agriculture and the peripheral regions derives from the failures of the pre-revolutionary governments, for historians to assume that economic backwardness is a legacy of colonialist interventions,[13] and for opponents of the régime in power to attribute failures in economic planning for the regions to the ineptness of the policies and administrative abilities of their rulers. The fact is that the Iraqi environment is not easily controlled, is subject to inherent fluctuations outside the aegis of the régime in Baghdad, and represents a poor resource base by any standard applicable to the Middle East area. Given a simpler option to sustain the country on oil income, it is hardly surprising that Iraqi governments are permitting the country to become an oil economy on a model not entirely different from that more maturely developed in Kuwait and other Arab oil-exporting states of the Persian Gulf.

Notes

1. D. Warriner, *Land reform and development in the Middle East* (RIIA, 1962), p. 113.
2. R.I. Lawless, 'Iraq: changing population patterns' in *Populations of the Middle East and North Africa* J.I. Clarke and W.B. Fisher (eds.) (London University of London Press, 1972), pp. 125-6.
3. 'Large areas – variously estimated as twenty to thirty per cent of the irrigated area – have already gone out of production.' *FAO Mediterranean Development Project*, 'Iraq', (FAO, 1959), p. 128.
4. Ministry of Planning, Central Statistical Organisation, *Annual Abstract of Statistics 1975*, pp. 61-78.
5. British Admiralty, *Geographical Handbook of Iraq and the Persian Gulf* (London, 1944), p. 449.
6. K.S. McLachlan, 'Iraq' in *The developing agriculture of the Middle East* M. Donovan and K.S. McLachlan (eds.) (Graham and Trotman, 1976), p. 46.
7. Lawless, 'Iraq: changing population patterns', p. 100.
8. C.S. Coons, *Caravan: the story of the Middle East*, (New York, 1951).
9. Lawless, 'Iraq: changing population patterns', p. 116.
10. Ibid.
11. Lord Salter, *The development of Iraq* (London, 1955).
12. Dr Majid al-Badri quoted in *Baghdad Observer*, 19 November, 1975, p. 2.
13. See the theme elaborated by M.S. Hasan, 'The role of foreign trade in the economic development of Iraq, 1954-1964: a study of a dependent economy' in *Studies in the economic history of the Middle East*, M.A. Cooke (ed.) (London, Oxford University Press, 1970), pp. 346-72.

9 INDUSTRIAL POLICY AND PERFORMANCE IN IRAQ*

Edith Penrose

The 1958 Revolution and the policies pursued by Abd al-Karim Qasim had a much smaller impact on the industrial sector of the Iraqi economy than on the agriculture and oil sectors. In both oil and agriculture Qasim initiated fundamental and irreversible changes in policy and the immediate result was a disruption and stagnation that could only be remedied by further far-reaching changes. The country has still not been able to escape from agricultural stagnation and it had to await the conclusion of agreements between the oil companies and the governments of other Middle East countries before it could effectively solve its problem with its own oil company. But in the industrial sector few important changes were made by Qasim's government.

Qasim shifted the emphasis of government development plans to favour housing, health and education, and to promote industry over agriculture. Although government-controlled industry was expanded at the expense of the private sector, which was thus faced with increasing uncertainty, there was no radical change of policy. The decisive step was taken by the government of Abd al-Salam Arif when the major part of large industry was nationalised. This brought over one-third of the net national income originating in manufacturing under government control, created a complete state monopoly in some industries and severely restricted the role of the private sector in a number of others.

Abd al-Salam Arif, like the military régimes before and after him, announced that his government endorsed 'socialism', but he did not include the nationalisation of private industry in his original version of the doctrine. Eventually, he was persuaded by the Nasserites that nationalisation was an appropriate action for the protection of the public and the advancement of Arab unity as well as for the more rapid development of the economy. In 1964 thirty large industries and all of the banks and insurance companies were nationalised. Other decrees

* This paper draws heavily on Chapter XVIII of *Iraq: International Relations and National Development,* Edith and E.F. Penrose (London, Ernest Benn, 1978).

were promulgated allocating 25 per cent of corporate profits to workers, providing for worker representation on boards of directors, limiting the size of individual shareholdings in larger companies, and creating an overall Economic Organization to own and operate the nationalised establishments in the public sector. All of this was on the Egyptian pattern.

Just as the agrarian reforms of 1958 introduced a sharp discontinuity in the development of Iraqi agriculture, disrupting the existing productive relationships and necessitating the introduction of entirely new forms of organisation, so the nationalisation laws of 1964 created a similar discontinuity in the development of Iraqi industry and necessitated the creation of new forms of management and control. Twenty years have passed since the agrarian reform and the organisational problems are by no means solved; similarly, the new organisation required for the development of an efficient and dynamic industry in Iraq has not yet materialised after fourteen years and there is no sign that it will do so in the near future. The primary motive for both the agrarian reform and the industrial nationalisations was political, but in both cases it was also confidently assumed that an improved economic performance would result. Industry did not suffer as badly as agriculture, but the rate of growth of industrial output has been commensurate neither with the amount of investment poured into it nor with the rate of growth of demand. The reasons for the unsatisfactory results are much the same in industry as in agriculture: the heavy hand of bureaucracy and the lack of co-operation from a dissatisfied population.

Iraqi statistics of industrial performance, and especially the reporting of financial results, must not be taken too seriously, for Iraqi accounting procedures have been and still are extremely defective. At the time of the nationalisations few firms had any real record of their invested capital, this term often referring simply to paid-up share capital, and the 'capital' reported for many enterprises was apparently largely arbitrary. Further investment in companies after their formation was often not recorded at all and reported profits were often little more than the difference between direct expenses and receipts in a given period. In an industry where demand was growing rapidly this could well lead to the reporting of very large profits. Most companies lacked book-keepers trained in modern methods, and some lacked even the simplest ideas of keeping accounts. Machines were often expensed, and sometimes even whole factories. When a factory was handed over in finished form, especially by an Eastern European contractor, the government often had no idea of the capital value to put on it. Commonly, depreciation accounting was primitive or entirely ignored. In these circumstances, any figures, including those derived from a study of company accounts, must be suspect.[1]

Clearly these accounting and statistical difficulties not only cast much doubt on the reported profits (or lack of them) for individual enterprises, but also on all figures of costs and value added in industry. By the same token, it is not possible to feel much confidence in appraisals of the economic results of the nationalisations; but we have little choice than to use the figures available. A recent careful non-governmental attempt to construct indices of the volume of output in manufacturing shows that there was a fall in the rate of growth of all manufacturing in the period 1964-9 compared to the period 1960-4, and that in twelve industries where nationalisation had been extensive the growth rate also declined in all but four, in some instances severely (see Table 9.1). Official statistics also indicate a decline in the annual rate of growth of manufacturing output in constant prices after 1963, and in the period 1964-9 compared with 1958-62. Over the ten years 1953-63, manufacturing output (including oil-refining) grew at an annual compound rate of 11.5 per cent, but between 1964 and 1971 output grew at only 6.7 per cent.[2] Similarly, manufacturing output (including oil-refining) grew between 1958 and 1962 at a compound annual rate of 15.7 per cent (1956 prices) and between 1965 and 1969 at 5.7 per cent (1969 prices).[3] In the short period such figures can be seriously distorted by a variety of factors which affect the end years, but in this period only 1963 seems to have been an unusually poor year, due probably to political uncertainties.

Thus the evidence does not support the contention that the nationalisation of large industry in Iraq brought about any improvements in output or investment; rather it indicates that output fell in the short run and that the rate of growth did not increase in the longer period. One cannot of course know whether or not the political uncertainties under which private enterprise operated would in any case have led to similar (or worse) results; but there is no doubt that government was ill-adapted to run industry.

In a study for the United Nations, Dr Khair al-Din Haseeb, who was himself largely responsible for bringing about the nationalisations, discussed the inefficiencies characteristic of the economic policies and controls of the government.[4] Ministers in charge were frequently changed. For example, between 1964 and 1968 there were eight Ministers of Industry and Transport, seven Ministers of Public Works, six

Ministers of Agrarian Reform, and six Ministers of Planning. This led to change in programmes and plans and very often also of the subordinate personnel. Political changes in countries without a secure, professional and stable civil service are always disruptive. More generally, government consultants and committees often paid close attention to technical aspects of industrial projects but little to economic aspects, including marketing – a persistence of the engineering 'bricks and mortar' bias. There were also long delays due to the need for import permits, labour permits, residence permits; deliveries would be made with no one to take them. Delays occurring in periods of inflation led to increased costs at a later date, which thus caused cancellation of projects and the need for subsequent retendering. Installation of imported equipment might take over two or three times longer than had been expected, or be delayed indefinitely. Personnel difficulties arose because of inflexible government regulations (e.g. personnel on government projects were required to be government employees but there was a regulation which prevented storekeepers from being classed as government employees; there was no way around the impasse). Another example of poor planning: a factory designed to employ 220 college graduates and 130 foreign experts was put in a town with less than 10 modern houses – more delay, greater costs.

Table 9.1: Growth in Volume of Output of Selected Industries 1960-4 and 1964-9 (1965 prices)

	1960-4 Annual Increase (per cent)	1964-9 Annual Increase (per cent)
Grain-milling	8.8	7.7
Vegetable oil	11.9	9.1
Cotton textiles	2.9	4.1
Wool textiles	5.0	8.6
Jute and rope	20.5	8.2
Footwear	8.6	2.3
Soaps and detergents	40.9	19.0
Matches	6.0	8.3
Asbestos	25.1	9.6
Cement	8.0	7.5
Paper and paper products	17.7	6.5
Cigarettes and tobacco products	.6	8.8
All manufacturing	7.3	6.6

Source: Calculated from the indices constructed by Zeki M. Fattah, 'Production, Capital Stock, Productivity and Growth in the Industrial Sector of an Oil Economy: Iraq 1960-1970) (unpublished Ph.D. thesis in the University of Oxford, 1976). Includes establishments employing ten or more persons in each industry.

The 1970-5 Development Plan was designed to promote an even faster rate of industrial investment, yielding a 75 per cent increase in value added in manufacturing between 1969 and 1974, or a 12 per cent annual rate of growth. Financial implementation was rapid, and between 1971 and 1975 85 per cent of the allocations for industry had in fact been spent.[5] Before this plan had been completed, however, the rise in oil prices and the nationalisation of the oil industry made large additional funds available to the economy and the financial allocations to the plan were greatly increased. The structure of imports reflected the rapid rate of capital formation and imports of capital goods rose rapidly. Machinery, iron and steel and non-ferrous metals alone increased from around ID 102 million in 1973 to over ID 1,000 million two years later as the investment effort intensified. And imports of food more than doubled between 1973 and 1975.

In the type of project (and even the rhetoric) the new plan for industry was not qualitatively very different from those of the past quarter of a century;[6] the scale, of course, was much larger not only because of increased oil revenues and planning resources but also because prices were very much higher and correspondingly greater expenditures were required to obtain the same goods and services. Projects comprised petrochemicals (including fertilisers), pulp and paper, vehicles and assembly of vehicles, electrical appliances, intermediate and finished synthetic textiles, paints and plastics. The contracts for the construction of the factories were made with foreign firms from a wide variety of countries in Europe (both East and West) and from Japan and the United States. New factories for electronics (radios, calculators, television sets) were opened in 1976. Iron and steel projects and a glass factory were also put in hand. A preference for 'turn-key' projects persisted. Altogether the revised plan after the rise in oil revenues allocated ID 391 million for the manufacturing sector.

After the settlement with the IPC following nationalisation, the uncertainty over how the oil companies and their parent governments would react and the effect any reaction might have on Iraq's revenues was eliminated, and the government moved ahead rapidly. The volume of contracts with foreign firms and governments increased very fast for the construction of factories, the importation of goods, the design and execution of transportation, electricity, port and other infrastructural projects. Moreover, there was a marked shift in the proportion of contracts granted to countries other than those of Eastern Europe. A rough analysis of published information indicates that whereas in the early 1970s somewhat more than half of the development contracts went to the Eastern European countries, from 1974-5 well over two-thirds were going to other countries. But the Minister of Industry and Minerals, Taha al-Jazrawi, denied that this implied any shift of political orientation: he noted that 'it would be a mistake to interpret Iraq's awarding of major development contracts to Western Governments or firms as a sign of Iraq's reorientation towards the West. The fact that Iraq is turning to the Western companies is not a sign of change but of the speed and volume of development.'[7]

The results of the new 'big push' to create very rapidly a large modern manufacturing sector with an export potential will not be clear for at least ten years from the time of writing. The Iraqi planners were naturally aware that they would continually run into serious 'bottlenecks', as indeed they have, and there is little point here in going into the details of the various problems encountered in the attempt to force the pace of industrial development. The general outlines are well known and afflict in varying degrees all the oil-exporting countries making similar efforts. Common to all is the problem of shortages and rising prices as local expenditures create an excess demand for local resources which cannot easily be fully substituted for by imports. Land prices rise, housing becomes very short and there is often difficult in importing construction materials rapidly enough. Transport and port facilities become congested. And labour, especially skilled labour, becomes very scarce. Such problems became particularly intractable in Iraq as oil revenues and expenditures rose with the increase in oil prices. Foreigners brought in their own resources to build factories and even their own labour on occasion. By 1977 some of the bottlenecks were substantially eased (for example, port congestion) but others continued to tighten (for example, labour shortages).

In addition to these 'normal' difficulties, however, Iraq faced special problems arising from her government's commitment to a type of socialism which required that all of the larger new enterprises should not only be owned by the state but also run by government departments. This enhanced the urgency of appropriate organisation for which by 1977 no solution was even in sight, and compounded the strains on management and workers. The Iraqi government shows no sign of being able to produce a reasonably efficient and stable organisation for the control and operation of its state enterprises.

Organisation and Efficiency

In 1964 the newly nationalised banks, insurance companies, trading companies and industries had been grouped under four public organisations: the General Organization for Banking, the General Insurance Organization, the General Trade Organization and the General Industrial Organization, the last three of which were placed under the umbrella of the Economic Organization. The Governor of the Central Bank and one of the chief architects of the system, Khair al-Din Haseeb, was appointed acting chairman of this new giant organisation.

Predictably, the structure was unwieldy, and it was reorganised in the following year when a General Organization for Industry, which took over insurance companies, manufacturing establishments and general industrial services, was created. Some regional rationalisation of industries was also attempted. This new and similarly unwieldy organisation was again reorganised in 1970 with the abolition of the General Organization and the establishment of six State Organizations, one each for spinning and weaving industries; clothing, leather and cigarettes; chemical and food industries; construction industries; engineering industries; and planning and industrial construction. Further organisations and reorganisations have taken place, but none has overcome the bureaucratic inefficiency of the state industrial sector.

In 1973 a paper presented to a conference of an expert group of the United Nations Economic and Social Office in Beirut described the chief characteristics of the management of public industrial enterprises in Iraq and analysed the problems.[8] It showed that state industrial enterprises were, in effect, organised as part of the state bureaucracy and were given very little autonomous power of decision. There were several levels of authority over the enterprise, including not only the State Organization to which it belonged, but up to at least four Ministers (Industry, Economy, Finance, Planning) and a variety of sub-Ministerial agencies. Nearly all decisions had to go through several layers and many of them had to go high up in the relevant Ministries. The drawing-up, evaluation and implementation of investment decisions required approval from a number of sources, and even the implementation might be undertaken by an agency outside the enterprise. Pricing decisions were made by the State Organization, and were subject to Ministerial approval, giving the enterprise very little flexibility to meet market conditions. Even to sell off obsolete inventories, surplus raw materials, etc., managers of enterprises had to obtain authorisation from higher authority and then sell at public auctions according to procedures laid down. Full cost pricing was commonly imposed, leading to excess capacity and unwanted stocks. Distribution and marketing were often separated from the productive enterprise; procurement of materials was subject to lengthy procedures and to numerous approvals regardless of the value of the material. In the larger enterprises compensation of personnel was regulated and transfers of workers between enterprises had to be approved by the State Organizations. (In general, resignations from the public sector to transfer to the private sector are not permitted without special authorisation; lay-offs are illegal.)

The disposal of profits is regulated by law, but enterprises are allowed to retain some of their profits and depreciation reserves for expansion. The forms of finance available to the enterprises are regulated and procedures must be followed with long advance notice. In practice, there is a reluctance on the part of individuals in the hierarchy to make decisions even if empowered to do so and in consequence decisions are commonly passed to a level higher than necessary.

Thus, not only are there many levels of decision-making, but the process is highly centralised; delays are long, and are made longer by the reluctance of officials to assume authority. Moreover, there is generally little weight given to the value of time. This is characteristic of any bureaucracy which is not under some sort of external pressure, and is notoriously common in state bureaucracies; it is especially damaging when extended to 'business' enterprises.

The United Nations Report drew attention to a number of consequences of the methods of organisation adopted in Iraq: long lags between proposals and final decisions, which are especially serious in the procurement of goods, including imports (it should be remembered that the prompt availability of imports is about the only way in which Iraq can keep the rate of inflation down in present circumstances); inflexibility in using labour, even including restrictions on overtime arrangements; undue interference and overruling of decisions by higher authorities and even reversal of the normal direction of the lines of authority; the very low premium attached to the value of time 'so that it does not matter how long it would take between the initiation of a decision and its implementation'.[9] All these cause great losses while at the same time unnecessary routine procedures must be observed. This last consequence is made worse by the fact that the costs of administration and control have no direct economic consequences for individuals or enterprises. Thus, evaluation of the results of the operation of individual state enterprises has no important role in the system. The cost of capital is largely ignored, and there is no effective provision against the inappropriate use of fixed assets. There are large holdings of inventories because of the time-consuming purchasing system and there is excess involvement of high-level managerial staff in routine decisions.

As might be expected from this brief description of the inefficiencies inherent in the methods of control, state enterprises frequently find themselves at a competitive disadvantage *vis-à-vis* the private sector.

All of this is reminiscent of the problems of the Egyptian industrial structure on which the Iraqis originally modelled their state organisations. It is now widely recognised in Egypt that the bureaucracy and the methods of managing the public sector have been among the most serious obstacles to the country's industrial revival. In Egypt, the public sector accounts for an overwhelming proportion of gross value added in industrial establishments employing 10 persons or more (90 per cent in 1966-7 and not much changed in the succeeding decade) and observers report very similar difficulties: the pricing system tended to insulate state firms from the market and capacity utilisation tended therefore to be inefficient; lack of direct access to foreign markets entailed economic losses; import delays led to emergence of idle capacity and costly excess inventories; overmanning is serious in plants and offices; and incentives are inadequate. The heavy burden of administrative controls created obstacles to efficient and dynamic performance.[10]

Iraqi labour policies are also similar to those in Egypt and give rise to the same inadequacy of incentives, overmanning and poor deployment of the labour force. Many graduates are not employed in the areas of their specialisations and their jobs are not necessarily consistent with their qualifications. Yet they cannot easily be moved without their consent.[11] In the autumn of 1976 the low productivity in Iraqi industry was the subject of a number of discussions and 'seminars' in the country. *Al-Thawrah* (the Baath official organ) reported the proceedings of a 'seminar' in September 1976 at which members of the Revolutionary Command Council, Members of the Regional (Iraqi) Baath Party, Ministers, heads of institutions and trade union heads were among those present. The group considered a working paper on the causes of the fall in productivity which had been prepared by representatives of labour and government.[12]

The working paper listed factors which affected productivity adversely. It emphasised labour laws which prevented management from giving a worker a job different from that mentioned in his contract and hence made it difficult or impossible to teach new skills or to train workers for other kinds of work according to the demands of industry. It criticised administrative organisation, especially in the productive sector, which was considered to be of low standard because of ignorance and lack of specialisation on the part of those responsible, the inability of administrators to control and supervise inefficient workers, and the unproductive efforts of management and small administrators to please workers, who were too often resentful, bitter and indifferent. The 'umbrellas' of the State Organizations which were used to protect top administrators and trade unionists were criticised. Inappropriate wage policies, inadequate incentives, competition for workers without regard to productivity and the shortage of primary products, especially evident in food industries, were all brought up.

In general, the impression was of poor co-ordination, tension between workers and managers, particular tension between 'inspectors' and the private sector, and an underlying tone of political discontent. The Iraqi Vice-President, Saddam Husain, addressed the seminar, insisting that 'there should be no increase in wages if there is no increase in productivity. The quantity and quality of Iraqi productivity needed to be improved in industry, agriculture, services.' He pointed to the disorder at the airport, in the telephone, water and electricity systems and asked who was responsible. He then denounced all who did not work and all who did not criticise those they found at fault, whether they were managers, workers or directors.

In the discussion on the report, representatives of the workers defended the labour law as necessary to safeguard their position against management, and they cited many instances of managerial 'mal-administration', shortages of material for production, excessive inventories with inadequate storage space, inadequate supplies of spare parts, etc. – in short, very many of the same problems which had been outlined in the 1973 United Nations Report.

When attempts to control markets, including labour markets, are inefficient, they usually create at least two problems for every one solved; the Iraqi attempts seem to provide no exception. Wage restraint has not been very successful, especially in large industries where the pressure of demand is very heavy (like brick-making), and in the private sector where higher wages naturally cause difficulty for the public sector in a variety of ways. Badly administered controls, badly designed administrative structures, ineffective incentives, inadequate provisions for training and retraining, etc., adversely affect the morale of workers and create conflicts between the individual interests of workers and industrial productivity.

The labour laws give a worker almost complete security in his existing job and thus provide no immediate personal incentive for him to exert himself unduly or to accept change which would increase the effort demanded of him. The government now offers financial inducements and bonuses to increase productivity but also relies heavily on slogans and exhortation which are evidently not convincing to a sufficient number of workers. It is also likely that the unpopularity of the régime with large sections of the population, especially the Kurds and the Shiis (which form the majority of the working class) increases workers' resistance to government attempts to persuade them to work harder and to accept personal inconvenience in the interests of the Iraqi state, the 'broad masses', or even of the 'Arab Nation' which, according to the Baath government's 'National Action Charter', was 'the frame of reference' for Iraq's planners and 'not the limited aim of developing only Iraq'.

On the negative side, the continued attempt to trace the country's difficulties to the machinations of imperialists seems to have been having a somewhat diminished impact after twenty years of 'revolutionary' government. There is little evidence that the government and people feel united in a genuine common effort at economic and political development. The tensions between management and worker seems to be less in the private sector, where firms are relatively small, than in the large state firms where workers blame management for most of the inefficiencies that the system of control imposes, as well as for remoteness. The government invites criticism, but tales are common of people, mentioned by name, who criticised and quickly found themselves in prison or otherwise punished. The régime is ruthless in acting against or even eliminating any critic it considers dangerous and in these circumstances there is considerable scope for victimisation resulting from personal feuds. Administrators are safer if they can avoid taking decisions, and are cautious over those they do take.

The very high degree of job security given to workers is a severe obstacle to the kind of change required in the process of economic development. The workers see their interest in zealously defending the security and privileges given them by the labour laws, not realising that these very privileges are often among the greatest obstacles to the increase in productivity and standards of living that they also want. Thus, the rhetoric of Baath socialism leaves the régime little scope to deal with one of the major sources of severe inefficiency in the economic system. Individual workers gain more in the short run from resisting change, and they have little incentive to put forth their best efforts unless the system of productivity bonuses can be made successful. That the government is concerned about the problem is evident from the widespread use of exhortation – a notoriously ineffective method of motivating workers, for any positive effects wear off quickly. But the growing labour shortages are pushing up wages in all sectors where control is absent or difficult to enforce, and especially in the services sector. Here, not only are wages rising very rapidly, but it often becomes necessary to make special side payments to retain a driver or hire a taxi, etc.

As we have noted, migrants from rural areas often go first into the services sector, where entry is easy, special skills are not needed and where relatives and friends who have come from the same areas in the past are likely to be found. Moreover, in many service occupations the reach of the government is likely to be easily evaded. The industrial companies are not supposed, for example, to hire a worker whose occupation is listed as 'farmer' on his identity card but the application of this type of control to, say, drivers may be very difficult to enforce. As labour scarcity spreads and the wages or other forms of remuneration in the service industries rise, the differential between incomes in the rural areas and that in the cities widens further, especially in view of the stagnation of agriculture. Migration is therefore further induced, and labour shortages become greater in rural areas without diminishing the shortages of skilled workers in the cities.

Planned Growth and Structural Change

At the end of the 1970-5 Development Plan, Iraq had completed 25 years of development planning. Although its plans had steadily grown in scope and in technical proficiency, very few of them had been allowed to complete their full course. Uncompleted plan succeeded uncompleted plan as changes in government policy (often because of unexpected increases in oil revenues) or successful *coups d'état* intervened.

From 1951 through 1964 a total of about ID 1,250 million had been allocated for expenditure on development but only about 46 per cent of it was actually spent; over the next decade through 1974/5, ID 2,256 million was allocated and 60 per cent spent, over three-quarters of the expenditure taking place in the five years 1970/5.[13] In part this increase reflects not only the very substantial rise in oil prices and revenues, but also the general rise in the prices of goods and services purchased.

The objectives of all of the plans were very similar; industrialisation and diversification of the economy; reduction of dependence on oil and development of alternative exports; greater processing of the country's raw materials, including oil; the local manufacture of increasing amounts of local consumption needs; the improvement of productivity in agriculture; and a large expansion of education, health services, water supplies, urban amenities, rural electrification and other social needs.

The relative distribution of funds among the major sectors – agriculture, industry and construction – changed without obvious reason from plan to plan, although there was a steadily increasing emphasis on education and health expenditure. There was extensive carry-over of projects from one plan to another since actual expenditure always fell far short of allocations. Investment grew rapidly (and the number of civil servants employed in the Ministry of Planning grew even more rapidly, the numbers rising from 639 to 2,932 in 1976), but the 'overall, integrated, and balanced' approach that planning was designed to ensure never materialised.

As the Baath government consolidated its power after 1968, considerable effort was put into the elaboration and articulation of economic development policy and the 1970-5 Plan was the most ambitious and the most advanced of all the plans. But this time Iraq had accumulated a large number of economists, statisticians, planners and engineers, many of whom had been trained in some of the best institutions of Europe, including Eastern Europe and the United States; in addition, the government imported, often under United Nations auspices and on the United Nations payroll, many foreign experts, prominent among whom were a number of experienced Egyptians. This group expounded with great expertise the theory and practice of 'scientific' and 'comprehensive' planning and outlined a 'stage theory' of industrial development. Iraq's past development efforts were considered to be defective because the problem had not been approached in a 'scientific', 'comprehensive' and 'integrated way'; this was now to be changed.

The new Plan was hailed as an example of 'scientific planning': its feasibility studies, its estimates of demand and supply, its input-output calculations and commodity balances all used modern econometric and computer techniques; the crude capital-output estimates and 'rule-of-thumb' judgements of earlier plans were gone forever. The euphoria induced by the nationalisation of the Iraq Petroleum Company and the end of the austerity programme which preceded it encouraged very expansive development policies. After 1973 the plan was much enlarged, but still in the belief that the country was safely embarked on scientific planning – on a scientific road to development through planning. Iraqi and foreign observers were much impressed; the planners appeared to grasp the important economic issues and to know how to deal with them; the government appeared to be very firmly established in power. Political stability, economic expertise and rising oil revenues appeared to many to be exactly the combination required to transform the Iraqi economy rapidly into that of a modern industrialised economy.

In spite of the planners' expertise, however, nothing effective was done to grapple with the really important problems; how to implement *any* plan, given the real shortages of effective managers, supervisors, office workers, and skilled factory workers; how to overcome the social, organisational and other institutional barriers in the way of rapid increases in productivity; and how to mobilise an enthusiastic commitment of the people. These fundamental weaknesses remained. The gap between the ability to plan and the ability to implement was still wide indeed, and the rising oil revenues, leading to larger plans, may well have widened it. And the Plan itself was built on the same shifting base as the preceding ones – the expected availability of foreign exchange. Thus, in spite of official statements to the contrary, the constraint on the size of the plan was simply the money expected to be available, rather than the rate at which appropriate resources could be mobilised in the economy. But in spite of the rise in the prices of goods and services, including a very sharp rise in contracting services, less than two-thirds of the allocations could in fact be spent, and inflation (or shortages) accelerated in the economy as it became increasingly 'overheated'.

The then Minister of Planning noted that the plan integrated 'investments, consumption, production, employment, exports, imports and other economic activities so as to achieve the defined economic and social targets. For the first time, this plan included a set of coordinated monetary, fiscal and trade policies.'[14] Certainly the plan attempted this, but the planners soon found that the binding constraint was not the availability of oil revenues and finance, but rather the availability of real resources, including adequate supplies of the local resources that were required in combination with the imports of foreign goods to establish and maintain efficient production.

Oil revenues are nothing more nor less than the power to purchase foreign goods and services; they cannot buy 'development' like a commodity. 'Turn-key' factories can be purchased from foreigners, but not the ability and experience to run them efficiently with local management; workers can be imported but not all the skills required, and in any case large-scale importation of labour creates social problems; accommodation and housing can rarely be expanded fast enough. The heavy reliance on foreigners has encouraged a large expansion of what might be called an Iraqi 'quasi-private' sector – the contractor-intermediary. Foreign firms which want to secure contracts for projects in Iraq need to be associated with and have the co-operation of domestic Iraqi contractors, or agents. These provide many services ranging from guidance around the ministries and through the regulations, to the organisation of supplies of domestic materials and labour and the securing of the goodwill of local politicians and administrators necessary to facilitate their work. All such contractors must be registered with the Planning Board and are classified into groups according to the value and type of their resources. Major contractors use subcontractors and the value of contracts can be considerable at every level.

The larger contractors are naturally close to the high officials in government and in the Ministries since they perform the role of intermediaries for firms seeking or executing government and public sector contracts. The 'conspicuous consumption' of some of the contractors which is taken as evidence that their incomes are considerable is a matter of widespread comment among Iraqis. Obviously there is much scope for the corruption of officials and politicians, which is again widely rumoured to have spread far, but which in any case has become serious enough to have led the government to issue draconian decrees in an attempt to deal with it. Penalties for illegal activity are severe (including death and life imprisonment) – which implies that the problem is serious.

One of the major difficulties of planning in Iraq, as in other parts of the less developed world, is the absence of adequate information about the economy. Iraqi efforts to provide sound data on which to base economic analysis and build economic policies have had considerable success. As the government took control over – or at least responsibility for – more and more aspects of economic life, the need for better information grew increasingly urgent, and accordingly the collection of statistical information was accelerated.

But solid statistical series from which reasonably firm conclusions can be drawn can only be established over considerable time. As late as 1968 the United Nations experts could write:

> In the absence of detailed relevant information, it is difficult to measure the degree of improvement or otherwise in the standard of living of the Iraqi population. The most commonly used indicators of per capita consumption/spending, or of individual wealth/properties, of educational and cultural factors, etc., are not being compiled.[15]

Hence all estimates of trends over time in the major economic sectors of the economy are of necessity very rough. And, as noted earlier, much of the basic accounting data from which statistics relating to the productive units in the economy can be compiled are not available because there have been so few qualified book-keepers and accountants. The collection of statistics requires extensive organisation and large numbers of skilled enumerators, estimators and reporters. This kind of service is not provided by Ph.Ds in statistics and to meet this need there has been a large expansion of vocational training in commerce. In 1969 Iraq had 5 schools of commerce, 64 teachers and 1,246 students; five years later these figures has risen to 21,368 and 7,782 respectively. Although a rate of increase of this magnitude cannot have produced very well trained people, especially in accounting and statistics, it is evidence that the problem has been taken seriously.

The absence of adequate statistical data regarding the economy implies, of course, that the planning of an integrated investment programme was necessarily built on a very shaky empirical basis. In consequence, the impressive technical and conceptual advances in planning and the elaborate planning mechanisms and procedures with their numerous logically connected stages were to a great extent irrelevant. That industrial projects in the obvious directions – processing of petroleum, including petrochemicals, and of other raw materials, expansion of investment in consumer goods and in the more suitable capital goods – would be pressed, could have been predicted without regard to 'comprehensive planning'. Similarly the expansion of schools, health facilities and housing were obvious necessities. 'Planning' was expected by Iraqi economic planners to provide integrated approaches which would avoid bottlenecks and excessive calls on resources, and lead to co-ordinated changes in the structure of the economy. These it has not produced. Not because the planning as a technical exercise was either incompetent or incomplete: it was simply unrealistic, and given its technical targets and methods, was unavoidably so in the absence of better information about the economy.

For example, Kamal Hameed, an International Labour Office Consultant, reported in 1974 that very few reliable studies of labour requirements had been made in spite of the large expansions planned, and that there was a severe shortage of training capacity. Migration from agriculture was not, and could not be, controlled, so that there are already severe seasonal labour shortages in agriculture, although agriculture contains half the work force of the economy.[16]

In spite of its 'sophistication', Iraq's planning, and even more the execution of the plans, not only tended to favour the obvious investments, but also the easier ones – easier because, being capital-intensive, they minimised the number of workers which had to be organised and trained quickly. It is always simpler and quicker to make large capital investments where relatively little labour is required and to hire foreign contractors to install turn-key plants than to invest in industries which require the recruitment, training and organisation of a large labour force. Much large capital-intensive investment is of course unavoidable given the fact that the industries which process oil are of this type – especially petrochemicals. But a similar preference is displayed in other industries as well. Large capital-intensive plants require highly skilled labour, where the shortages are greatest. Training programmes are being developed rapidly but to the extent that one of the major objectives of planning was to co-ordinate the rate and type of investment in Iraq with the size, composition and rate of development of the skills of the labour force, it has not been effective.

Iraq can expect a rapid rate of growth of the urban labour force as population expands, as an increasing proportion of the population, notably women, enter the labour force, and as migration continues from the rural areas. After the nationalisation of industry in 1964 the role of the public sector became of central importance from the point of view of national planning and of the implementation of national plans. But in spite of the rapid expansion that took place in the public sector it had absorbed only about one-quarter of the employed labour force by 1974.[17] A survey of manpower in the State Organizations undertaken in 1972 showed that about 42 per cent of all public sector employees were recruited between December 1968 and May 1972; in 1974 all unemployed university graduates were taken into the public service. The failure to provide employment on an adequate scale in the directly productive sectors of agriculture and industry reflected the failure of these sectors to grow at the planned rate. As industrial demand grew, however, the services of those absorbed into government service were needed in industry, but it was often difficult to squeeze them out of government.

Planning was also intended to bring about a co-ordination of monetary, fiscal and trading policies, one of the effects of which should have been to control inflation. Again there is no evidence that Iraqi planning has been effective in this respect. Although the plan made ample provision for the expansion of the transportation, ports and other infrastructure required to handle the high level of imports, shortages were bound to develop. The enormous pressure on resources that resulted from the very large expenditure seriously strained the internal transportation facilities and thus even large imports could not prevent the inflation of prices; the prices of goods were heavily protected by import tariffs, and prices of goods which could not easily be imported, like bricks, rose substantially more than the planners had counted on. For this reason special efforts have been made to increase production of items like bricks.[18]

The official indexes of prices do not reflect the underlying pressures, partly because of their statistical deficiencies and partly because of the extensive subsidisation of food. Iraq could not, of course, escape the general world inflation of prices in the period after the middle 1960s, but its attempts to control food prices led to severe shortages of a number of food-stuffs, especially vegetables, dairy products and meat. The prices of construction materials nearly doubled between 1969 and 1975, and those of some locally produced materials increased even more. In 1974 there was an especially rapid increase of prices and complaints of shortages of fruit, vegetables, meat and other consumer foods seemed to rise in volume. The price of bricks increased nearly three times between 1973 and 1975; exports of cements had ceased under pressure of local demand and wages rose rapidly.

The steep rise in the price of oil defeated Iraq's attempts to reduce its dependence on oil, but was hardly unwelcome to the country. The Iraq government has always claimed that it wanted to become more independent of the crude oil industry by reducing the proportion of the national income, the proportion of export receipts, and the proportion of government revenues attributable to crude oil. What was wanted, of course, was simply a growing and substantial increase in the production of other commodities for domestic consumption and for export, and of other sources of revenue for the government. There has been a rapid increase in industrial output even though it has been low in relation to the increase in investment; total manufacturing output at constant prices rose by 25 per cent between 1971 and 1974 as recorded in the accounts and reached 10 per cent of the gross domestic product in 1972 before the rise in oil revenues reduced it to less than 5 per cent.[19] But since agricultural output lagged badly and food imports increased, while dates and petroleum products were the only remaining exports of note, together accounting for over three-quarters of the total non-oil exports, any significant reduction of dependence on crude oil was not yet in sight.

But efforts in this direction must inevitably struggle against perverse economic forces. Large oil revenues from the export of oil imply a strong currency on the foreign exchange markets. A strong currency is by definition expensive for foreign importers who must buy it in order to buy the country's exports. This discourages exports. The development of export industries capable of competing on world markets is, in consequence, handicapped by the very strength of the country in other directions. But if the chief export commodity is an exhaustible resource which must eventually be replaced by the development of other export industries, then it behoves the country to take especial care to ensure that its domestic cost structure does not become inordinately inflated and that the prospects of achieving international competitiveness by its newer industries are favourable when eventually helped by falling exchange rates. This it shows no signs of doing – but neither does any other major oil-exporting country.

Notes

1. The observations on the state of Iraqi accounting procedures are based on discussions we held in Baghdad in 1968 with officials of the State Organization of Industries and foreign expert consultants. We were given many examples of the inefficiency of government-run plants and were told that there was a great deal of unplanned excess capacity in them. One Iraqi study indicating a 70 to 80 per cent utilisation of capacity very much over-estimated the true situation, which was nearer 30 to 40 per cent, according to some foreign experts. One foreign engineer reported that the Iraqis who were making the estimates had no training in how to estimate the capacity of a plant. Moreover, over-manning was almost endemic; one spinning and weaving factory, which required some 700 workers, employed nearly 1,200; the management in some factories was extremely weak and the factories were virtually run by the workers with appalling productivity, while for other new ones the estimates of local demand far exceeded any possible rate of increase in the foreseeable future.

2. The 1953 to 1963 figures are the estimates of Khair al-Din Haseeb, widely published in Iraqi official series; those for the later period are those of the Central Statistical Office of Iraq.

3. Calculated from the figures given in United Nations, Economic Commission for Western Asia, 'National Account Studies, Bulletin No. 1. Economic Growth of the ECWA Countries throughout the period 1960-1975' (mimeo., May 1977), pp. 72-7.

4. See *Studies on Selected Development Problems in Various Countries in the Middle East, 1969* (United Nations, 1969).

5. Jawad Hashim, 'Development Planning in Iraq; Historical Perspective and New Directions', six lectures (Baghdad, mimeo., April 1975), and the *Abstract of Statistics 1975.*

6. See, for example, the discussion of industrial plans in K. Langley, *The Industrialisation of Iraq* (Cambridge, Mass., 1961) and F. Jalal, *The Role of Government in the Industrialisation of Iraq, 1950-1965* (London, 1971).

7. Quoted in *Middle East Economic Digest,* 25 July 1975, p. 16.

8. United Nations Economic and Social Office in Beirut, 'Review and Appraisal of the Process of Decision-Making and Management in the Public

Industrial Enterprise in Iraq' (Beirut, mimeo., October 1973).

9. Ibid., p. 29.

10. See Robert Mabro and Samir Radwan, *The Industrialisation of Egypt, 1939-1973* (Oxford, 1976), p. 96.

11. See the Report of K.A. Hameed, 'Manpower and Employment Planning', Beirut, United Nations, 1975, mimeo.

12. *Al-Thawrah*, 8, 9, 10 September 1976.

13. Calculated from the *Abstract of Statistics*, 1975, p. 257.

14. Hashim, *Development Planning*, p. 62.

15. United Nations Special Fund Project, *The Economic Status of Iraq*, Report prepared under Assistance in Development Planning and Execution (Baghdad, April 1968), p. 8.

16. Hameed, 'Manpower and Employment Planning'.

17. Ibid.

18. The brick industry in Iraq is a very old one with many small, old and labour-intensive factories. These are being replaced by large capital-intensive factories using the newest technology. It was reported in May 1977 that the old factories were being closed as new ones, ten of which were planned or coming into production in 1977, were built to replace them. See *Middle East Economic Survey*, 6 May 1977.

19. *Annual Abstract of Statistics*, 1975, pp. 162 and 163.

Figure 9.1: Gross Domestic Product at Constant Factor Cost 1953-75 (million dinars)

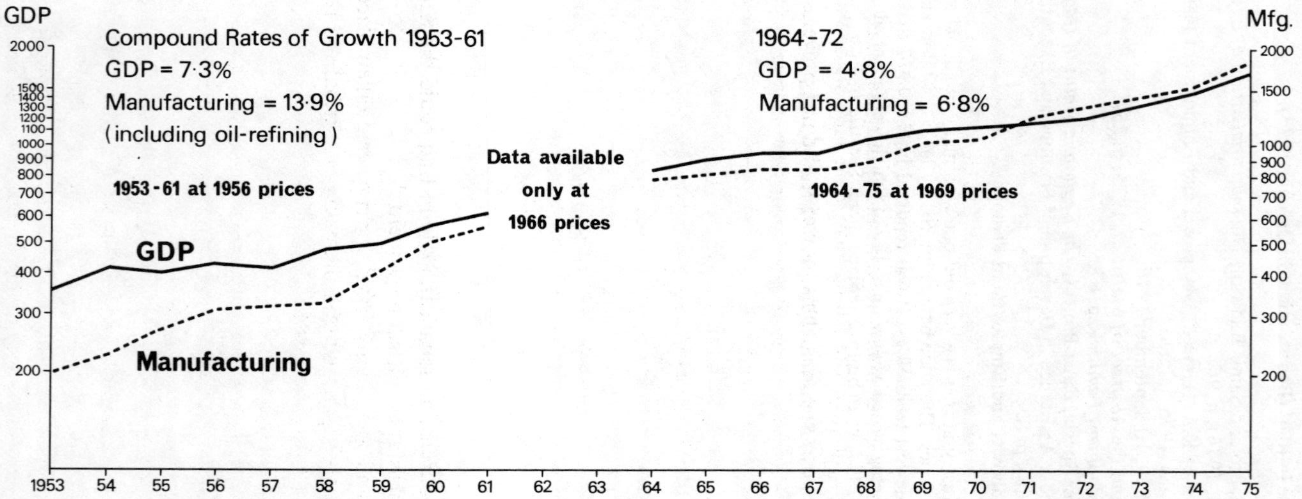

Source: ECWA.

10 THE KURDISH PROBLEM IN IRAQ

Sa'ad N. Jawad

By far the most critical problem that has faced modern Iraq is the Kurdish question and the failure to solve it peacefully. Being of a different ethnic origin, the Aryan Kurds, who spoke a language of an Indo-European origin, always wanted to have a free hand in dealing with their own affairs. They argued that in order to preserve this freedom, as well as their national identity, the Kurdish areas should be granted autonomy, Kurdish should be made the official language and only Kurds should be given government appointments in these areas.

Throughout their history, the Kurds have been subjects of the empires that dominated the area. This, however, did not prevent some Kurdish tribal leaders from taking advantage of the weakness of the central government to establish their own autonomous principalities.[1] These principalities were always short-lived as the central government, depending on Kurdish tribal divisions and feuds, were able to crush them and assert direct rule. In 1920 the Kurds' hope for independence was boosted by the declaration of the Treaty of Sèvres, which promised them autonomy and independence. This hope again was short-lived, as in 1923 the Treaty of Lausanne replaced that of Sèvres. As a result of the new treaty, Kurdistan was divided between Turkey, Iran, Iraq, Syria and the USSR. In Turkey and Iran, where the majority of the Kurds lived,[2] immediate measures were taken by the central government to suppress Kurdish nationalism. Only in Iraq could the Kurds claim to have a consistent political movement.[3]

Between 1919 and 1932 many tribal uprisings had taken place in Iraqi Kurdistan. Sheikh Mahmud of Sulaimaniyya, a tribal and religious leader, was the first to rise against the Iraqi government and the British. He was followed in the latter part of the 1920s by Sheikh Ahmad of Barzan, another tribal and religious leader. However, these revolts fell short of being nationalist ones. Both sheikh Mahmud and Sheikh Ahmad were more interested in gaining the sort of 'autonomy' which tribal leaders of the remote areas had enjoyed during the disintegrating period of the Ottoman Empire. As the main reason behind the revolts of that time was the expanding authority of the central government, the latter was justified in crushing them. But the Iraqi monarchy made the mistake of attempting to assimilate the Kurds, taking advantage of their success in militarily ending the tribal Kurdish opposition. This policy created a breach between the nationalist Kurds and the government, and consequently the government's attempt to foster a new Iraqi identity did not appeal to the Kurds. However, the Kurdish nationalists were too weak to stage any effective opposition. The tribal leaders, who through commanding the loyalty of their followers were able to gather fighting forces, remained the only active element among the Kurds.

Eventually Kurdish nationalists began to feel the need to utilise and manipulate Kurdish tribal loyalty and leaders, and indicated their readiness to subordinate their organisations to tribal leadership. They hoped that they could change tribally motivated uprisings into national revolts. Needless to say, they have not succeeded. The subordination of the intellectuals to the tribal leadership was best demonstrated in 1943, when members of the newly established Hewa Party (the first Kurdish party to be established in Iraq), failing to organise an effective opposition to the government, helped a tribal and religious leader, Mulla Mustafa al-Barzani, to escape from his exile in Sulaimaniyya to lead a rebellion against the central government.[4] Shortly after he declared his revolt, Mulla Mustafa was joined by the two Kurdish parties of that time: Hewa and Rizgary.[5] Although these intellectuals had succeeded in influencing Mulla Mustafa in the sense that they made him submit broad national demands to the government, they had failed to change the tribal structure of the revolt, and were in the end relegated to a secondary position within it. The government, taking advantage of the tribal divisions amongst the Kurds, crushed Mulla Mustafa's revolt. Late in 1945 he was forced, together with his supporters and members of his tribe, to take refuge in the Soviet-sponsored Kurdish Republic of Mahabad in Iranian Kurdistan.[6] In 1947, however, the Iranian army crushed the Republic of Mahabad and drove the Barzanis back into Iraq. Upon their return to Iraqi Kurdistan they were attacked by the Iraqi army. Sheikh Ahmad was arrested, four Kurdish officers were hanged and the Barzanis' land was confiscated and bestowed on tribes that took part in defeating them. (This was to give the Barzanis another reason for future revolts seeking revenge from their enemies.) Mulla Mustafa escaped punishment by walking, with 400 of his fighting followers, the distance between Iraqi Kurdistan and the Soviet Union, a march which made him a national hero and a legend to the Kurds. Up to 1961 Iraqi Kurdistan was more or less a trouble-free region. Nevertheless, the success of the government's military solution was to augur ill for Arab-Kurdish relations. Even since that time, the central government has resorted to force in dealing with demonstrations of Kurdish nationalism, ignoring the reasons behind them. Thus the government failed, in peacetime, to propitiate the Kurds or to expel their increasing fear of assimilation.

However, not only the differences between the government and the Kurds that were increasing, but the differences between the Kurds and the Iraqi Arab nationalists were also on the increase. In the absence of a well organised national movement, the educated Kurds found their way into the bigger Iraqi political parties, like the National Democratic Party and the Iraqi Communist Party. These parties have also failed to establish a solid Arab-Kurdish platform or to help the Kurds achieve their national demands. More significant was the failure of these parties to give the Kurdish national movement and problem the attention it needed. This was apparent in the fact that up to the 1960s no profound study of the ramifications of the Kurdish question was undertaken by any of the parties, and the Kurdish national movement was treated by the various parties as a secondary ally. This attitude remained the same even when the Kurdistan Democratic Party (KDP) was established in 1946 and managed, ten years later, to successfully challenge the position of the other parties among the Kurds. The only positive move made by the different parties was to declare in the first half of the 1950s that Kurds and Arabs were partners in the country. But the Kurds' jubilation over this declaration was soon to appear misplaced when the application of the KDP to join the secretly established Front of National Union in 1957 was rejected by the parties involved. (The Front included the Iraqi Communist Party, the National Democratic Party, the Arab Baath Socialist Party and the Istiqlal Party. In its programme the Front had also stated that Kurds and Arabs were partners in the country.)

On 14 July 1958 the Iraqi monarchy was overthrown by a group of army officers, known as the Free Officers, and a republican régime was established. Brigadier Abd al-Karim Qasim became the first republican premier, and Colonel Abd al-Salam Arif became his deputy. The Kurds hailed the revolution, believing that the new régime would be more sympathetic to their cause, and indeed the new régime responded positively. Although the first communiqué which declared the republic did not mention the Kurds as such,[7] the second declared the establishment of the 'Sovereignty Council' to undertake the responsibilities of President. It was composed of three members, one of them a Kurd. Another Kurd, Baba Ali, the son of Sheikh Mahmud of Sulaiymaniyya, was included in the first Cabinet, and all Kurdish political prisoners, and those who were under arrest, were released. More important was the declaration of the new constitution, in which the Kurds were mentioned in a separate article as partners with the Arabs in the Iraqi homeland.

Meanwhile, the Front of National Union was reorganised to include the KDP. However, neither this move nor the favourable measures taken by Qasim were to indicate a change in the official attitude, or that of the political parties, towards the Kurdish national movement. The different parties were simply emotionally and tactically motivated. The fact that the new Front was soon to be dissolved and the Kurdish demand for autonomy rejected by Qasim tend to confirm this view. As for the measures taken by Qasim, they were only to indicate his call for equality within the Iraqi state. He thought of no special position for the Kurds and was convinced that the Kurdish objectives were partly achieved by the removal of the monarchy. He failed to see the national substance in the Kurdish demand for autonomy, and continually reminded the Kurds of his policy of equality.[8] In this respect Qasim was representing a view shared by a great number of people in Iraq. People of this view, when discussing the Kurdish problem and demands, always compare the situation of the Iraqi Kurds with that of the other Kurds living in Turkey and Iran, and by concluding that those living in Iraq were far better off, they argued that Kurdish nationalism in Iraq was not justified in continuing its demonstrations in favour of national rights. These people failed to differentiate between the rights of citizenship and the national rights of a minority. True, as Iraqis the Kurds were not discriminated against, but as a nationality they were denied the simplest and most precious right, that of learning in their own language.

However, the KDP supported Qasim, and the latter's need for allies to strengthen his position pushed him more towards the Kurds. He allowed the return from the Soviet Union of Mulla Mustafa, together with his Barzani followers, armed and subsidised them, and allowed the KDP, whose politbureau had immediately surrendered the presidency of the party to Mulla Mustafa, to act more or less freely. Kurdish newspapers were legalised and the Kurds were allowed to celebrate their national feasts.[9] Meanwhile, Qasim made use of the Kurdish nationalists and the Barzanis to curb the influence of the other parties. It was now the turn of the Kurdish national movement to make the mistake of separating itself from the general Iraqi national movement by indefinitely and unreservedly supporting Qasim's oppressive measures against the other parties.

However, two years later Qasim was to realise the extent of Kurdish political aspirations and showed a marked reluctance to have them accommodated. Having dealt with the position and influence enjoyed by both the pan-Arabs and the Communists, Qasim turned against the Kurds. Qasim's rupture with the Kurds could be dated to 1960, when the KDP was legalised. Although he granted the KDP a licence, a Qasim amended the programme of the party, omitting any reference to autonomy and to the need for a special status for the Kurds. He also suggested that the name of the party should be changed from the United Kurdistan Democratic Party to the Kurdistan Democratic Party.[10] Qasim's amendments were final. Mulla Mustafa, who showed no interest in the fate of the KDP, did not object, and the politbureau accepted the changes arguing that the need for acting freely and legally was more important than the wording of the programme. As a consequence to this confrontation, Qasim was to become familiar with the willingness of the Kurdish leadership to compromise on ideological questions, as well as the sharp division between them and Mulla Mustafa. He was encouraged to go ahead with his attempts to curtail Kurdish influence.

From that date Qasim began to withdraw the privileges which his régime had bestowed on the Kurds. What made Qasim determined to completely curtail and ultimately destroy the Kurdish political movement was the manner which both Mulla Mustafa and the KDP had misused their influence and started to liquidate their enemies and rivals. Qasim thought that he could depend on tribal rivalries to balance the influence of Mulla Mustafa and the KDP. He failed to realise that both Mulla Mustafa and the KDP had in their possession sufficient arms, which ironically enough Qasim himself had bestowed on them, to stage an effective resistance protected by the Kurdish mountains. Moreover, Qasim's move against the KDP and Mulla Mustafa had coincided with the implementation of the Agrarian Reform in Kurdistan and the introduction of a new land tax and restrictions on the cultivation of tobacco, the main crop in Kurdistan.[11] Thus Qasim was also deprived from the support of tribal landlords, who often sided with the old régime against the Kurdish nationalists. The other warning which Qasim had failed to heed was the continuing departure of Kurdish leaders, such as Mulla Mustafa and the KDP leaders, to the Kurdish mountains. Mulla Mustafa was the first to do so in April 1961. In fact Qasim had not only failed to assess the situation but he went on in his policy of offending the Kurdish nationalists. He cancelled Kurdish conferences, changed Kurdish names of public places, closed down the Kurdish newspapers and some branches of the KDP, and put leading Kurdish nationalists in prison.[12] What offended the KDP and Mulla Mustafa most was Qasim's insinuation that the Kurds were not a nation, and that all previous Kurdish revolts in Iraq were instigated by imperialism. The KDP's protests against this policy, and the appeals of the Kurdish landlords to Qasim to reconsider his agrarian policy in Kurdistan went unheeded. Failing to attract Qasim's attention some Kurdish landlords rebelled in June 1961, refusing to pay the new tax or to allow the implementation of the Agrarian Reform. Other anti-republic Kurdish tribal leaders were quick to leap at this opportunity and raised their followers against the régime. Qasim's failure to respond firmly and with understanding encouraged the tribal forces to attack army convoys and police posts. In this Qasim saw the proper time to strike. He immediately blamed the troubles in Kurdistan on Mulla Mustafa and the KDP, who until that time had taken no part in the tribal activities. In fact the KDP had even condemned the tribal revolt and called for it to be crushed. In September Qasim committed the fatal mistake of ordering the bombardment of Barzan, Mulla Mustafa's home village, and the closure of the KDP. Mulla Mustafa was left with no other alternative but to join and foster the Kurdish tribal revolt.

As the tribal revolt gathered strength the KDP began to feel isolated and its claim to be the vanguard of the Kurdish national movement was seriously challenged. By that time the relations between Mulla Mustafa and the politbureau of the KDP, headed by Ibrahim Ahmad, the Secretary-General, and Jalal Talbani, member of the bureau, were deteriorating. The KDP leaders, who were dissatisfied with Mulla Mustafa's lack of interest in the party's affairs, were working to restrict his influence on the party's organisation. Mulla Mustafa, who always valued people according to the number of fighting men they could muster in time of crisis was not expected to take the KDP's challenge very seriously. His confidence in dominating the party had risen when an increasing number of party members began to join the tribal revolt after he himself had decided to assume its leadership. Ahmad's instructions to the members to desist were ignored. In order to contain the crisis, the politbureau decided to join the revolt so that the members could fight under their party's banner. They failed to realise that by taking this decision they were risking the 'independence' of their organisation and putting its destiny under the mercy of Mulla Mustafa and his tribal alliances.

However, the participation of the KDP added a national substance and an element of organisation to the revolt, the two factors that previous revolts had lacked. The KDP's effect was clear in two directions: first in the formation of a regular and trained forces, the Peshmarga,[13] and the submission of defined national demands and objectives. Mulla Mustafa and his tribal allies were quick to follow the examples of the KDP.

In order to justify its participation in a tribally motivated revolt, and to make substantial its claim for its leadership, the KDP had to reintroduce the revolt in a new national shape. This, the KDP thought, could be done through the adoption of national and wide-ranging demands. Thus, as soon as it joined in, the KDP began to speak about the revolt as a national one which was aiming not only at achieving autonomy for Kurdistan but also to establish democracy in Iraq. Although these objectives were accepted and acclaimed by all nationalist Kurds, the different factions inside the Kurdish national movement had different, and at times vague, ideas about autonomy and its extent. They often took advantage of the weakness of the central government to expand this objective and made it look like virtual independence. Yet the second objective, democracy for Iraq, had failed to gather support for the Kurdish national movement from the rest of the Iraqi people. Apart from the fact that they themselves had set a poor example for democracy in the area under their control, both Mulla Mustafa and the KDP did nothing constructive to indicate their belief in this objective.Yet the readiness of the Kurdish leadership to co-operate with elements hostile to Iraq and Arab nationalism not only alienated Iraqi public opinion from the Kurdish revolt, but also gave support to the military point of view, and in the end military rule was perpetuated. Moreover, the Kurds made the mistake of insisting on achieving all their demands, thus making it increasingly impossible for fruitful negotiations to take place. Between 1961 and 1968 the Kurdish revolt continued to simmer, despite the four truces, which varied in length, and the four changes in the régime. Apart from their general reluctance to grant the Kurds self-rule, successive military governments made use of the Kurds' ambiguous concept for autonomy and accused them of seeking separation. The Kurdish demands to maintain the Peshmarga forces, the demarcation of the Kurdish areas and the inclusion of the oil-rich province of Kirkuk in the autonomous region were the issues the military relied on to justify their point of view. On the other hand, the Kurdish leadership justified their excessive demands as guarantees against the increasing military desire to crush their movement. The failure to find a peaceful settlement to the question, of which the two sides shared responsibility, complicated the issue and increased the lack of trust between the two sides.

As the Kurdish revolt progressed, Mulla Mustafa's leadership over it and over the whole of the Kurdish national movement became undisputed. The only challenge to his position came from the politbureau of the KDP headed by Ahmad and Talbani.[14] In 1964, however, taking advantage of the second truce with the government, Mulla Mustafa expelled the Ahmad-Talbani faction from the party and from Iraqi Kurdistan. He replaced them by people loyal to him. Despite the subsequent co-operation of the Ahmad-Talbani faction with the central government against Mulla Mustafa, the latter's domination over the movement remained unaffected.[15]

In opposition to the military idea of solving the Kurdish problem by force, civilian leaders were calling for a peaceful settlement to the problem. The civilians believed that the continuity of the war would strengthen military domination and deepen the split between the Arabs and the Kurds. They argued that the problem could be peacefully settled by giving the Kurds a degree of self-rule to enable them to deal with their own local affairs. These views were represented by premier Abd al-Rahman al-Bazzaz, who in 1966 overruled the military domination and concluded an agreement with Mulla Mustafa's leadership.[16] His idea was to recognise fully Kurdish national rights and to give the Kurds certain decentralised powers. His emphasis was on cultural demands. But before he could put any clause of his 29 June Programme into practice, al-Bazzaz was forced by the officers to tender his resignation. He was followed by another army officer. Al-Bazzaz's experience had failed because he had neither an organised popular base nor the power needed to enforce his solution.[17] Moreover, al-Bazzaz's conservative views had antagonised and in the end deprived him from the support of the other radical political groups in the country. Nevertheless, al-Bazzaz's successors declared their adherence to his programme as it was the only way to maintain the shaky peace in Kurdistan, and to take advantage of inter-tribal struggle inside the Kurdish national movement between the faction of Mulla Mustafa and that of the Ahmad-Talbani. Nothing constructive, however, was done to carry the programme out.

In July 1968 the Arab Baath Socialist Party made a successful comeback to power. Armed with the support of its cadres, and realising that with a smouldering Kurdish problem the régime would remain weak, the Baath Party declared its intention to find a fundamental solution to the Kurdish problem. This intention, however, met with the same old obstacles. First there was the increasing confidence of the Kurdish leadership under Mulla Mustafa. He was determined not to come to terms with the central government before obtaining all his demands. Second, there was the problem of convincing the party members and the Iraqi and Arab public opinion that autonomy was not equivalent to separation. Finally, there was the continuing opposition by the military to a peaceful settlement. It seems that the Baathist leadership, taking advantage of the five years of reorganisation following their party's removal from power in 1963, had fully considered the Kurdish problem before coming back to power. This was clear in their quick and conciliatory approach to the issue immediately after they have dominated the régime in 1968. Their policy was to combine diplomacy with the use of force in tackling the Kurdish problem, the emphasis being upon conciliation when the Kurds showed a readiness to talk. To give a sign of their good intentions, the Baath government began to implement the still outstanding programme of al-Bazzaz; beginning, significantly enough, with the secret clauses. The other positive step was to open the issue for public and frank discussion by publishing in the official newspaper a series of articles about the Kurdish question, its ramifications and the ways to settle it.[18] A helpful factor in changing the official attitude towards the Kurdish question was the gradual replacement of the military by civilian influence, and the continuing foreign attempts to take advantage of the Kurdish issue to weaken Iraq. As for the Kurdish leaders, they began to feel that the continuing application of armed resistance would only weaken the central government, but it would not force it to come to terms with the Kurds. Thus they responded positively to the government's appeals. Negotiations began in January 1970, and on 11 March an agreement was concluded.

Unexpectedly, the March Manifesto, as the agreement became to be known, touched upon fundamental demands which no other government had dared to talk about. The Manifesto included no secret clauses; it promised the Kurds full recognition of their nationality, autonomy within four years of its declaration, a Kurdish vice-president for the republic, and five Kurdish Ministers, compared with two in previous Cabinets, were included in the Cabinet. The Kurdish language was made an official language and was to be taught, together with Arabic, all over Iraq. Kurdish was also made a primary language in Kurdistan. Moreover, the Kurds were granted the right to form their own political and professional organisations, and a number of the Kurdish Peshmarga were kept as border guards, and were included in the Iraqi armed forces.

The government have also ordered the reinstatement in their previous posts of all those dismissed because of the Kurdish revolt. More important was the government's declaration that the Kurds were part of the divided Kurdish people and Kurdistan, and that the Kurdish national movement was part of the general Iraqi national movement.[19] As for the problem of Kirkuk, the two sides agreed that it should not be included in the autonomous region until a plebiscite would determine its nature. As it met with their major demands, the Kurds acclaimed the Manifesto as a historical and national achievement. On the other hand, the fact that it resulted in an immediate peace in Kurdistan made the government hail the Manifesto as its major achievement. Hence the fact that the Manifesto was so far-reaching and progressive aroused some fears, later justified, that it would be above the level of the political maturity of the Iraqi bureaucracy and the Kurdish cadres who were to carry it out. (This is what made the need for a programme to explain the Manifesto and to convince both sides concerned with its fulfilment so imperative.)

However, between March 1974 and March 1975 the Kurdish Peshmarga took to arms again, despite the fact that the government had declared, in March 1974, the Kurdish areas as an autonomous region. Differences over the interpretation of the Manifesto and the Kurdish claims that the plan for autonomy did get their approval were the main reasons behind the eruption of fighting. Other reasons were the Kurdish continuing claim for the oil-rich province of Kirkuk to be included in the autonomous region, over the extent of powers to be given to the autonomous region, and over the Kurds' participation in the central government. Interesting to note that despite this rupture both sides kept on claiming their adherence to the March Manifesto. Thus one could conclude that the need was not for another agreement but for more flexibility, realism, deliberation and tactfulness.

As the Kurdish revolt of 1961 had managed to outlive four Iraqi regimes, in which it was a major factor contributing to their overthrow, the Kurdish national movement began to acquire an international status. The international press gave the revolt a great deal of coverage and foreign countries showed readiness to maintain it. Mainly it was Iraq's rivals and opponents who welcomed the opportunity to exploit this perennial problem in order to weaken Iraq. Thus Iraq's foreign policy and her international and regional disputes were the main factor in determining the extent and nature of assistance reaching the Peshmarga. The foreign involvement in the Kurdish national movement increased as the Kurdish leadership under Mulla Mustafa saw in it the only effective method to force Iraq to give more concessions. He failed to realise that by doing so he was surrendering the fate and destiny of the whole national movement to elements which have no interest in Kurdish nationalism, if they were not deadly against it, such as Iran. However, in the present international setting, the Kurds may come to realise that they stand a greater chance of achieving their national objectives by co-operating with the progressive elements in the country, and by trying to build on any achievement they could get through this co-operation.

Notes

1. For a history of these principalities see M.A. Zaki Beg, *Mulakhas Tarikh al-Kurd wa Kurdistan, (A Short History of the Kurds and Kurdistan)* (Cairo, 1939).

2. In an estimation made in 1967 C.J. Edmonds put the total number of Kurds at about 7,000,000, divided as follows: Turkey 3,200,000; Iran 1,800,000; Iraq 1,550,000; Syria 320,000; and the Soviet Union 80,000. See C.J. Edmonds, 'Kurdish Nationalism', *Journal of Contemporary History*, Vol. 6, No. 1 (1971).

3. Ibid.

4. After taking a leading part in the revolt of his eldest brother Sheikh Ahmad of 1927-30, Mulla Mustafa was exiled, together with members of his tribe, to th south of Iraq, only to be transferred to Sulaimaniyya a few months later. See Hamza Abdulla, 'Thawrat Barazan', *al-Muthaqaf*, Baghdad, No. 11-12 (August-September 1959).

5. Hewa, which was founded in 1939, did not appeal to the majority of educated Kurds. Some Kurdish intellectuals refused to join, regarding Hewa as a right-wing organisation. In 1944 these leftist Kurds were encouraged by the Iraqi Communist Party to form the Rizgary Party, a coalition of Communist and leftist Kurds. See Jalal Talbani, *Kurdistan wa al-Haraka al-Qawmiyya al-Kudiyya (Kurdistan and the Kurdish Nationalist Movement)* (Beirut, 1971), pp. 120-1, 136-41.

6. For details about the Mahabad Republic see Archie Roosevelt, Jr., 'The Kurdish Republic of Mahabad', *The Middle East Journal*, Vol. 1, No. 3 (July 1947) and W. Eaglton, Jr., *The Kurdish Republic of 1946* (Oxford University Press, 1963).

7. It only spoke about creating equality in a new Iraq.

8. See Ureil Dann, *Iraq Under Qassem*, for Qasim's views and beliefs.

9. See I.O. Vanly, *Le Kurdistan Irakien Entite Nationale*, pp. 81-5, for Qasim's pro-Kurdish measures.

10. It seems that Qasim's rejection of the word united stemmed from his fear that this word might have implications for Turkey and Iran.

11. The Agrarian Reform Law, which was declared in September 1958, decreed the expropriation of privately owned land holdings in excess of 625 acres in the south and 1,350 acres in the north.

12. See D. Kinnane, *The Kurds and Kurdistan* (London Oxford University Press, 1964), Vanly and Dann for the breach between Qasim and the Kurdish nationalists.

13. Peshmarga in Kurdish means those who face death.

14. Ahmad became a Secretary-General in 1953. Talbani became a member of the Politburo in 1957. See Talbani for the history of the KDP.

15. In fact the Ahmad-Talbani faction was more effective in the ideological struggle between the two factions. Being more educated, their faction's members were dedicated to the party's ideology. The faction was also more consistent in its general policy.

16. He took advantage of the army's failure to complete its operation to occupy the administrative headquarters of the KDP in north-eastern Kurdistan.

17. This weakness was apparent in the fact that al-Bazzaz, although agreeing to most of the Kurdish demands, declined to make his acceptance of them public, and included some secret clauses in the agreement because of fear of public protest.

18. See *Kaifa al-Sabil li Hal al-Masala al-Kurdiyya*, al-Thawra Publications, Baghdad, No. 3.

19. See the March Manifesto and *Kaifa al-Sabil.*

11 AZIZ AL-HAJ: A COMMUNIST RADICAL

A.R. Kelidar

It is recognised that the Iraqi Communist Party (ICP) has been one of the best-organised and widely supported political movements in the Arab world. It has survived many crises and overcome several attempts to destroy it by the authorities but nothing has shaken its confidence and alienated its supporters like the split which occurred in 1967. The events which led to the split can be traced back to 1959 when, following the massacres at Mosul and then in Kirkuk in which Communist partisans played a prominent role, the leadership of the ICP indulged in the familiar exercise of self-criticism and censured what they called 'the leftist and adventurist tendencies of their comrades'. The main cause for what happened was simply blamed on political inexperience, and calls were issued to party members to exercise restraint and proper control. The burgeoning membership of the party was purged and the speed with which new members were recruited slowed down.

One man who has thrown some light on the inner controversy, which lasted for about ten years, is Aziz al-Haj, or to give his full name, Aziz al-Haj Ali Haidar. He figured prominently on three occasions, all of which have been regarded as marking important turning-points in the brief and chequered history of the ICP. In 1948 he was arrested with practically the whole membership of the ICP and was sentenced to a twenty-year term of imprisonment, only to be released in 1958, following the overthrow of the monarchy by a military coup led by Brigadier Abd al-Karim Qasim. In 1969 al-Haj appeared on Baghdad TV and renounced his Communist past and condemned the movement to whose success he had contributed so much. Until then he had been one of the main purveyors of Marxist ideas in Iraq, and a chief populariser of Communist motions in politics as well as economics. He did this in an elegant style with forceful eloquence, especially in putting over the concept of the united national front under the leadership of the Communists.

Aziz al-Haj is a highly educated Marxist – one of the few intellectuals which the Communist movement in Iraq has produced who has shown that he is capable of independent thought and judgement. He is by no means an armchair revolutionary, but a revolutionary who, faced with the appalling and continuing prospect of severe torture and in a depressed state of mind after 25 years of struggle, decided to give up. This paper is primarily concerned with the affair that caused the schism in the Communist ranks in Iraq between the Central Committee group led by Amir Abdulla and Zaki Khairi and the Central Command led by Aziz al-Haj and Muzafar al-Mawab. It is based on a collection of articles written by Aziz al-Haj defending the revolutions of 1958 in Iraq against the press campaign mounted against it in Egypt by the late President Nasser entitled 'Our Revolution', two essays published in Prague, one under the title 'Non-Capitalist Transformation in Iraq' and the other 'Neo-Colonialism: How do we Fight it?' In addition extensive reference has been made to the Memorandum which al-Haj's group submitted for discussion to the rank and file of the ICP, evaluating the role of the ICP in Iraqi politics in order to oppose the new policies advocating co-operating between the ICP and the nationalist groups in Iraq (parts of which have been translated and published in *Towards Revolution* edited by John Gerassi, vol. 1 pp. 238-51.

Being of recent creation and inhabited by a conglomeration of minorities, the state of Iraq failed to develop a political community with a uniform focus of political loyalty. There is little doubt that the founders of the ICP were determined to take advantage of the fragmented nature of Iraqi society. They sought support and recruits amongst the disaffected minorities which showed little sympathy for the irredentist campaigns of the pan-Arab nationalists who have dominated Iraqi politics ever since the establishment of the modern state. The intelligentsia among these minorities rallied to the ideologically orientated parties which did not distinguish between them on the grounds of religion, sect or ethnicity. It is not surprising, therefore, to find that something like 30 per cent of those arrested in 1948 and accused of belonging to a subversive organisation were Jews. It has been this fact, for instance, that led, amongst many others, Dr Fadil al-Jamali, a former Prime Minister and an important politician and publicist under the monarchy, to establish a link between Communism and Zionism. However, if the account given by Malik Saif in his latest book – *My Experience in the Communist Party of Iraq* – is correct, then there is no doubt that it was Fahad's policy (Fahad being the pseudonym of Yusuf Salman Yusuf, the Secretary-General of the ICP, hanged in 1949) to marshal support and seek adherents for the party among the social communities that did not feel an integral part of the political establishment of the new state, like the Kurds, the Shii, the Jews or the Christians (of whom Fahad was one). Indeed there is evidence that Fahad was so aware of this problem that he deliberately sought the promotion of young Shii and Kurds in the party ranks. Saif goes so far as to suggest that Fahad was in fact grooming Husain Muhammad al-Shabibi, who was also hanged in 1949, for the leadership. I suppose it could be said that Fahad had his wish fulfilled in about 1956, when Salam Adil emerged as the Secretary-General of the ICP. The other distinguishing mark was the proletarian nature of the leadership.

What is important in al-Haj's case is that he was not only a Kurd but a Shii Kurd as well. He was born into a poor Fuaili Kurdish family from Badra in the Kut district and educated at state schools. When he finished his secondary education he went to a teachers training college in Baghdad, and joined the party in 1945 while a student at the college. After completing the course he was appointed a teacher at the secondary school in Kut; while there he also became the organiser of the Communist Party in the district, recruiting his own students and writing in their wall news-sheet. He also took part in such annual celebrations as the Prophet's birthday, or the commemoration of Ashura, an annual event marking the martyrdom of Imam Husain, and other public meetings where expression of his political attitude to the prevailing conditions in the country was made. The authorities in Kut became concerned and al-Haj was transferred to Baghdad and then to Sulaimaniyya. But rather than go to Sulaimaniyya, he preferred to resign. The reason he gave for his resignation was that he wanted to remain close to his family in Baghdad, but the family in fact saw very little of him. The real reason was that he was devoting all his time to becoming the main publicist of the ICP; another factor was that he had contracted tuberculosis and did not want his family to know about it.

It was in his capacity as a publicist that he acquired national fame. He became the editor of the Communist organ, *al-Qa'ida*. After his arrest and trial in 1949, when he was sentenced to twenty years in gaol he became a legendary figure with schoolboys whose political attitudes were being highly radicalised as a result of the Arab failure in Palestine, and the negotiations with Britain about the Anglo-Iraqi treaty of alliance. Following his arrest he was candid, even arrogant, in his admission of being a member of the ICP and proud of writing its pamphlets and leaflets. He joined the Communist Party, he told the investigating magistrate, of his own free will, because it was the only movement that cared about 'the pains and aspirations of working people and the liberated intelligentsia'. He concluded his statement to the magistrate with a reproach to the security officials that torture and strong-arm methods employed by them would not deter Iraqis from flocking to the cause. He closed with the customary greeting 'long live our party and its great leader' ('al-Mausu'a al-Sirriyya' an extensive report compiled by the investigating magistrates on the activities and membership of the Iraqi Communist Party).

Aziz al-Haj was to spend the next ten years of his life incarcerated in the maximum security prison of Nuqrat al-Salman in the western desert. He emerged following the *coup* of 1958 which overthrew the monarchy. In the trials of the political leaders of the monarchy that followed in Mahdawi's Peoples' Court al-Haj was often seen as a witness for the prosecution. He also resumed his vocation as one of the leading publicists of the ICP, but was not an enthusiastic supporter of the co-operation which ensued between Qasim, the leader of the *coup*, and the Communist Party. This became clear in 1964-5 when al-Haj's conviction of the validity of the traditional role of the CP as the vanguard of the proletariat and the instigator of revolutionary action was to cause a split in the ranks of the ICP in which he led a radical faction advocating armed struggle to bring about the revolution. His career as an armed revolutionary was rather short-lived. He was arrested in 1969 in a suburb of Baghdad charged with organising a communist insurrection in the Marsh region of southern Iraq.

In his public pronouncements and 'confessions' he abandoned his earlier insistence on the distinction between the movement for national liberation 'democratic revolution' organised by nationalists as a preliminary stage leading to the introduction of socialism under a Communist régime, and the socialist revolution led by Communist parties. His earlier slogan that there could not be socialism without Communists was to give way to an express willingness to acknowledge the Baathist régime in power in Baghdad since 1968 as a revolutionary vanguard capable of introducing socialism. In short, Aziz al-Haj condemned the Communist concept of international proletarianism for which he fought so hard and led Communists to fight Communists in Iraq. His warnings against the danger of over-emphasising the independence of the Communist parties on the basis of nation states, lest they become nationalist, was thrown to the wind. At fifty, and after 25 years of imprisonment, torture and exile, it became obvious that al-Haj was no longer the arrogant young Communist of 1948-9. He had mellowed and was prepared to recant. Indeed, it is reported that he told the authorities following his arrest, 'I can no longer bear torture, I will co-operate.' In his public statement he likened himself to 'a bull charging a concrete wall to break it, but could not make an impression on it'. He did not add, it seems, that 'the bull was broken', as he supplied the authorities the names and addresses of his supporters, many of whom were killed following clashes with security forces or were tried and executed. His collaboration with the Baathist régime continued and he was to assist in the establishment of a school to train a professional political cadre. Later he was appointed Iraq's representative at UNESCO in Paris, where he has remained, making the occasional contribution to the official press of Baghdad in support of the régime.

None the less, the radicalist notions of Communism expressed by al-Haj have continued to reverberate in the halls of Communist politics in Iraq. Al-Haj has not been alone: his was not a peculiar phenomenon. The question that has bedevilled Communists in the Third World is what should their role be when the objective conditions for a proletarian revolution have not been attained, and when economic development has only given rise to a class of bourgeoisie which has come to lead nationalist revolution against Western domination and influence. This question has led Soviet theorists to introduce some important alterations to Marxist dogma in order to accommodate certain processes in the modification of the social structure. This was manifested in the 20th Congress of the Soviet Party and the pronouncement by Krushchev on the role of the national liberation movement in the Third World and endorsed by the World Communist Parties Conference of 1960. Until then Communist parties in the Third World, and the Iraq one was no exception, had insisted on being the dominant partners in the promotion of the United National Front. This alliance was to be concluded bilaterally with the other groups, whereby Communists would infiltrate these groups, gradually disarm the suspicions of the bourgeoisie, thus dominating them. In Iraq this method had not been successful. Front organisations like the Peace Partisans and Democratic Youth Movement have often been suppressed or controlled by the state. Moreover, practically all parties in Iraq have been rather wary of Communist objectives and have refused to merge their organisations with that of the Communists. There are numerous examples which indicate the reluctance of these parties to co-operate with the Communists, perhaps the most famous one being the decision by the National Democratic Party to suspend its activities in 1959 rather than join the Front.

The implications of the Soviet pronouncement on the role of the national liberation movement was that CPs should no longer regard themselves as an independent and separate vanguard but as a segment of the movement conducting the war of liberation as a preliminary stage to the introduction of the socialist revolution. It should subordinate its role to that of other parties. However, the position of Aziz al-Haj in the politics of the ICP would indicate that Communists found it difficult to decide when a bourgeois government had completed its task, and whether the imperialist influence had been eradicated and economic emancipations achieved. Thus, when Communist parties in the Middle East were being pressed to adjust their position accordingly, as was indicated by the Egyptian party which decided to disband itself and called on its membership to join the Arab Socialist Union, Aziz al-Haj led a faction in the ICP that sought to maintain the radical traditions on which he was brought up as a Communist. In the acrimonious debate that followed, al-Haj defended the purity of his Marxist upbringing and condemned the leadership of the ICP as being 'revisionist' and 'rightist', particularly when calls began to emanate for co-operation with the Arif régime following the nationalisation decrees of 1964 and the agreement with Egypt to have a unified political command and the introduction of the ASU to Iraq.

This debate came in the wake of the serious blow which the ICP suffered in 1963, following the overthrow of the Qasim régime. The party was practically decimated, its leaders either dead or imprisoned and its organisation badly shaken and hardly functioning. It is not surprising therefore that the debate should have taken place in Eastern Europe, and Prague in particular, where most of the remnant of the Iraqi Communist leadership found its way. At the beginning the argument followed the attempt to appraise the role of the ICP since 1958, and to identify the faults which had occurred. It was very much the self-criticism ritual which Communists and other radicals indulge in from time to time – mainly to justify their failure. In this process al-Haj and his followers were alienated by the prognosis which the leadership of the ICP proper, namely Zaki Khairi and Amir Abdullah, was to arrive at. This conclusion was that the ICP udner the leadership of Salam Adil was too leftist and adventurous and did not take into consideration the fundamental changes that occurred in the politics of Iraq as a result of what they called 'the spirit of the age', 'ruh al-'asr wa ta'thiratuhu al-hasima'. This seems to be a reference to the balance of power between East and West and how favourable the balance has been to the forces of Communism as a result of the appeal and popularity of socialist thought, and that the mere presence of a socialist camp in the world had contributed to the struggle of the countries of the Third World for national liberation. Nasser's conversion to socialism was cited as another contributing factor. Al-Haj does not dispute the increasing weight of the Communist camp. Where he parts company with the ICP is to use this factor coupled with the disintegration of the colonialist system in order to conclude in favour of the priority of the peaceful struggle. He rejected and reprimanded the ICP, and by implication the Soviet Union, since the CPSU approved this policy at its 22nd Congress in 1963, namely, to allocate to the party and the democratic movement at large a secondary role – secondary to that of the bourgeois and nationalist leadership such as that of Nasser or Ben Bella. He insisted that to do so would be an abdication of the leading role of the working class in the revolution, political democracy and the dictatorship of the proletariat. To accept that the principle of armed struggle could be substituted by any other means was irreconcilable with Communist teaching, since it was placing too much emphasis on the importance of external factors which bore no relation to the internal conditions and contradictions that existed in Iraq. The analysis should be based on the strength of the enemy, and that of the democratic movement; the level of revolutionary consciousness among the masses, the Kurdish revolution, Iraq's strategic location, oil companies and other historical conditions; and not on the fact that a bourgeois régime like Nasser's and its own political organisation, the ASU, was to be introduced to Iraq in order to buttress the tottering rule of Arif.

Al-Haj made it clear that Communists should not rely on such régimes, nor should they play a secondary role in their non-capitalist politics. He insisted that the bourgeoisie would hold and exercise power to serve its own narrow interest, not that of the working class. Helped by Communists, it will only consolidate its hold on power and proceed to destroy any political organisation that may challenge its authority. Moreover, in a brief review of the history of the relationship between the Qasim régime and the Communists, he provided sufficient indication as to what the result of co-operating with the national bourgeoisie would be.

He insisted that despite the major role played by the ICP in bringing about the revolution of 1958, the part was circumscribed by the fear of a counter-revolution against Qasim to such an extent that co-operation with Qasim had rendered its revolutionary role completely impotent. The concern of the ICP was no more than to protect the Qasim régime even when that régime had showed itself to be hostile to the aspirations of the masses and the ideology of the Communists. He had no qualms in declaring the ICP to have been wrong in its characterisation of Qasim as a petty bourgeois, since when in power he showed all the signs of the conscious representative of the national bourgeoisie. While he was as fearful of the increasing influence of the ICP and the upsurge of working class and peasant militancy, the ICP was pursuing a policy of seeking an alliance with him, dubbing him the sole leader, a revolutionary democrat, who was bound to join the camp of the working class.

Aziz al-Haj was concerned with the central question of political power in any revolution. Economic and social measures taken to transform society could not be implemented or consolidated if the apparatus of the state remained in the hands of groups that were hostile to the working class. Thus he evidently wanted the ICP to adopt a revolutionary plan to radicalise the Qasim régime and overthrow it if it stood in the way. The party should have adopted the tried method of class struggle in the realisation of revolutionary democratic demands. Communists must rely on the masses working from below, from the streets, and should not fear to alienate their ally, the bourgeoisie, but what the ICP did was to conduct secret negotiations with Qasim on the participation of the ICP in the government. 'Such methods do not educate the masses through the practical revolutionary struggle, nor do they develop the revolution and push it forward.' Al-Haj declared the exercise to be based on 'immediate, narrow interests which are alien to the Party's basic goals'. He wanted the party to go beyond agitation and propaganda in its attempt to transform the *coup* Cabinet into a genuine national coalition.

Following the failure of the Shawaf *putsch* in 1959, al-Haj believed that the ICP should have seized power from Qasim. He also thought that the party should have taken the initiative to topple Qasim before the Baathist-led *coup* of 1963. He states:

> We resolved not to initiate armed struggle in defence of the Qasim régime when faced with a military *coup*. In other words, we decided not to initiate civil war, but to avoid it at all costs – at a time when the other forces were preparing for it, sharpening their knives to butcher us. Indeed we resigned the initiative to the counter-revolution to choose the most appropriate moment to realise its dream of liquidating our party and crushing the revolutionary movement.

He condemns the party leadership for that and for calling the masses to arms on 8 February 1963 without providing them with sufficient arms and ammunition. He is not criticising the armed resistance but the party's failure to provide the means for it through its reliance on the bourgeoisie. He rejected the strategy of the party for disbanding the popular resistance groups, the armed peasants' movement, the failure to set up revolutionary organisations inside the armed forces when they had thousands of sympathisers in deference to Qasim, and in favour of protecting the Baghdad district for Qasim. He thought there should have been contingency plans to pursue the armed struggle outside Baghdad, and a long-term defensive plan. There was no doubt in his mind that the lack of military organisation was a consequence of the political line which refrained from furthering the workers and peasants' revolution, but limited itself to defending the revolution or ameliorating the situation in alliance with the bourgeois forces inside and outside the government. He suggests that it never occurred to the ICP to organise the agrarian revolution or push it forward by encouraging the peasants ot enforce the land reform law as a *fäit accompli* by confiscating the lands of the feudalists or refusing to pay rent.

Aziz al-Haj found the rationale that led the ICP to see the Arif régime in a favourable light unacceptable. Arif's agreement with Nasser to co-ordinate his policy with that of Egypt and set up the ASU in Iraq was condemned as tantamount to the importation of revolution irrespective of the objective conditions existing in Iraq. He did not think that the dissolution of Communist organisations and the integration of Communists into an amorphous organisation like the ASU ('full of reactionaries'), marked by ideological disunity and political apathy, and constituting an integral part of the régime, to be a solution in the interest of the revolutionary movement. Moreover, he did not accept that the nationalisation measures in Egypt and the decrees taken in Iraq in 1964 had led these countries to the accepted norm of non-capitalist transformation because of the lack of popular control in the case of Egypt, and the continuity of the traditional economic relationship in the case of Iraq. Besides, he questioned Egypt's motive in concluding the agreement with Iraq as part of Nasser's quest to dominate the Arab world and a facet of inter-Arab politics. 'Cairo will collaborate with any Iraqi government that is not openly hostile to Egypt.' And in open reference to the position of the Soviet Union, al-Haj warned in a pamphlet against 'neo-colonialism', the changing nature of imperialism where influence could be exercised in various and devious manners. He pointed out the overthrow of Ben Bella and Nkrumah to drive the point home that a bourgeois organisation of the ASU type could not protect a régime that is truly opposed to imperialism.

Thus, there was no alternative to the establishment of a revolutionary, national-democratic régime which was required in order to sustain a resolute struggle against imperialism and to successfully defeat counter-revolution. In Iraq's case, al-Haj concludes, this régime can only come to power through the active and efficient, if not leading, role played by the working class and its party controlling the state apparatus. Communists should not be asked to idealise bourgeois nationalism and ought not to help in the consolidation of nationalist rule – not even in the name of the fight against imperialism and counter-revolution. Such slogans should be replaced from the outset by the demand for a revolutionary, national-democratic régime, would seek to educate the masses about the need for the participation of the ICP in power, constantly exposing the ambivalence of the national bourgeoisie and its political organs. It should marshal public support to impose the implementation of revolutionary democracy through the escalation of the class struggle in order to establish the dictatorship of the proletariat.

The debate within the ranks of the Iraqi Communists continued from 1964 to 1967 with an increasing amount of recriminations, charges and counter-charges and frequent threats of expulsion. However, in 1967 a conference was held – it was the third ever – a highly important meeting of delegates designed for cases where a national congress would be impracticable. The conference resolved to expel Aziz al-Haj and his revolutionary supporters. Amir Abdullah and the veteran Communist Zaki Khairi kept a tight grip on the organisational establishment in all its ramifications. However, the long and acrimonious exchanges between the leaders of the ICP left its mark. By 1967 supporters of Aziz al-Haj, men like Ibrahim Allawi, Kazim al-Saffar, Muzafar al-Nawab and Mu'in al-Nahar had already taken to the countryside to organise a peasant uprising against the government of Arif. In June 1966 the Front for Popular Armed Struggle began operations in the Marsh region of southern Iraq under the command of Khalid Ahmad Zaki, an ex-President of the Iraqi Students' Society in the UK and a former member of the Secretariat of the Bertrand Russell Peace Foundation. Government forces soon surrounded the base of Zaki and he was killed in the subsequent clash. The Communist guerrillas al-Ansar, never could hold a compact territory like Barzani. In 1968 a Peoples Army was formed under the command of Mu'in al-Nahar, but this came to grief when al-Nahar was killed in a clash with the security forces in a suburb of Baghdad. Remnants of the army still exist but hardly effectively, particularly after the capture and subsequent execution of five leaders of the movement in Sulaimaniyya two years ago. However, there is no doubt that the moving spirit for this kind of revolutionary political action was Aziz al-Haj, whose career as an activist Communist came to an end in February 1969.

CONTRIBUTORS

M.M. al-Adhami is a Lecturer in History at the College of Arts at Baghdad University, and has written a PhD thesis at the School of Oriental and African Studies, on Parliamentary Elections in Iraq.

Paul J. Hemphill has been working on a PhD thesis at the School of Oriental and African Studies.

Shakir M. Issa was formerly Director of the National Statistics Office in Iraq. He has completed a PhD thesis at the School of Oriental and African Studies, on the Distribution of National Income in Iraq.

Sa'ad N. Jawad is a Lecturer at the College of Law and Politics, Baghdad University. He has written a PhD thesis on the Kurdish question in Iraq.

Atheel Al-Jomard is an Iraqi economist currently writing a PhD thesis at the School of Oriental and African Studies.

Abbas Kelidar is a Lecturer in Politics with reference to the Near and Middle East, School of Oriental and African Studies.

Heino Kopietz is a Lecturer in International Politics, School of Oriental and African Studies.

Keith McLachlan is a Lecturer in Geography with reference to the Near and Middle East, School of Oriental and African Studies.

Edith Penrose, formerly Professor of Economics with reference to Asia in the University of London, is now at the Institut Européen d'Administration d'Affaires in Paris.

David Pool is Lecturer in Politics with reference to the Middle East at Manchester University. He wrote a PhD thesis at Princeton and taught politics at the University of Khartoum for four years.

A. Shikara is an Iraqi scholar working on a PhD thesis at the University of Southampton.

INDEX